Ireland and the Global Question

Ireland

and the

Global Question

Michael J. O'Sullivan

CORK UNIVERSITY PRESS

First published in 2006 by
Cork University Press
Youngline Industrial Estate
Pouladuff Road, Togher
Cork, Ireland

British Library Cataloguing in Publication data
A CIP catalogue record for this book is available from the British Library.

ISBN 1-85918-402-2
ISBN-13 978-1-85918-402-8

A CIP record for this publication is available from the Library of Congress.

Printed by ColourBooks Ltd., Baldoyle, Dublin.

Typeset by Redbarn Publishing, Skeagh, Skibbereen, Co. Cork

www.corkuniversitypress.com

Contents

To Hélenè

Acknowledgements

I owe a great deal of thanks to the staff of Cork University Press, to Mike Collins and Caroline Somers, for their help in turning the manuscript into a book, and to Tom Dunne for his guidance and support. In addition, the book has been greatly improved by the comments from two referees.

The encouragement of both friends and family has carried me through this endeavour and I am very grateful to all for their help. In particular, I would like to thank Michael O'Brien, Tom Farrell and Daniel Keohane for their detailed comments on the manuscript and, within my family, Michele Dufour, Mícheál Ó Suilleabháin and my parents have been enthusiastic and incisive contributors to the process.

Finally, more than a little acknowledgement is due to my wife and daughter, especially to Hélenè for giving me the peace of mind to write this book in the first place.

Introduction

'To the unfettered control of Irish destinies, to be sovereign and indefeasible.' Irish Proclamation of Independence, 1916

'Small states must rely heavily on the quality of their strategic thinking to counter their vulnerability to international influences.' J. J. Lee[1]

In broad terms, globalisation refers to the increasing interdependence
and integration of economies, markets, nations and cultures. It is difficult to measure, a fact that probably contributes to the wide range of
interpretations that are given to it. Despite this, most economic indicators of globalisation,[2] such as the extent of a country's trade with the outside world and the investment funding it receives from abroad,
combined with indices of globalisation like that produced by AT Kear-
ney/*Foreign Policy* magazine, place Ireland at the head of the 'most globalised' league table.

It is the origin and dramatic nature of the turnaround in Ireland's
economic and political fortunes, combined with its title as 'most globalised', that makes it an interesting test case of the process of globalisation and the manner in which a small country can manage this. What
is also noteworthy is that it is not yet clear whether the enormous economic and social changes[3] that have taken place in Ireland during the
current period of globalisation have occurred by design of domestic policy-making, or simply by coincidence with external factors. Other countries are already beginning to take note of the globalisation experiment
going on in Ireland. Government officials from Bulgaria[4] to China[5] have
commented on the economic success enjoyed by Ireland in the last
decade and pondered on whether they can replicate its success.

This book examines the challenges that globalisation presents to Ireland in the context of international trends in economics, foreign affairs and
politics, and in doing so aims to stimulate and provide a framework for the
debate on Ireland's experience of globalisation. The overall view expressed
here is that globalisation has so far been kind to Ireland, but that more
demanding times await it, especially regarding the ways in which economic growth can be sustained and foreign policy refined to fit a new
international order and, most importantly, the way in which the state can
intermediate the effects of globalisation on society and public life. In this

context Ireland should prove a very interesting test case of globalisation for other countries, though Ireland itself still has much to learn.

Then and now

Though many of the artefacts of globalisation, such as technological advances, make it look and sound new, it does have a precedent. There are two generally recognised waves of globalisation, the first having taken place from 1870 to 1913, and the current one, which effectively began in the late 1980s. What makes the case of Ireland more interesting is its journey from a state of seclusion and poverty during the first wave of globalisation to a position of economic and political wellbeing during the current period.

The essential difference between the Ireland of the nineteenth century and the one that we now examine is that Ireland today is both sovereign and independent. This change mirrors one of the significant differences in the world during the first and second waves of globalisation. Compared to the second half of the nineteenth century, a great number of nation states have now been established and democracy, though still evolving, is widespread in the western world. Though the causality between them is unclear, there does seem to be some relationship between democracy and globalisation.

The broad basis for this relationship is that the current wave of globalisation effectively dates from the collapse of Communism and the subsequent erosion of political, cultural and economic barriers across the world. In response to this trend, some political scientists have optimistically and perhaps prematurely heralded the triumph of liberal democracy over totalitarianism as the 'end of history'. In this sense there is also a broad parallel between recent Irish history and events in the wider world. The ending of Ireland's history of economic underdevelopment and the relative calm that has followed the Good Friday Agreement could also be seen to mark the end of a period of history and the beginning of a new era in Ireland.

The National Question

Until the current wave of globalisation came upon Ireland, the dominant framework in public life has been what is referred to as the 'National Question', the pursuit of sovereignty and independence from Britain. The argument of this book is that, if the globalisation of Ireland does represent a new epoch, this is still likely to be guided by the same principles that motivated key events in modern Irish history: namely, a desire to maintain the sovereignty and independence of the nation in the face of powerful external forces.

The utter importance of the values inherent in the National Question to Irish public life is underlined by two of the prominent figures of the 1916 Rising. First, James Connolly, who was executed for his part in the rebellion and was a leading socialist at the turn of the nineteenth century, defines a free nation as:

> one that possesses absolute control over all its own internal resources and powers, and which has no restriction upon its intercourse with all other nations similarly circumstanced except the restrictions placed upon it by nature. Is that the case of Ireland? . . . NO![6]

Second, Eamon de Valera, the key figure in twentieth-century Irish politics, in a response to an attack by Churchill on Ireland's policy of neutrality during the Second World War, underscored the enduring nature of the National Question in Irish history:

> There is a small nation that stood alone, not for one year or two, but several hundred years, against aggression; that endured spoliations, famines, massacres in endless succession; that was clubbed many times into insensibility, but that each time, on returning consciousness, took up the fight anew, a small nation that could never be got to accept defeat and had never surrendered her soul.[7]

Even after the establishment of the Irish state in 1922, the issues of independence and sovereignty persisted in the form of the partition of Northern Ireland from the Republic. The Good Friday Agreement, which was made possible by an improving geo-political climate, has now brought some closure to the National Question.

One of the achievements of the Good Friday Agreement has been to reduce the role that territory plays in the way we define sovereignty. Whether intentional or coincidental, this is consistent with the process of globalisation, where traditional links between nation states are being replaced by networks that are not territorially based and over which traditional nation states have less control than they used to, such as in the transfer of ideas, information and financial flows. Reflecting this trend, Ireland's relations with both Northern Ireland and the European Union are now based less on traditional notions of sovereignty and independence and more on integration and complex interdependence.

The example of the Good Friday Agreement illustrates the way in which Ireland and the world around it are changing, and helps to make the point that, although the National Question is not yet fully resolved, it no longer captures and describes the multiple changes occurring in Irish society, politics and economics. Globalisation is presenting the Irish state with a new defining question, the Global Question.

The Global Question

In Ireland's case the Global Question asks how a small open nation can independently manage the effects that globalisation has on its economy, society and public life. For larger countries like the US, the Global Question relates to how it can continue to direct the process of globalisation in its favour, while for others, like France, it may relate to the way a counterbalance to the Anglo-Saxon form of globalisation can be constructed. Most small developed countries share the same predicament as Ireland. Finland, Singapore, Switzerland, Austria and New Zealand join Ireland at the top of the most globalised league table. Their dilemma lies in balancing the impact of powerful external forces with independence of choice over the kind of society, identity and public life they desire.

The challenges presented to Ireland by the Global Question are similar to those posed by the National Question. How can it maintain some independence of action in the face of forceful global economic, political and social forces, or, to paraphrase the quotes at the beginning of this chapter, how can a small country use strategic thinking to remain sovereign and indefeasible? To recycle the earlier quotes from Connolly and de Valera, is Ireland a free nation in a globalised world, one that can 'possess absolute control over all its own internal resources and powers, and which has no restriction upon its intercourse with all other nations', and is it 'surrendering its soul' to globalisation? Essentially, the Global Question asks how Ireland can preserve its independence in a world that is more integrated and interdependent.

One way of addressing the Global Question is to use the framework of republicanism, the most influential political idea to be imported to Ireland. As a framework it remains relevant today, and more so in a globalised world. A republic, to use the definition of the philosopher Philip Pettit, is a state where citizens are free from domination, by which he means 'not being subject to the arbitrary sway of another or being subject to the potentially capricious will or the potentially idiosyncratic judgement of another'.[8] This definition is particularly relevant in the case of a globalised society, because the social and political aspects of the Global Question centre on whether globalisation emasculates, taking away the power of sovereign states and citizens, and leaving them in thrall to powerful market forces. In globalised Ireland, it is hard to escape the feeling that people are dominated by the 'Celtic Tiger', its causes, effects and the expectations it gives rise to.

The Global Question is posed primarily to the state. The state's role as the intermediary between the external trends driving globalisation and the domestic economy and society is likely to become more important because of globalisation, and not less so, as neo-liberals might wish. In this respect, Ireland is unique amongst the small globalised economies of the world in that the size of its government (e.g. government spending as a share of GDP) is relatively small. Typically, there is an inverse relationship between the size of government and the openness of an economy because a high level of government involvement counterbalances the large external risks posed to small open economies. In Ireland, the nature and magnitude of external risks to the Irish economy have become more serious in recent years, but government spending has not grown in tandem with the pace of globalisation. On a broad basis, this leaves both the domestic economy and society vulnerable.

Economics, or rather geo-economics, is a good case in point. Outside of a few large countries, most nation states have little power over financial markets and are in fact dwarfed by them. Global financial markets now exist above the borders of nation states, not between them. A counter reaction to this has been the creation of the euro-zone, where twelve European countries have surrendered their respective sovereign currencies and monetary policies, in addition to accepting restrictions over fiscal policy, in return for an altogether more robust collective currency.

Though loss of sovereignty is balanced by more powerful collective action, it also means a loss of independence. Given the poor stewardship of the Irish economy up to the late 1980s it could be argued that this loss of control is no bad thing. Though some free-market liberals argue that globalisation should and does make the state less relevant, the contention here is that its role is even more important in a globalised world. By having fewer economic policy instruments at its disposal and being more exposed to policy and market events abroad, a premium is put on the ability of domestic policy-makers to be more inventive in the way in which they use the policy options available to them. Specifically, if broad tools like monetary policy are no longer available, policy must increasingly take the form of surgical strikes to tackle specific problem areas like wealth and income inequalities and high property prices.

To some extent the response of a small country like Ireland to the Global Question is pre-determined. It is simply neither large nor powerful enough to have a direct and lasting bearing on the globalisation process. At the other extreme, the economic successes of Ireland's experience of globalisation, such as the fall in unemployment from over 15% to below 5%, leave it understandably unreceptive to the arguments of anti-globalists who demand the slowing or even ending of the globalisation process. It must accept globalisation, but adapt to it with innovative strategic thinking and policy-making.

Why Ireland?

The case of whether Ireland can manage the effects of globalisation should prove noteworthy for several reasons. First, it is not yet clear whether the benefits (mostly economic) that globalisation has brought to Ireland have occurred by design or by default. If they have occurred largely by design, then the consequences of globalisation should be easier to manage. However, Ireland's economic boom coincided with the second longest American economic expansion of the twentieth century, one that was crowned by massive amounts of investment spending in high technology sectors. This was partly driven by the drop in long-term interest rates in both the US and Europe. Moreover, the 1990s were arguably the most successful period in the history of the EU. The magnitude of these and other trends suggests that external factors have had a great influence on the Irish economy and that Ireland merely succeeded in hitching a ride on the coat-tails of globalisation.

The contribution of domestic policy-making to Ireland's economic success is also put in doubt by the fact that many of the factors that are accepted as being the determinants of the 'Celtic Tiger' (such as the education system and plentiful supply of labour) were in place during some of the worst as well as the best years of Irish economic performance.

A second point is that the factors that have driven the Irish economy, such as low interest rates, social partnerships and a booming property market, amongst others, seem to have reached levels where their future contribution, if positive at all, can only be marginal. Global interest rates look to have bottomed, social partnership is likely to be more difficult in the face of already low taxes and rising inflation (what is popularly referred to as 'rip-off Ireland'), while property prices look stretched on a number of fronts. Therefore, the ability of Ireland to sustain and to draw growth from new sources should prove an interesting exercise to watch.

Has globalisation gone too far?

Globalisation in Ireland is also interesting because of its uneven nature, and the extremes that some aspects of globalisation have reached. This is evident in the growing disparity between a neo-liberal economy and a still developing society, in the growing influence of the Anglo-Saxon world (effectively the English-speaking world, though predominantly the US and the UK) on Irish identity, in the unimaginative way in which the central pillar of foreign policy, neutrality, is practised, and above all in the way globalisation has raised the expectations of Irish people. The tensions aroused by these extremes are already beginning to manifest themselves and beg the question as to whether globalisation is going too far in Ireland, or at least whether it needs to be better managed.

Related to this is the fact that there is a growing strain between Ireland's role as a modern European nation and its increasing adoption of Anglo-Saxon political, economic and cultural norms. Globalisation, which is largely Anglo-Saxon in nature, has contributed to this. The first wave of globalisation was spearheaded by British merchants and the second by American corporations. As the most globalised country in the world, it is almost inevitable that Ireland has become more Anglo-Saxon. Despite frequent assertions that Ireland is a European country, the parts of globalisation that have taken root in Ireland have left it looking more and more like an Anglo-Saxon society than a continental one. Even the much-vaunted 'social partnership' agreements have as their motivation the goals of tax reduction and inflation stabilisation, rather than income equality.

Another phenomenon is the move away from the public (i.e. the state) and towards the private. There are several tell-tale signs of this. In the past ten years, adherence to the fiscal guidelines of the EU has shrunk the public debt, though at the same time private debt (i.e. mortgage and credit card debt) has expanded faster than ever before. This marks a transfer in risk from the public to the private sphere and this shift reflects a greater change in mindsets, part of which is manifest in the increasing privatisation of state enterprises and also in the creeping privatisation of public goods like healthcare and education.

What is also interesting is that Ireland has largely made a success of the facets of globalisation that anti-globalisers most complain about, such as large multinationals, and the economic model of the neo-liberal Washington consensus. For instance, the leading trade economist Jagdish Bhagwati[9] outlines a trilogy of popular discontents with globalisation, stressing that 'globalisation's enemies see it as the worldwide extension of capitalism, with multinational corporations as its far-ranging B-52s'. Yet, this is precisely the sort of globalisation that has taken hold in Ireland. His comment draws attention to the fact that the aspect of globalisation that has proved most important to the Irish economy has been the presence of large multinationals, up to three-quarters of which are American.

Given this backdrop, Ireland is in effect a member of the 'New European' group of countries referred to by US Secretary for Defence Donald Rumsfeld in 2003. Consistent with this distinction, and similar to other New European states in Eastern Europe, is the pace and scale of social change in Ireland. The eruption of social change in Ireland tallies with the views of some social scientists that globalisation in general, and economic shocks in particular, lead to great transformations in public and social life.

The way we live now
In particular, globalisation is beginning to be strongly associated with a more liberal, materialistic and less cohesive society. In Ireland unemployment has collapsed, though crime, and especially violent crime, is rising. It seems that a trade-off for greater personal wealth has been a decrease in personal security in the physical, psychological and social senses. The position of women has changed for the better, while the power of religious institutions has waned. The flow of emigrants from Ireland has turned around, bringing new cultures, nationalities and religions into what had previously been a starkly homogenous society.

The above are some of the overt effects of globalisation. A less clear but equally profound and underestimated effect of globalisation is the way in which it changes people's expectations of the world in which they live. The case of Ireland, with its successful economy and transforming society, is no exception to this.

The enduring problem with expectations is that they are rarely met. For instance, few commentators or policy-makers had forecast the extent of the change in Ireland's economy and society over the past twenty years and, even if some did, fewer politicians and policy-makers acted on these forecasts, as the woeful state of Ireland's physical infrastructure attests. Predicting the rise and fall of nations is a precarious business, especially in an increasingly unpredictable globalised world. Like Japan in the 1980s, the Asian economies in the mid-1990s and the US technology sector in 1999, it seems that there are now few people who believe Irish economic growth will fall below the levels of the last ten years. As in the above cases, this is foolish.

The effect of globalisation on the Irish economy has radically changed expectations about productivity, incomes, growth and education in Ireland. The most dangerous effect on expectations that globalisation can have in an economic sense is to support the notion that the very high level of economic growth enjoyed by Ireland in the last ten years, together with surges in private wealth and incomes, will continue into the long term. The sustainability of such high rates of growth is doubtful and any view that sees them lasting well into the future would be very optimistic. A history of asset bubbles going back to the Crusades[10] shows that humans are prone to over-confidence, a phenomenon that is normally bred by periods of expansion, and this in turn generates complacency in consumers and policy-makers. It also draws people into asset bubbles and provides them with the justification to take on debt.

What is crueller is the strain of relative expectations. In a country where income and especially wealth inequalities prevail, rising national wealth creates the expectation that all will benefit, but in reality only relatively few actually do. In this way, globalisation has the potential to make people less happy, because most people find it difficult to match rising benchmarks of wealth and achievement.

In general, the title of 'most globalised country' and the awkward cliché of the 'Celtic Tiger' mask the fact that a great part of Irish society is unused to, or untouched by, globalisation. In comparison to the Asian Tiger states of Singapore and Hong Kong, Ireland's infrastructure looks anything but globalised. When measured against the Nordic countries, its education system, levels of human development and equality are mediocre. When matched against foreign companies, the domestic economy is pedestrian. Globalisation in Ireland is a lop-sided process, with the country being much more globalised in terms of trade and investment than in terms of domestic industry, politics, foreign policy and society.

Overall the economic globalisation of Ireland seems to have gone as far as it can go, such that new goals and a new approach to policy-making are required if economic growth is to be sustained. The side-effects of globalisation on society need to be buffered by a bigger and more responsible role for the state. Finally, the globalisation of foreign policy has not gone far enough, and it needs to be projected globally in a more defined way.

Tone and approach

The aims of this book are to provide a top-down view of the process of globalisation in Ireland, to set out the challenges facing the Irish economy, society and public life in the context of the broader world, and to highlight future issues regarding the Global Question. The focus is on the political, social, economic and international affairs aspects of globalisation. Other worthy aspects, such as culture, environment, legal issues and gender, are outside the scope of this book. The commentary here tries to steer away from accounts of modern Irish history, about which there is a large literature, though it does use the analysis of well-known thinkers like Karl Marx to throw light on important periods of history. Two specific time periods are referred to here: Ireland before and during the first wave of globalisation, and then the period from the late 1980s to the present that marks the second period of globalisation. The book also tries to avoid prescriptive doctrines as to how the world should be ordered, so that it does not necessarily reflect the dogma of any particular 'ism'.

In presenting a view of globalised Ireland in the light of events in the wider world, the book also attempts to stick to the tight parameters of the globalisation framework, however tempting domestic issues like corruption are to write about. In recent years there have been a number of publications aimed at the 'New' Ireland, which, though they may pick up the effects of globalisation in Ireland, do not use it as a specific framework. Tying the story of Ireland in the last twenty years down to a specific framework makes it easier to analyse and to identify lessons for other countries.

Specifically, Chapter One examines the definitions of globalisation and isolates the growing integration and interdependence of markets, economies and societies as the common themes running through the prominent conceptions of globalisation. Globalisation is not new, as the late nineteenth century also witnessed a period where international trade and finance expanded dramatically, the costs of transport and commodity-type goods fell, and cross-border human migration reached record levels. This period of globalisation came to an end with the rise of nationalism, economic crises and the beginning of the First World War.

Chapter Two tackles the measurement of globalisation, which is a difficult exercise, partly because its definition is still contested or misunderstood. Economic data proves the most straightforward means of quantifying globalisation and on this and similar bases Ireland is now regarded as one of the most globalised countries in the world. This fact coincides with survey evidence that shows Irish people to be strongly in favour of globalisation.

Before examining the nature of modern-day globalisation in Ireland, Chapter Three takes a brief detour through the nineteenth century. Though there is a considerable literature on Irish history during this period, this book does not try to contribute another account to this growing cottage industry but instead highlights several of the lesser-known accounts of life in nineteenth-century Ireland as provided by some prominent thinkers, like Alexis de Tocqueville, whose work continues to infuse the debate on globalisation today. The purpose of these accounts is to emphasise how disadvantaged and unglobalised Ireland was before and during the first period of globalisation, a fact that in turn underlines the reversal in its fortunes in the late twentieth century.

This transformation in Ireland's economic performance is the subject of Chapter Four. Though it now labours under the cliché of the 'Celtic Tiger', Ireland's economic performance during most of the last hundred years was feeble. It had no discernible competitive advantage, an underdeveloped physical infrastructure, low levels of indigenous research and development and, until recently, sloppy policy-making. The chapter searches for the factors that have contributed to Ireland's economic success and questions whether any of these ingredients are uniquely Irish. It then plots the risks and challenges to the Irish economy in the future, and outlines the difficult environment facing policy-makers.

The economy is the most prominent aspect of globalisation in Ireland and, although Irish society and public life are not as globalised as its economy, the side-effects of globalisation are impacting on them. Using the idea of the 'republic' as a broad framework, Chapter Five examines the great transformation in Irish society during this period of globalisation and the way in which political ideals and institutions may have to adapt to the changes wrought by globalisation.

Chapter Six examines the effects of globalisation on foreign policy. The expression of independent Irish foreign policy has been exemplified by neutrality and the evolution of Ireland's place in the world can be read through the emergence and changing interpretation of Ireland's policy of neutrality. This chapter explores the range of reasons why the traditional understanding of neutrality is being challenged by globalisation and suggests several strategies through which neutrality can be adapted to a globalised world in a distinctive and meaningful way.

Finally, Chapter Seven highlights the lessons that other countries can learn from Ireland's great leap forward from developing to post-industrial economy. To any recommendations that follow from the Irish case must be added the caveat that globlisation in Ireland is still only half-baked, and that Ireland itself still has much to learn about globalisation.

Conclusion

This book was written with the aim of framing and stimulating the debate on the globalisation of Ireland. To date, this is a phenomenon that, although ever present in Irish life, has with a few exceptions yet to be the subject of a thorough and serious public debate in Ireland.

Like most policy issues in Ireland, globalisation has been treated with a far greater dose of pragmatism than it has with careful strategic thought. Ireland is at a crucial juncture with regard to the next stage of its economic development, its place in the world, the wellbeing of public life and the structure of its society. The present danger is that delaying a close examination of what Ireland's engagement with globalisation means could squander its recent successes.

In gauging the effects of globalisation on Ireland, the critical barometer must be whether globalisation permits a small country like Ireland to independently manage its economy and society. If the answer to this question is no, then globalisation has gone too far in Ireland.

This question was posed at a broader level some eight years ago by Dani Rodrik.[11] Globalisation is still thriving, especially in Ireland, but its side-effects are now becoming more apparent. Rodrik suggests that globalisation can be marshalled if 'policy-makers act wisely and imaginatively'[12] and writes that 'what is actually required to make progress . . . is political entrepreneurship, imagination, patience here, impatience there, and other varieties of virtu and fortuna. We need all of these, plus a good dose of pragmatism, to make progress on the challenges ahead.' Ireland is a case in point. Inventive policy will be the key determinant of its continued economic success, and to the orderly adaptation of society and public life to globalisation in the future.

Chapter One

Defining globalisation

'Society is undergoing a silent revolution, which must be submitted
to, and which takes no more notice of the human existences it breaks
down than an earthquake regards the houses it subverts.' Karl Marx[1]

As a concept, globalisation is difficult to define for a number of reasons.
The first is that it is broad based and its implications stretch across economic, social, cultural and political arenas. Second, it is sufficiently broad
that different constituencies have appropriated it for themselves and
accordingly define globalisation with reference to the issues that occupy
them. Many important issues such as poverty, inequality and the spread
of disease existed before globalisation, although they are often invoked as
side-effects of it. While these problems deserve the attention and scrutiny
of developed countries and institutions, their cause is often not furthered
by promoting them under the banner of anti-globalisation. A third problem is that some of the more emotive uses of the word globalisation in the
past number of years have resulted in the concept being less well understood. In particular, the anti-globalisation lobby, best known for public
demonstrations in places like Seattle, has done little to broaden the public understanding of globalisation. Fourthly, defining globalisation is also
confounded by the fact that there is no particular body prosecuting the
globalisation of the world's societies and economies; it merely represents
the outcome of a mixture of processes and events. The absence of a single
body on which to blame the ills of globalisation in turn makes it more
difficult to focus criticism of globalisation.

The lack of clarity about what globalisation means is not specific to
it as a phenomenon. Marx, Machiavelli and Adam Smith, for example,
today serve as intellectual fig leaves for ideas they themselves would most
likely not have supported. Equally, many of the ideas that have dominated Irish public life, such as republicanism, nationalism and neutrality,
have either acquired new meanings or departed from the meaning that
was originally intended for them.

A starting-point in clarifying what globalisation means is to stress
what it is not. Many of the changes that have occurred in Irish society
over the past twenty years have relatively little to do with globalisation.
An example is demographics, one of the significant factors behind the

growth of the Irish economy, which until very recently has had little to do with globalisation. The young productive tranche of the Irish population (20–45-year-olds) accounts for 38% of the total population, according to the last census (2002). This demographic segment is largely unrelated to globalisation, as most of the people in this range were born before the current wave of globalisation began, although coming behind them is a large group of over 824,000 'globalised' 0–14-year-olds (this group is greater than all of those aged 55 and over).[2]

Similarly, some commentators readily associate the widespread institutional failure in Ireland (from local to national politics, to the Church) with globalisation. Although the catalyst that globalisation delivered to the Irish economy may have enlarged the crock of gold from which politicians and businessmen helped themselves, globalisation was not the cause of the numerous cases of corruption in Irish public life. There is no sign, for example, that Microsoft or Intel, rather than domestic businessmen, bribed local and national politicians. If anything, globalisation provides a more open society where many of these issues can be scrutinised.

This chapter tries to clarify what globalisation means by examining a number of definitions from a wide range of sources. In addition, it outlines the prevalent Anglo-Saxon form of globalisation, as well as the forms emerging in Europe and Asia. It also underlines the role of institutions like the Catholic Church in the globalisation process. The current wave of globalisation is widely recognised as the second one, the first having taken place between the years 1870 and 1913. Some similarities and differences between the two waves are highlighted here, and their impact on both the developing and undeveloped worlds is considered.

Defining globalisation

In order to understand, adapt to and even change globalisation, it is first of all necessary to define what it is. There is a broad range of definitions of globalisation, though most tend to focus on the integration or interlinking of economies, perhaps because this is the most tangible form.

One of the more extensive efforts to define and understand globalisation has been undertaken by the House of Lords Select Committee on Economic Affairs.[3] This Committee, whose report was published in 2002, gathered together a varied and experienced cast of experts, policymakers and opinion-formers. They highlight a number of definitions, such as that adopted by the World Bank: namely, that globalisation is 'the rapid increase in the share of economic activity traded across national boundaries, measured by international trade as a share of national income, foreign direct investment flows and capital market flows'. This is similar to the definition that was supported both by Greenpeace and by Anita Roddick (founder of the Body Shop): 'the integration of national economies into the global economy through trade and investment rules and privatisation, with the help of technological advances'.

The United Nations Conference on Trade and Development (UNC-TAD)[4] offered a definition in a similar vein:

> In general terms, globalisation describes the process of increasing economic integration among nations through cross-border flows of goods and resources together with the development of a complementary set of organisational structures to manage the associated network of economic activities.

Stanley Fischer, the former managing director of the International Monetary Fund (IMF), has commented that 'globalisation is the ongoing process of greater interdependence among countries and their citizens, and is complex and multifaceted'.[5]

Other economic academics display a crisp understanding of globalisation. O'Rourke and Williamson,[6] whose research focuses on international trade, take globalisation to be represented by 'the integration of international commodity markets . . . the only irrefutable evidence that globalisation is taking place, on our definition, is a decline in the international dispersion of commodity prices or what we call commodity price convergence'.

Willem Buiter, Chief Economist of the European Bank for Reconstruction and Development (EBRD), focuses principally on the breakdown of boundaries.[7] Globalisation is, he said:

> A process of diminishing importance of distance, geography and national boundaries in shaping all kinds of human activities. It therefore refers to trade liberalisation, trade integration; it refers to increased capital mobility. It refers in certain regions to increased labour mobility; and it also refers to the enhanced mobility of just about everything and anything that is permitted by the combination of technological change, lower transportation costs and communication costs that have been going on for a long time.

The political scientist Joseph Nye defines globalisation as referring to networks of interdependence at worldwide (multi-continental) distances.[8] He expands on this definition in his book, *Governance in a Globalizing World,* by stating that 'these networks can be linked through flows and influences of capital goods, information and ideas, people and force, as well as environmentally and biologically relevant substances'.[9]

Despite the above and many other efforts to define globalisation, the popular usage of the term remains so poorly defined that Anthony Giddens, formerly Director of the London School of Economics, is quoted as saying that 'there are few terms that we use so frequently but which are in fact as poorly conceptualised as globalisation'.[10]

Nevertheless, it is not difficult to distil a couple of core characteristics from the many definitions that are offered of globalisation. One is that globalisation involves the increasing integration of markets, economies and societies, as borders become less relevant. The other is that integration brings increased interdependence between nations.

A borderless world

Some academics have sought out further distinctions in the definition of globalisation. This trend is reflected in the work of Jan Scholte, who has written in depth on defining globalisation. He defines it as 'processes whereby many social relations become relatively delinked from territorial geography, so that human lives are increasingly played out in the world as a single place'.[11] He sees globalisation as occurring more above national borders rather than as an intensification of activity between them. His overview of globalisation finds it emerging from four trends that have moulded international relations in recent decades: internationalisation, liberalisation, westernisation and universalisation.

Internationalisation involves growing relations between nations across borders and is easily mistaken for globalisation. The difference is that globalisation involves the exchange of ideas, capital or information above borders rather than across them. It is paralleled by the spread of goods and services across the world. Some of these goods and brands have become so well known that they are universal (Scholte's definition of globalisation conceives of this as universalisation). Global brands such as McDonalds and Coca-Cola fall into this category, as do popular culture and sports events (e.g. the World Cup).

Liberalisation refers to the free market ethos that has sprung from thinkers like Adam Smith and has provided the intellectual force for those who have sought to lower barriers to trade and capital flows. The assertion that a rational and liberal approach to trade will inspire both prosperity and liberty is one of the primary factors that grants globalisation its western, if not Anglo-Saxon, character. In theory, this philosophy rails against barriers, be they national or regulatory, that stand in the way of the efficient allocation of capital and is perhaps the reason why many on the left instinctively find the notion of globalisation threatening. With the fall of Communism, liberalism has acquired a dangerous and unedifying triumphalist tone, which in turn may help to explain some of the popular and more militant revulsion for it.

Comparative and competitive advantages
One reason for the growing acknowledgement of liberalism as the orthodoxy of globalisation, by both its proponents and critics, is the rise of the corporation. In sympathy with this trend, an increasing number of perspectives on globalisation come from the relatively new academic discipline of business studies.

In this respect, one of the first and more prescient definitions of globalisation came in 1983 in a paper by Theodore Levitt, professor of marketing at Harvard. Levitt wrote that:

> The globalization of markets is at hand. With that, the multinational commercial world nears its end, and so does the multinational corporation. The multinational and the global corporation are not the same thing. The multinational corporation operates in a number of countries, and adjusts its products and practices in each – at high relative costs. The global corporation operates with resolute constancy – at low relative cost – as if the entire world were a single entity, it sells the same things in the same way everywhere.[12]

His distinction between multinational and global companies is crucial to understanding how globalisation differs from internationalisation. A multinational company tends to replicate itself on a regional or national basis, building planning, marketing, production and distribution operations in each area. Conversely, a truly global corporation can locate its production operations in one country, its marketing in another country and be headquartered in yet another. These parts are integrated by technology and communications systems that permit the easy flow of information and capital. The ability of firms to quickly switch the production of goods and services to the lowest cost location is already being seen in the rising use of India and China as low-cost service and production bases. An offshoot of this is that the low cost of manufacturing in China is affecting the global economy by exporting deflation (falling prices) to the developed world through the goods it manufactures, while also causing commodity price inflation by virtue of the huge amounts of oil, cement and steel it needs to drive its industrial expansion.

The first wave of globalisation revolved very much around trade between nations and was governed, theoretically at least, by Ricardo's concept of comparative advantage, which states that a country will always have a relative cost advantage in the production of something and that it should stick to the production of those goods or services in order to maximise the benefits of international trade. However, as Levitt's definition of globalisation suggests, the current wave is led more by corporations than countries. As this has passed, a concept related to comparative advantage, called 'competitive advantage', has been developed by Michael Porter of the Harvard Business School.

The theory of competitive advantage is aimed at the corporate world and states that the only way for a corporation to earn adequate or excess rates of return is to pursue either a policy of low-cost production or one of differentiation and niche-based businesses. A strategy that tries to combine these will be unsuccessful, according to Porter, and can result in the failure of the corporation.

There are strong similarities between the concepts of competitive and comparative advantage, although it is worth pointing out that Ricardo rightly assumes that countries will always have a comparative advantage, and therefore a productive function in something and, unlike companies, will not disappear if they have no competitive advantage. For countries, comparative advantage has been a driver of trade flows, while, for firms, competitive advantage is a key determinant of profitability.

Ireland's advantage

The pursuit of competitive advantage by corporations in the form of a global business strategy has driven them to look beyond national borders. The increasing fragmentation of the production chain means that competitive advantage is now exploited within the vertical chain of production of any particular goods, instead of just between different final goods.

The definition offered by Levitt and the supporting concept of competitive advantage from Porter are of great relevance to the Irish case. The Irish economic miracle is a very global and corporate one, in that growth, productivity and capital flows have been significantly driven by the arrival of foreign (largely American) firms in Ireland. The ability of global companies to slice up their 'value chains' (other terms are outsourcing or delocalisation) means that they can locate production facilities in Ireland, while keeping more important functions like headquarters and research in their country of origin. Most of the economic indicators that point towards the globalisation of the Irish economy (such as the high level of exports relative to GDP, or the level of profits repatriated out of the Irish economy) are significantly affected by the activities of foreign multinationals. This makes the corporate perspective on globalisation particularly relevant to the Irish case, and the fact that many of these corporations are Anglo-Saxon in their nature also tells us something about the character of the prevailing form of globalisation.

This is one of the few facts upon which there is close agreement from both the critics and proponents of globalisation. The historical structure, or architecture as some call it, of globalisation is indisputably western, and its heritage is largely Anglo-Saxon. This is principally due to the economic and financial nature of globalisation and the fact that the pillars on which it has so far been built – capital markets, corporations and multilateral bodies such as the WTO (World Trade Organisation) – are chiefly western or Anglo-Saxon in character.

The Anglo-Saxons
The term 'Anglo-Saxon' refers to the English-speaking world, notably the countries of America, Australia, Canada and the UK. Globalisation was born out of two Anglo-Saxon empires – the British trade and land-based empire of the nineteenth century and the American hegemony of the twentieth and early twenty-first centuries. Though the British empire was undemocratic and sought to transfer value from the rest of the world to its core, it did at least set up transport routes and cultural, legal and linguistic structures that globalisation still travels by today. As a result of this, most facets of globalisation have a strong Anglo-Saxon flavour, especially if we think of globalisation as a legal/political/economic, and perhaps cultural, network.

The original free-market philosophy that has spawned globalisation has been propagated by thinkers like David Ricardo and Adam Smith, and spread by US and British policy-makers. It is safe to assert that the notion that free markets are the most efficient mode of economic activity is now one of the intellectual pillars of the pro-globalisation camp. This spirit lives on in academia, in that many of the world's leading economists have trained or worked in the large universities of the US east coast which supply many of the staff for organisations like the World Bank and IMF (one critic of globalisation has accused these institutions of employing third-class graduates from first-class universities).[13]

Also, many international financial institutions, such as Germany's central bank, the Bundesbank, a significant chunk of the Japanese financial system and economic restructuring programs in Latin America, to name just a few, can claim Americans as their architects. The dollar remains the world's reserve currency, the US Federal Reserve is considered the most powerful central bank in the world and, importantly, the investment banks that drive activity in the global financial system are American, and where they are not they often mimic the behaviour of the large American houses.

Were globalisation more European in its ethos, then we might expect that degrees in philosophy, physics or languages would be among the most prized educational qualifications. Instead, the Masters in Business Administration (MBA) now appears to be the most valued form of post-graduate degree. The MBA is a very American creation, and is a far more practical than academic qualification. It teaches and preaches the skills necessary to inhabit large global corporations. The MBA template travels relatively easily and is now very popular in countries like India. Generally speaking, it is laden with the values and rationale of a liberal free-market approach to the world, although there are some moderate exceptions, such as the Iese school in Madrid and Insead in France.

The diffusion of this value system and the assumptions it makes about the world are very important for the way it exerts an influence over the officer/executive class of large corporations.[14] Together with incentive mechanisms like stock options, it aids the spread and entrenchment of a very neo-liberal form of globalisation.

The Asian way

An alternative to the Anglo-Saxon approach is taking root in Asia, where, since the 1970s, the Asian Tiger economies, Singapore, Hong Kong, Taiwan and Korea, have outperformed the rest of the world economy and are now all highly globalised. Singapore and Hong Kong, whose economic growth in the past thirty years easily outstrips that of Ireland, have become entrepôt economies, importing and then exporting huge quantities of goods and services. The example of these small Asian economies is now being followed by the bigger players in the region, notably China and India.

Broadly speaking, what these countries have in common in the ways in which they have globalised is heavy government control and only a passing interest in the idea of an open society. Their approach is distinctive enough to have been labelled the 'Sinatra' doctrine (i.e. do it my way). While open trade with these countries has been sponsored by the US (China has enjoyed Most Favoured Nation trading status), it has occurred against a backdrop of weak human rights and often feeble democratic accountability. In this sense, the rise of Asia represents a counterpoint to the triumphant liberals who hold that western-style democracy is a prerequisite for strong economic growth.

In addition, the complex nature of Asian social and cultural life, as well as the growing international political and military power of China and India, point towards a potential balance to what some regard as rampant western liberalism. At the same time, it seems that critics of globalisation should have more to complain about regarding Asian-style globalisation rather than the Anglo-Saxon approach in terms of its demo-cratic, political and environmental credentials.

While the globalising Asian countries do not follow the economic and political prescriptions of the received Anglo-Saxon model, what they do have in common are well-developed systems or architectures of gov-ernance, in addition to intricate social and cultural norms. For instance, China's deep-seated culture and the political structures built up during Communism have allowed its authorities to promote pro-growth eco-nomic strategies while at the same time maintaining a high degree of con-trol over both economy and society. These superstructures, as Marx referred to them, give the Asian countries the ability to engage in global-isation in a controlled manner.

By contrast, political structures and institutions in many African and Latin-American countries are weak and in many cases do not extend beyond key strongmen or regimes. Unlike Singapore, for example, polit-ical uncertainty is high and the conditions under which business is done are variable. The lack of a stable political legal infrastructure is a likely reason for some countries' failure to benefit from globalisation.

Europe

Between the Anglo-Saxon model of globalisation and the Sinatra doctrine of the Asian countries lies the European approach. Its brand of capital-ism is less aggressive than the Anglo-Saxon model, and it is far more democratic a region than Asia.

The European project has the breaking down of barriers and the building of permanent peace as its aims, and is a more considered form of globalisation than the Anglo-Saxon version. The creation of the euro-zone is an example of this. It was a managed, consensual process, in part motivated by a desire for increased and cheaper trade, but it also had a wider political imperative and proceeded in a manner that was mindful of the consequences that Europeanisation would have for its members. In addition, the creation of the EU was driven by governments and not by corporations. It has succeeded in eliminating borders between its members but nevertheless still operates behind a more resolute border.

While the EU has not directly taken on the task of remoulding globalisation, largely because it has been rightly preoccupied with its own destiny (i.e. its new constitution and new members), trade and competition negotiations in recent years have shown that in the eco-nomic arena it is now the equal of the US. The exchange of sovereignty by Member States for economic security makes the EU a very powerful player in the global economy, and in turn creates a bulwark against the predominantly liberal form of globalisation that is prevalent today.

In turn, despite significant differences between European countries in terms of their levels of globalisation, the creation and deepening integration of the EU leads the way towards increased regionalisation in other parts of the world, with NAFTA and MERCOSUR in the Americas, and ASEAN and APEC in Asia.[15]

The Catholic Church

Long before the advent of the European Community, Europe was periodically united and divided by religion. In particular, the Catholic Church has played an enormously significant role in the social and political history of Europe. It has withstood the challenges of the Reformation, the French Revolution and the Industrial Revolution, and more recently two world wars. Beyond Europe, the missions of the Church followed, and in many cases preceded, the stream of European traders and conquistadores throughout the world. In Ireland, it has left a heavy imprint on social, political and cultural life. Moreover, the central role that the Catholic Church has played in Irish life makes the response of the Church to globalisation important to the way in which many Irish people interpret it.

The Catholic Church is perhaps the longest established global organisation in the world, having been 'global' well before the first period of economic globalisation. Although the structure of the Catholic Church is strictly speaking more multi-national than global, in that it tends to replicate its hierarchical system within countries, it is global in the way this hierarchy is controlled from Rome, and in the universal nature of its doctrine. Today, the presence of the Catholic Church is felt in almost every country in the world. Unlike the Protestant and Muslim churches, its reach is not restricted to specific cultural or geographic regions.

The Catholic Church has a unique place in the discourse on globalisation in that its teachings and its practical involvement in issues like education, NGO (non-governmental organisations) activities, the alleviation of poverty and debates on modern science (e.g. genetics) and philosophy bring it into close contact with what are generally perceived as the ill-effects of globalisation. The scope of the Church and its appreciation of the damaging elements of globalisation make its views on globalisation of particular importance.

The Church has occasionally entered the debate on globalisation. Near the height of the first wave of globalisation in 1891, an encyclical from Pope Leo XIII[16] sought to address the poor labour conditions that resulted from the trend towards the growing industrialisation of commerce, and which were increasingly highlighted by the rise of socialism and militant labour organisations.

On the centenary of Pope Leo's encyclical, the last Pope, John Paul II, issued an encyclical (Centesimus Annus, May 1991) which acknowledged the potential for economic development in the light of the collapse of Communism, but also underlined the risk of an ideological vacuum in its absence. Pope John Paul II highlighted the Church's well-balanced judgement of the need to both create and distribute wealth in a just manner. In recent years, Pope John Paul II addressed globalisation more specifically, in particular in an address in April 2001. He held that:

> Its prime characteristic is the increasing elimination of barriers to the movement of people, capital and goods. It enshrines a kind of triumph of the market and its logic, which in turn is bringing rapid changes in social systems and cultures. Many people, especially the disadvantaged, experience this as something that has been forced upon them, rather than as a process in which they can actively participate.[17]

While clearly mindful of the uneven consequences of globalisation, especially for the weak, the late Pope John Paul II also appeared pragmatic, seemingly regarding globalisation as the spirit of our times ('globalization, a priori, is neither good nor bad. It will be what people make of it'). At the same time, he did sanction that the logic of globalisation should not ultimately take priority over humanity: 'Ethics demands that systems be attuned to the needs of man, and not that man be sacrificed for the sake of the system.' In this spirit, Pope John Paul II stressed that economic globalisation should be followed by the globalisation of human rights and that 'globalization must not be a new version of colonialism'. Further, he has called for new approaches to policy-making that will safeguard solidarity, the principle that the weak and the poor be valued and protected.

Although the Catholic Church is important to the debate on globalisation as both a 'global' organisation and as one of the few authoritative and powerful antidotes to the free-market logic that lies behind globalisation, it is ironic but at the same time understandable that, in the Western world at least (Ireland again being a good example), active participation in the Catholic Church has waned as globalisation has spread. Like other fallible institutions, the Church has suffered institutional failure in the way in which it has handled the abuse of children by priests,[18] amongst other issues. Demographics will also present some interesting challenges to the Catholic Church. The very low levels of recruitment of priests and nuns in America and Europe, coupled with relatively low population growth in Europe, will gradually tilt the balance of political power within the Church's hierarchy towards developing nations. While expanding populations in the Third World will give it the potential for expansion, the economic and social problems associated with population growth (from the spread of disease to malnutrition) may in time sharpen its response to globalisation.

The first wave of globalisation

It is difficult to associate the advent of globalisation with any one event, although the end of the Second World War and the setting up of multilateral institutions like the IMF and the GATT (General Agreement on Trade and Tariffs) certainly formed a loose structure that gave globalisation a foundation. In addition, the breakdown of the Bretton Woods system, and most importantly the fall of Communism, cleared the geopolitical climate for the onset of liberalisation and the growth of financial markets. Since then, the spread of contemporary globalisation has been so awe-inspiring in its magnitude that it is difficult to imagine that it could have existed before, and more so that it imploded. However, it does have a precedent.

The period from 1870 to 1913 is widely considered to have marked the first wave of globalisation, until it was encumbered by economic crises and the First World War. It was not until the end of the Cold War in the late 1980s that a period of peace was established between developed nations which allowed the flow of capital, information and ideas into parts of the world they had not reached in over forty years.

The first period of globalisation was a buccaneering, conquering and land-grabbing one, not unlike the original voyages of discovery launched almost four hundred years before. Some writers like the French economist Daniel Cohen[19] hold that there have been three waves of globalisation, the first beginning with the conquest of America by the likes of Pizarro in the sixteenth century. Cohen relies heavily on the thesis of Jared Diamond's book *Guns, Germs and Steel*,[20] that the domestication of animals and plants and the exchange of flora, diseases, animals and customs played a key role in determining the wealth of nations.

However, the suggestion that globalisation began in the fifteenth and sixteenth centuries is refuted by O'Rourke and Williamson in their article entitled 'When Did Globalization Begin?'. They find little evidence in the fifteenth and sixteenth centuries of the form of price convergence that would be associated with the building of international markets and the commoditisation of trade. A supporting fact is that world trade grew at only 1% per annum between 1500 and 1800, but by 3.5% thereafter. On the other hand, a critique of the O'Rourke and Williamson paper echoed some of Cohen's points, namely that globalisation began with the explorers, and its trail is reflected in the price and exchange of silver.[21]

At very least, Cohen's argument highlights the role of the environment and the migration of disease as important issues in the debate on globalisation. Indeed, environmental globalisation is perhaps its oldest form, going back to the time of the Black Death, which originated in Asia but whose migration to Europe killed over a quarter of the population in the middle of the fourteenth century. Modern-day concerns over the rapid spread of diseases like SARS[22] and avian flu reflect this.

The fantastic power that capital markets seem to wield makes it difficult to appreciate that the world could ever have been as developed as it is now. Yet, research shows that a number of countries (especially those outside the US) were more financially developed in 1913 than they were in 1980.[23] For instance, in proportion to GDP (gross domestic product), the market capitalisation of the French stock market was nearly twice that of the US in 1913, but fell to a quarter of it by 1980. Generally speaking, financial market development over the course of the last hundred years reached its nadir in 1980, from which point it has increased towards and beyond the levels of development seen at the turn of the last century. Yet, a lesson to globalised countries like Ireland is that the countries that were the most financially developed in 1913 (such as Argentina) have not necessarily remained so.

The nineteenth-century period of globalisation was one of extensive commodity market integration. According to O'Rourke,[24] the London–Cincinnati price differentials for bacon fell from 93% in 1870 to 18% in 1913, the London to Bombay cotton price spread fell from 57% in 1873 to 20% in 1913, and the London–Rangoon rice price spread fell from 93% to 26% over the same period. During this time, transport (boats and trains) costs fell dramatically in much the same way as communication and air travel costs have dropped sharply over the last twenty years. Against this backdrop, the level of trade surged, so that by 1913 merchandise exports as a share of GDP in western European economies reached a level of 17%, from 14% in 1870 (subsequently falling to around 6% by 1938 and climbing above 17% again in the 1990s).[25]

As the now well-worn quote (below) from Keynes shows, the first period of globalisation placed an array of goods and services at the disposal of (wealthy) people that they could acquire with new-found speed. The confidence and optimism reflected here are emblematic of the outlook of many on the 'new' economy of the 1990s:

> The inhabitant of London could order by telephone, sipping his
> morning tea in bed, the various products of the whole earth, in such

quantity as he might see fit, and reasonably expect their early deliv-
ery upon his doorstep; he could at the same moment and by the
same means adventure his wealth in the natural resources and the
new enterprises of any quarter of the world, and share, without exer-
tion or trouble, in their prospective fruits and advantages, or he
could decide to couple the security of his fortunes with the good faith
of the townspeople of any substantial municipality in any continent
that fancy or information might recommend . . . Most important of
all, he regarded this state of affairs as normal, certain and permanent
except in the direction of further improvement, and any deviation
from it as aberrant, scandalous and avoidable.[26]

The 1870–1913 period of globalisation was also remarkable for the levels
of emigration that were witnessed. Over sixty million people migrated to
the New World between 1820 and 1913. It is estimated that from the
1880s to the early 1900s 6% of the population of several European countries migrated overseas. In the Irish case this figure was closer to 14%. In
1913, about 10% of the world's population were immigrants, although
that figure is now closer to 3%.

However vibrant globalisation was at the turn of the century, bur-
geoning levels of trade, finance and technological advances (in transport
and communications) soon led to imbalances in the European, Latin-
American and American economies, which in many cases were dealt fatal
blows by poor policy-making. Openness quickly gave way to protectionism and the application of tariffs. The rise in poverty and unemployment that was brought about by inflation in the price of goods and
deflation in asset prices forced an eventual response from governments
who had come to fear the greater say that the poor had in politics
because of the expanding franchise. Where small government had previously been in vogue (in 1912 government expenditure in developed
countries was about 13% of GDP), governments were now expected to
spend and protect their way back to prosperity. Thus, protectionism, economic decline, nationalism and finally war brought down the curtain on
the first period of globalisation.

Parallels and differences

There are many parallels between the first wave of globalisation and the
current one. The main ones are the rise in trade, the growth of financial
systems and the rapid diminution in the cost of doing business as transportation and communication costs fall. It is also interesting to note that
stock-market bubbles arose during both periods of globalisation, driven
by the advent of new technologies. In the early twentieth century it was

primarily the railway, telephone and radio stocks that led the rise in share prices, while in 1999 information technology was the chief culprit.

Still, there are crucial differences. Chief amongst these is that today more countries and more people are touched by globalisation, and in most cases are better off as a result. Globalisation today has a much greater reach. This is partly due to the fact that, compared to the twentieth century, more people than ever before enjoy electoral franchise and the freedom of democracy, and today popular opinion has a greater say in politics, at least in developed countries. Within the majority of developed countries, the role of government is greater than it was one hundred years ago and the notion of welfare insurance is now well accepted in the developed world.

Advances in technology are now more rapid and in fields like communications have sped up the transfer of ideas and information and made globalised forms of production more feasible. Corporations have grown in size and influence over the last one hundred years, to the extent that the corporation is the dominant force behind globalisation today. As a result there are now many more 'global' products or brand names than there were in the period 1870 to 1913.

Baldwin and Martin (1999) explicitly address the question of the differences between the current and the nineteenth-century wave of globalisation. They hold that, while there are similarities in trade and capital flows, the roles of multinational corporations and foreign direct investment (FDI) are much greater now. In general, the period 1870–1913 saw foreign direct investment flowing mainly from developed countries to other developed countries, whereas now more of it has flowed from developed to developing countries. In addition, the state of the world before both periods of globalisation, or what Baldwin calls initial conditions, was different: 'before the first wave, all of the world was poor and agrarian. When the second wave began, it was sharply divided between rich and poor nations.'[27]

A final difference between globalisation now and that of the nineteenth century is the growth of institutions and transnational governance. While the nation state is still very much a viable entity, power is increasingly placed in the hands of unelected policy-makers. This is reflected in a number of quarters, such as the standardisation of accounting and financial measures. Institutionalisation increasingly seems to be replacing the role played by the gold standard, Pax Britannia and the ideological consensus that prevailed in the nineteenth century. It is manifest in bodies like the EU or IMF and has, broadly speaking, been beneficial in preventing and resolving crises, and in particular in placing a premium on negotiating skills rather than military power.

Critics of globalisation
Henry Kissinger is known to have complained that that there was never a single foreign policy chief in Europe on whom the Americans could call in times of need. Equally, there is no one person or institution that directs the process of globalisation, although well-known figures like George Soros,[28] and the IMF, World Bank and US Federal Reserve, are frequently called on to answer for its ills.

Institutions, and the growth of institutionalisation, make easy and often just targets for the critics of globalisation, mostly because they are run by unaccountable technocrats (though the purpose of institutions like the European Central Bank [ECB] is to take politics out of policy-making), and are often late on the scene of humanitarian, economic and geo-political crises. A further and perhaps better justified criticism of world institutions is that the policies they recommend are simply not appropriate for fledgling economies. This criticism echoes the contention that globlisation is effectively a western if not Anglo-Saxon process and that its many foot soldiers (investment bankers and policy-makers) view the world through Anglo-Saxon tinted glasses. What makes Ireland an interesting example of globalisation is that the aspects of globalisation that have proved beneficial to Ireland, such as international institutions and multinationals, are also the favourite targets of the critics of globalisation.

Has globalisation helped the developing world?
The debate about globalisation and its merits is at its most intense when the effects of globalisation on the Third World are discussed. When confronted with the current socio-economic problems of the African continent, it is hard to argue that globalisation has been kind to under-developed and developing countries. A counter-argument states that many of the problems of the world's poorer countries are not the direct effect of globalisation and that colonialism, disease, despotism and exploitation all thrived on the African continent before the arrival of globalisation.

The question of whether globalisation is good or bad for the developing world centres on the issues of trade, inequality, health and poverty. The evidence employed in this debate is heavily skewed by the recent growth of the Chinese and Indian economies. Though both of these countries are having a major impact on the global economy and on the globalisation process, they could not yet be described as globalised.

However, the experience of these Asian giants, as well as the Asian Tigers during the current phase of globalisation, has, broadly speaking, been positive. For instance, life expectancy has grown dramatically in some countries. From 1960 to 1999 it rose by 20 years in India, doubled in China to 70 years and has risen by 7 years (to 77) in the US.[29] Likewise, infant mortality in globalising countries has dropped dramatically, though it remains high in regions not touched by globalisation, such as sub-Saharan Africa.

With regard to trade, the evidence is less clear, and most likely confused by the issue of causality. One of the leading studies (Rodriguez and Rodrik, 1999) of the relationship between open trade and economic growth struggles to find a clear relationship between these variables. Alternatively, there is no strong evidence that increased openness of developing nation economies leads to a significant and prolonged deterioration in output.

On the issues of poverty and inequality, relatively optimistic results come from a study of globalisation conducted for the EU.[30] With regard to inequality amongst the world's nations, it states that the Gini coefficient (a measure of income inequality, from 0 to 1, the higher the more unequal) for the world moved from 0.5 in 1820 to 0.61 in 1910, and to 0.64 by 1950, and only to 0.657 in 1992. This suggests that, globally, inequality increased during the first wave of globalisation with the creation and entrenchment of the distinction between the first and third worlds, but that this level has effectively remained flat since 1950. Within developed countries, the study reports much lower Gini coefficients for Germany and France, and higher ones for Anglo-Saxon countries like the US, the UK and Canada. This supports the view that the European 'social model' leads to a less unequal form of society than the Anglo-Saxon one.

At the same time, the authors hold that the proportion of the world's population that lives on $2 per day (inflation adjusted) dropped from 94% in 1820 to 76% in 1910, and to 51% now. Despite this apparent improvement, the absolute number of poor has increased to 2.8 billion, owing to population growth. As mentioned above, economic growth in the Chinese and Indian economies has helped to make the world less unequal, though inequality still persists between Africa and the rest of the world. Specifically regarding the Third World, the authors state that:

> It is difficult to be sure whether the poor economic performance of some countries is due to their having been sufficiently open to the world economy, or whether they lacked the institutions and capacities that would have enabled them to benefit from the opportunities such openness might in principle provide.[31]

Evidence from Lindert and Williamson (2001) suggests that the latter holds true. They document the fact that inequality between nations has increased, but differentiate between globalising and non-globalising countries. Specifically, they hold that 'the dramatic widening of income gaps between nations has probably been reduced, not raised by the globalisation of commodity and factor market, at least for those countries that integrated into the world economy',[32] but conclude that those countries that did not 'liberalise' gained least from globalisation. Their statement 'that nations that gained most from globalisation are those that changed their policies to exploit it, while those that gained the least did not, or were too isolated to do so'[33] is consistent with the recent Irish experience, though it offers little comfort to many Third World countries.

A more recent study from the World Bank by Dollar also supports the view that poverty reduction and economic growth have tended to pick up faster in countries that integrate rapidly and as fully as possible with the global economy. Broadly speaking, Asian countries have globalised rapidly (China, Bangladesh and the Philippines are amongst the countries with the biggest positive change in the trade to GDP ratio from 1977 to 1997), while African countries have globalised least (Zambia, Egypt and Nigeria are the countries with the biggest fall in the trade to GDP ratio from 1977 to 1997).[34] This study reports a net 6% difference in GDP per capita growth rates between globalising countries and the rest of the developing world in the 1990s. Following from this, poverty reduction has been highest in Asian countries like China and Vietnam.

Overall, Dollar cheerfully claims that global inequality has declined since 1980, reversing a trend of rising inequality over the past two hundred years, and moreover that the number of poor people in the world has fallen by 375 million. He concludes by saying:

> True integration requires not just trade liberalization, but also wide-ranging reforms of institutions and policies . . . As long as there are locations with weak institutions and policies, people living there (unglobalized developing countries) are going to fall further behind the rest of the world in terms of living standards.[35]

A study from the UN[36] supports this point by underlying the serious need for basic physical and human infrastructure – schools and teachers, hospitals and doctors – without which developing societies have little chance of engaging globalisation and profiting from global markets and trade.

An alternative view is provided by Robert Hunter Wade,[37] who takes careful aim at claims from the neo-liberal consensus that poverty and inequality are falling. He questions the accuracy of much of the data and methodologies that are employed to underline the decreases in cross-country inequality and world poverty. Many of his points hit home. For example, the assertion that poverty and inequality have fallen in the cohort of 'globalised' countries is heavily dependent upon the inclusion of China and India in this group, whereas in fact both are still large government-controlled economies that have low globalisation rankings (China ranked 54th and India 61st in the *Foreign Policy*/AT Kearney 2005 globalisation index).

In addition to his thorough discussion of data issues, Wade argues that the presumption that liberal economic policies are the only means towards economic development is disproved by the likes of Japan, Korea and Taiwan, countries that have benefited hugely from illiberal trade regimes. On the whole, he stresses that both inequality and poverty are worse than stated in official accounts and that they are underestimated as very serious social and economic problems.

Conclusion

Despite a wide range of interpretations of it, globalisation can be summed up as the increasing integration and resulting interdependence of markets, economies, societies and political systems. It places decreasing emphasis on territorial sovereignty, but arguably makes the role of the state more important, because its side-effects need to be managed, especially where small countries are concerned.

Globalisation is not new, given that the world has already experienced a wave of globalisation in the period 1870 to 1913. The current period has both similarities and differences to the nineteenth-century one, and can be seen to have begun after the fall of Communist regimes in Eastern Europe in the late 1980s. Some critics see globalisation as the triumphant expression of free-market liberal democracy over Communism, although it is probably too early to judge whether this is the case. What is very hard to dispute is that globalisation is Anglo-Saxon in nature, although competing forms are emerging in Asia and being constructed in Europe. It is hard to tell decisively whether globalisation benefits or harms poor countries, though the lack of institutional structures with which developing countries can harness globalisation seems to be a telling factor.

Chapter Two

Measuring globalisation in Ireland

'If the citizens themselves devote their life to matters of trade, the way will be opened to many vices.' St Thomas Aquinas[1]

'Money does not buy happiness.' Richard Easterlin, author of *Explaining Happiness*

Having defined globalisation in the previous chapter, this chapter sets about measuring it. In the case of Ireland, this is both an interesting and a difficult task, largely because, in the period in which it has become highly globalised, Ireland has changed dramatically, not just economically but also in terms of society and public life. Although these two trends are inevitably interrelated, the causality of this interplay is hard to square. Similarly, there are certain aspects of life in Ireland that have not changed anywhere near as much as expected (i.e. inequality), and others where changes have been more dramatic than expected (e.g. the increase in the suicide rate).

This chapter seeks to untangle some of these trends by first of all highlighting the lopsided manner in which Ireland has become globalised and then charting the parallel changes in human development in Ireland over the past ten years. On a more qualitative basis, the chapter examines survey evidence of Irish people's attitude to globalisation and draws upon the academic literature on happiness to examine ways in which globalisation could be used to make Irish people happier, as well as better off.

Finally, the chapter tracks changes in the Irish identity. As mentioned earlier, the type of globalisation that has taken hold in Ireland is Anglo-Saxon in nature, and this is beginning to leave its trace on social and cultural life. For a country that is widely regarded as an enthusiastic member of the EU, Ireland seems to be gravitating away from the European model of society and moving towards the Anglo-Saxon one. In many respects, it is now the leading 'New European' country in the EU.

Measuring Ireland

Measuring and understanding globalisation on its own is difficult enough. Doing so in Ireland is more complicated, not least because of the dramatic nature of the economic and social changes taking place there, as well as the fact that the extent of many of these changes is only now becoming apparent.

Though significant progress has been made in data collection and distribution, mostly by the Central Statistics Office (CSO), considerable problems remain, such as the CSO's small size relative to other national statistics bodies, the weight of demands for EU standardisation of indicators, the postponement of IT upgrading and poor data integration.[2]

The pace of globalisation itself also raises challenges, especially where large multinationals are making creative accounting into an art form and where reliable statistics are needed to make sense of their impact on national accounts. Labour flows are also sowing confusion. For instance, official statistics show that between April 2003 and April 2004 over 50,000 immigrants came to Ireland, 8% of whom (say 4,000) were from Central/Eastern Europe.[3] However, between May 2004 and April 2005, over 40,000 Personal Public Service (PSS) numbers were issued to Polish nationals alone.[4] These shifts in population are not common and clearly take time to percolate through official figures.

While the accession of Ireland to the EU improved the ability of Irish statisticians to gather and analyse data, owing to their increased interaction with other statistics bodies, the accession of new Member States to the EU is one of a number of factors that makes data collection and analysis more difficult. For this reason and others, such as the relatively low level of data collected through the social welfare and taxation systems, the range of data available to researchers in Ireland has been relatively limited, though it is improving. As a result, while the straightforward economic impact of globalisation is not hard to judge, the business, demographic and social aspects are still not clear.

Measuring globalisation

In general, definitions of, objections to and perspectives on globalisation span many fields. In many cases, it is not easy to identify whether specific problems arise as a result of globalisation, or indeed if globalisation simply exacerbates them. Measuring globalisation, and in particular the causality of its effects, is difficult, though perhaps the least problematic aspect of analysing globalisation is to measure its economic effects.

Measures that economists often examine are the relationship between a country's savings and its investment activities, its current account relative to its output, and levels of foreign direct investment (FDI). A number of other more idiosyncratic measures can be examined as well, such as the change in the number of foreign firms located in a country, differences between domestic and national products and between the research and development activities of foreign and indigenous corporations. Measures of migration are useful too, though the flow of labour was more widespread during the first wave of globalisation than it is now.

Most globalised of them all

One survey that attempts to draw together the economic, social, political and technological aspects of globalisation is the AT Kearney/*Foreign Policy* magazine globalisation index.[5] In three of the past four years it has ranked Ireland as the world's most globalised country.

The AT Kearney/*Foreign Policy* index brings together thirteen indicators of global integration. The index measures economic integration by combining data on trade, foreign direct investment, portfolio capital flows, income payments and receipts. The importance of the economic element of globalisation is underlined by the fact that the index accords a larger weighting to the economic measures than it does to the technological, personal and political elements.

The personal aspect of globalisation is accounted for by data on personal contacts via levels of international travel and tourism, international telephone traffic, and cross-border transfers, including remittances. The index also gauges technological connections by counting the number of internet users, internet hosts and secure servers. Political engagement is assessed by counting the number of international organisations and UN Security Council missions in which each country participates, as well as the number of foreign embassies that each country hosts.

In the three years between 2002 and 2004, Ireland ranked as the most globalised country, being knocked into second place in 2005 by Singapore.[6] In the 2002–2005 surveys, Ireland ranked highly in terms of economic and personal rankings, with portfolio investment, international trade, travel and tourism all being particularly strong. Yet, on the basis of political and technological rankings, Ireland ranked outside the top fifteen, consistently falling behind most other European countries on the basis of technological variables like internet users, hosts and number of secure servers. Neither did it impress on the issue of political engagement, coming in 19th place.[7]

Some of the recent AT Kearney/*Foreign Policy* reports have considered globalisation in the context of various other factors, namely life expectancy and religious participation. In general, there is a positive relationship between the level of globalisation of a country and the life expectancy of its population, though on this basis Ireland is something of an outlier, being more globalised than its peers but having a lower average life expectancy. On gender-related development, Ireland is close to but still below its European peer group average.

In terms of religion, Ireland also sticks out. In general, there seems to be a small negative correlation between religious participation and a country's level of globalisation, but Ireland does not conform to this rule, as it outstrips other developed countries in terms of the religious partic-ipation of its citizens (based on the results of the World Values Survey from 1981 to 2001). Only the US, Portugal and the Slovak Republic even approach the level of religious participation that exists in Ireland. In the less globalised countries, religious participation is highest in Nigeria, Poland, the Philippines and Uganda.

Overall, the picture of Ireland that emerges from the AT Kearney/ *Foreign Policy* reports is of an economy very much open and attuned to the flow of trade and investment, but one that is not as politically or tech-nologically integrated as the rest of the world. The uneven nature of globalisation in Ireland is emphasised by the fact that it has ranked highly for economic integration, but is only moderately globalised in political and technological terms. This pattern is consistent over the past four years and is underlined by the fact that Ireland is an outlier when measures of human development (i.e. education spending) are matched against its high overall globalisation ranking. Across most countries, there is a positive relationship, causality notwithstanding, between globalisation and human development, though much less so in Ireland.

Globalisation and human development in Ireland
More detailed evidence on globalisation and human development comes from the UN Human Development Report,[8] which ranked Ireland in 8th place in terms of its Human Development Index. However, as with other studies, this comprehensive report shows development in Ireland to be irregular. It scores in second place (after Luxembourg) on GDP per capita (GNP per capita would of course leave it further down the rankings), though when other broader measures of development[9] are factored in it drops to 8th place overall.

As the AT Kearney/*Foreign Policy* reports note, Ireland does not rank as highly as other first world countries for factors like life expectancy or education spending. For instance, in terms of life expectancy at birth it ranks in only 28th place with an average life expectancy of 76.9, behind most other European countries and the likes of Hong Kong, Costa Rica and New Zealand. Also, the combined primary, secondary and tertiary education enrolment ratio for Ireland is 90%, ranking it in 25th place, behind countries like Lithuania, Korea, Sweden and Australia. Another noteworthy trend in the UN report is that the rate of population growth in Ireland is expected to be close to 1% per annum, with only the US and Israel displaying a higher rate in the developed world.

Consistent with the findings of the AT Kearney/*Foreign Policy* reports, on the basis of technology, Ireland is one of the least well developed countries, according to the UN report. Telephone connections (mainline and cellular), internet use, patents and research and development are all comparatively low, undermining the assumption that a globalised economy results in a high-tech society.

In short, the two prominent surveys mentioned above, the AT Kearney/*Foreign Policy* globalisation index and the UN Human Development Report, sketch a picture of globalisation in Ireland that seems to be driven largely by economic factors and, within this category, by the investment and trade activities of large foreign multinationals in Ireland. They also highlight the weaknesses inherent in Ireland's low level of political and technological globalisation, and its increasing vulnerability to the social side-effects of globalisation.

Happy global people
Another survey that reflects Ireland's generally positive experience of globalisation and its improving economic fortunes is the new Economist Intelligence Unit (EIU) quality of life report, which in 2004 ranked Ireland at the top of its 'quality of life' index, and proclaimed it the happiest nation in the world.[10] The EIU quality of life index is based on a range of factors,[11] some of which, like geography, family life and political stability, would arguably have scored higher in pre-1990s Ireland and others, like GDP[12] and unemployment, which have improved markedly since then.

The EIU survey comes at a time when happiness is enjoying a revival as a topic of interest to economists, and one of the clear conclusions of the literature[13] is that, with the exception of those on very low incomes, more money does not make people more happy. In the US, for example, despite the near continuous rise in incomes since the 1960s, reported levels of happiness have remained static. Unemployment and, to a lesser extent, inflation are the main economic variables that cause unhappiness, while health and family life (especially a good marriage) are key determinants of a happy life. Transparent political systems that encourage active citizenship are also found to increase happiness.

Richard Easterlin, whose early work on happiness is credited with having sparked academic interest in the issue of happiness by economic researchers,[14] sums up the literature: 'life events in the non-pecuniary domain, such as marriage, divorce and serious disability have a lasting effect on happiness', and adds that 'an increase in income and thus in the goods at one's disposal, does not bring with it a lasting increase in happiness'.[15]

One of the reasons that income does not bring about a commensurate increase in happiness is that expectations change as people get wealthier, acquire more possessions, become used to certain levels of wellbeing and in turn compare themselves to their peers. For example, Richard Layard quotes Marx: 'a house may be large or small; as long as the surrounding houses are equally small, it satisfies social demands for a dwelling. But if a palace rises beside the little house, the little house shrinks into a hut.'[16]

In the context of the above findings, Ireland's growing economy presents a number of challenges to the happiness of its citizens, and to the presumption that happiness is brought about by rising wealth. The dramatic fall in unemployment in Ireland in the past ten years is perhaps the biggest contribution that Ireland's experience of globalisation has made to the happiness of the nation. On the other hand, the rise in expectations that has been created by economic growth has probably led to more unhappiness than happiness, simply because this growth in income has not been equally spread, and because it is creating expectations that many feel stretched to match.

One area that lends support to the view that Irish people may not be as happy as some surveys suggest is health. That there has been a rise in suicides in Ireland is well known, and it is a sad but perhaps unsurprising coincidence that the rise in wealth in Ireland is associated with a rise in suicides during the 1990s to a level of 444 deaths recorded by the Central Statistics Office in 2003. From 1949 to 1970 the suicide rate (per 100,000 people) stayed at around 2–3, but from the 1970s to the 1990s the average rate was 6 people. Yet, by 1991 it had risen to 10 and peaked at 14 in the late 1990s.[17] In particular, the number of male suicides is high in both absolute terms and relative to Northern Ireland, England and Wales, as measured per 100,000 of the population. Though there is a multitude of motivations for attempted suicides and deaths by suicide, the concentration of suicides around the young male category – the section of society most challenged by rising expectations of what they can produce and how they must behave – seems to be closely related to the trend towards globalisation.[18]

Further, in recent years over 8,500 people annually have been admitted to accident and emergency departments with injuries consistent with attempted suicide.[19] On a broader level, there are at least 300,000 people in Ireland who suffer from depression.[20] Mental health does not seem to have improved during the globalisation of Ireland and, although the argument that it is only now being uncovered and exposed is a valid one, the rise in stress-related illnesses does not help the case that globalisation has been an entirely happy experience in Ireland. Moreover, physical health, as measured by the incidence of heart disease, infant mortality, cancer, alcohol consumption or indeed obesity,[21] remains at levels far in excess of EU averages, again suggesting that more is not necessarily better.

The issue of health is under-researched in the globalisation literature, a point that is powerfully made by Angus Deaton: 'The recent (2004) report of the World Commission on the Social Dimensions of Globalization, whose membership included globalization critic Joseph Stiglitz, gives only cursory mention to international health. Health is evidently not one of the discontents of globalization.'[22] He underlines the importance of technology and knowledge transfer to the eradication of disease and poverty, rather than policies that focus explicitly on increasing incomes: 'growth in income is not strongly predictive of declines in mortality . . . the transmission of health knowledge and technology is at least as important as changes in income'.[23] Although his comments are directed at poverty and ill-health in the Third World, they are also relevant to the Irish case, and suggest that more imaginative healthcare policies are needed to combat the range of health problems in Ireland. Not only is spending on healthcare in Ireland as a proportion of total social protection expenditure and GDP (7% in 2003)[24] low in comparison to other OECD countries, but there is a strong consensus that the quality of public healthcare in Ireland does not reflect this expenditure, suggesting that a serious rethink in overall healthcare policy is required.

In summary, there are aspects of Irish society, such as political stability and family life, that contribute to a happy society. What globalisation has done is to end unhappiness, primarily by eliminating unemployment. However, if Ireland is true to the findings of the economics literature on happiness, rising incomes are not guaranteed to make Irish people much happier, and in fact are more likely to lead to dissatisfaction and stress as people compare themselves to their peers, and to the costs associated with maintaining certain standards of living. Oswald sums up the implications of the literature:

> In industrialised countries, well being appears to rise as real national income grows. But the rise is so small as to be sometimes almost undetectable. Unemployment seems to be a large source of unhappiness. In a country that is already rich, policy aimed instead at raising economic growth may be of comparatively little value.[25]

If public policy in Ireland is to be focused towards the greater happiness of its citizens, as Jeremy Bentham suggested centuries ago, then it should look beyond income growth as a policy goal and address other issues, like long-term poverty, women in the workplace and healthcare, to name a few. J. K. Galbraith's well-known book, *The Affluent Society*, follows this line of argument, proposing that in wealthy societies too many productive resources are devoted to private needs which ultimately do not contribute to the quality of life, and too few to important public resources (i.e. education and healthcare) that would. This trend seems to describe life in Ireland today.

What do we think of globalisation?

For the moment, though, it appears that Irish people do not associate social problems and issues like health with globalisation, but instead dwell on the economic benefits that it has brought. This was made clear in a special Eurobarometer[26] poll on globalisation in the spring of 2004, where the attitude of Irish people to globalisation was strikingly, but perhaps not surprisingly, positive.

The Irish (71% as compared to an EU average of 63%), Dutch and Germans are most favourably disposed to globalisation, as defined as the 'opening up of markets', while Spaniards and Austrians (40%) are the most pessimistic. Irish people are well aware of the phenomenon of globalisation, as 77% of them responded that they had heard of it (though 38% in the UK apparently had not).

The view that globalisation is positive for the domestic economy was understandably highest in Ireland (72%), and 'negative for the economy' the lowest at 22%, though only 48% of Irish people believed that their economy is adapted to globalisation and 24% felt that it was too closed. Similarly, the view that globalisation is positive for employment in Ireland was unsurprisingly the strongest in Europe at 63%.

Faced with the question 'If globalisation intensifies in the future would it be more or less advantageous?', Irish people had the most positive score in Europe – 66% versus an average of 52% – and only 23% of Irish people said it would be less advantageous. Similarly, two-thirds of Irish people believe that globalisation represents an opportunity rather than a threat, compared to only 56% of Europeans. The French feel most threatened by it (58%).

Up to 70% of Irish people believed that it could be possible for the process of globalisation to be effectively controlled and regulated. At the same time, 69% of Irish respondents felt that Ireland has not enough influence on globalisation (54% in the EU, 78% in Austria and 68% in Finland). In addition, 75% of Europeans believe that the US has too much influence over the process of globalisation.

It is therefore not surprising that Europeans turn towards the EU to counterbalance globalisation, with 61% of Europeans trusting the EU to ensure that globalisation follows the correct course. In Ireland, 76% of Irish people trust in the EU to make sure that globalisation goes in the right direction, which, together with Portugal, is the highest in the EU. Trust is lowest in the UK.

When asked 'Who benefits most from globalisation?', the pan-European responses came out in favour of multinationals (87%), financial markets (80%), the EU (77%), the US (76%), farmers (35%), and small and medium-sized companies (38%). There is also some appreciation of anti-globalist movements, which get credit for raising points that deserve to be debated (EU average 73% – Ireland had the highest score here of 78%), which raise awareness of certain issues (EU 63%) but fail to slow down globalisation (EU 58%) and which do not succeed in influencing political decision-making (EU 61%).

Good Europeans, proud Irish

To a large extent, Irish people and some academics tend to associate Ireland's successful experience of globalisation with its membership of the European Union, and recent survey evidence suggests that Irish people are as positive about membership of the EU as they are about globalisation, most probably because of the economic benefits that it has brought to Ireland.

The Eurobarometer country report on Ireland (Autumn 2004) showed that 77% of Irish people regard membership of the EU as a good thing, versus 56% for the European average.[27] In fact, over the course of 2004 there was a notable increase in the percentage of people who believe that Ireland has benefited from membership of the EU – from 80% to 87% – which is not surprising, given Ireland's successful stewardship of the EU Presidency. Moreover, 61% thought that Ireland is more influential in the EU now than it was ten years ago and 60% said it was more economically stable as a result of membership. The image of the EU in Ireland is generally a positive one, with 59% of the Eurobarometer respondents saying that the image of the EU in Ireland represents hope (versus an EU average of 47%), and only 4% said it represents mistrust (EU 18%).

However, as positive as Irish people are about the EU, they are much more proud to be Irish (78% said they are 'very proud' of their nationality versus an EU average of 45%). In addition, Irish people are more attached to their homeland than Europeans. Specifically, their sense of attachment to their country is higher than the EU average (80% versus 56%), but their attachment to Europe is the same as the broad EU average (23% versus 20%).

On the broad issue of the further integration of the EU's Member States, Irish people are less willing than the average to permit joint decision-making in the areas of immigration and refugees, and their two biggest fears arising out of integration were a transfer of jobs to other member countries and an increase in drug trafficking and crime. Conversely, there was a high level of support on the part of Irish people for joint decision-making on international terrorism, exploitation, foreign policy and humanitarian aid, though not on the issue of defence (59% believe that the government should control this).

Who are we now – European or Anglo-Saxon?

The previous sections of this chapter showed that Ireland is one of the most globalised countries in the world but that this trend is skewed towards economic factors and that Ireland's sharp economic upturn has not been matched by a commensurate improvement in social and development factors. At a very broad level, this kind of imbalance is emblematic of the image of an Anglo-Saxon country – a vibrant economy built at the expense of social development and cohesion, or the inverse of the European social model. It is a trend that suggests that Ireland is becoming more Anglo-Saxon than European.

Yet, the embrace of the Anglo-Saxon form of globalisation by Ireland and Irish people's positive attitude to the EU has yet to register as a contradiction, nor has it triggered a crisis of identity. The inconsistency in Irish people's resoundingly positive views on both globalisation and Europe is that in many continental European countries the path that Ireland has pursued in its economic progress would be regarded as neo-liberal and contrary to the European social model. However, Irish people display very little of the aversion to globalisation that is manifest in some other European states, and their attitude does not reflect the concerns of those who are discontented with globalisation. One such concern is that globalisation changes a country's identity and exports an Anglo-Saxon cultural and sociological orthodoxy.

Whether Ireland is influenced more by the European or Anglo-Saxon world is a crucial distinction and an important question. The emphasis on this distinction is not to ignore the presence of an indigenous Irish culture and way of life, but merely to track the influence of external factors on it. The next section describes how, because of its geography and history, Ireland has been less influenced by the key shared experiences of European history, while at the same time it is increasingly influenced by the social and cultural aspects of the Anglo-Saxon world.

Boston or Berlin?

The issue of the competing influences of the Anglo-Saxon and continental European worlds on Ireland has received scant attention in Irish public life. At the popular level, this issue is referred to as the 'Boston or Berlin debate', which questions whether Ireland is politically and culturally closer to the US or to Europe. What is missing from this question is whether Ireland is in fact closer to Britain than it is to either the US or to continental Europe, and where in the future it would like to be.

Ireland is a European country in terms of its geography, democracy and ancient and medieval history. Most of its cities were built by either the Norse or the Normans. The monasteries and scholarship of ancient Ireland were an integral part of the flow of ideas and religion in Europe. Despite this, Ireland has missed out on many of the crucial shared experiences that define the European project and mindset, and in this sense it is relatively less 'European'.

From the medieval period onwards, the occupation of Ireland spelled isolation, and the reality that it did not play a part in the significant European historical and intellectual movements from the fifteenth century onwards. Hale writes that, despite its acknowledged contribution to the early fortunes of Christianity, around the sixteenth century 'the Irish were coupled with the Russians as representing the parts of Europe into which the civilised virtues of decorous manners and rationally organised government had scarcely reached'.[28]

In his account of the new world (dis)order, Tzvetan Todorov[29] lists the following as marking the key events that European countries have in common: the civilisation of Greece and Rome, Christianity, common technologies, the Renaissance, colonial conquests, world wars, totalitarianism, Communism and Nazism. Further, Valéry Giscard D'Estaing, in drafting the new EU Constitution as President of the European Convention, emphasised the following as defining 'Europeanness': the cultural contributions of ancient Rome and Greece, the creative enthusiasm of the Renaissance, Europe's religious heritage, philosophy during the Enlightenment, and contributions of rational and scientific thought.[30] With the exception of a golden period in the seventh and eighth centuries, when scripts and missionaries from Irish monasteries maintained the vibrancy of the Christian and classical traditions around Europe, few of the above movements have had as profound an impact on public life in Ireland as they have in most other European countries. In fact, Ireland's Christianity is the main factor linking it to the European world. Excluding nationalism and the revolutionary examples of the American and French republics, Ireland has (thankfully in most cases) been inured to forces like totalitarianism that have dominated recent European history.

Daniel Cohen makes a similar point about the isolation of the Islamic world and China from the western world from the sixteenth century onwards, when he says that 'renaissance, reformation and scientific revolution went unseen',[31] with the result that innovations in politics, technology and philosophy failed to prosper. The same argument could be applied to a long stretch of Irish history. Ireland has missed out on these experiences largely because of its occupation, something which in turn has left a heavy Anglo-Saxon footprint on cultural and social life. The point here is that globalisation is exacerbating this effect.

Boston, or just Birmingham?

A telling benchmark is to examine policy-making. Economic policy in Ireland has broadly followed the Anglo-Saxon framework (e.g. deregulation, credit growth and tax reduction), foreign policy has followed the paths beaten by the large Anglo-Saxon countries and Ireland much more resembles the Anglo-Saxon countries than the continental European ones when issues like labour market regulation and inequality are taken into consideration.

Given these trends, placing Ireland in the Anglo-Saxon camp is appropriate, though to compare it to Boston is to flatter it. Boston is known for the excellence of its well-funded educational institutions, the high levels of research and development of its industries and its excellent transport infrastructure, all of which are notably absent in Ireland. Instead of drawing parallels with Boston, perhaps a more accurate comparison is with a middle-ranking region of Britain.

It is one of the great ironies and disappointments of Irish life that, while anti-Britishness has often been widely and loudly expressed, independent Ireland has continued to imitate British life, no more so than in the past decade, when many of the things that are unattractive in English society have been willingly imported into Ireland. It could be argued that what Britain and Ireland have most in common are excesses like binge drinking,[32] poor diet, large income and wealth inequalities, anti-social behaviour, drug-related crime, house price bubbles and rampant consumerism, to name a few that are not manifest to the same extent in most continental European countries.

Irish city centres increasingly resemble those of Manchester or Glasgow rather than Paris or Madrid, choked by the spread of UK chain stores. There is a strong sense that Ireland is also becoming more materialistic, a trend that is supported by evidence from consumption patterns and levels of indebtedness. The Irish and English have an increasingly shared popular culture. From boy and girl bands, to the intake from the Murdoch media, and a common appetite for the output of the US entertainment industry, the differences between these cultures are closing.

In sport, the preponderance of Irish players playing in the English Premiership and the huge extent to which English football (as opposed to other leagues in Spain and Italy) is followed in Ireland is one of many shared tastes. With notable exceptions,[33] Irish footballers seem to share the aversion of English players to European leagues, and tend not to succeed in these 'foreign' lands. While the rising popularity of other Anglo-Saxon sports amongst the Irish sporting audience, rugby for example, has much to do with the success of Irish athletes in these events, it nevertheless cements a common cultural bond. It must be said of course that neither domestic sports (GAA) nor the Irish language seem to have suffered as a result of the encroaching Anglo-Saxon element into Irish culture and may in fact have been spurred on by the competition from abroad.

Again at the government level, the Irish and English governments share an aversion to spending money on important public goods like healthcare and education, relative to their European peers. In these areas, France, Germany and Sweden all spend twice as much as Ireland and the UK. Also, both governments' ability to spend sensibly and efficiently on infrastructure is unconvincing.[34]

Social, labour market and economic policy in Ireland largely resemble those of its closest neighbour, in that taxes are low, the tax wedge (effectively the tax and social contribution of both employer and employee) is the lowest in the EU 15, social welfare payments are heavily means-tested, social spending is low compared to continental European countries, the labour market is lightly regulated and there remain barriers to the full participation of women in the economy.

In addition, on many key issues Ireland is becoming less compliant with broad EU policy and in recent years has given the impression of being Britain's lieutenant in Brussels, as the policy stances that the two nations have adopted on a range of issues (legal issues, crime and economic policy) are very similar.

Through Irish Eyes

Cultural, political and social similarities are reflected in attitudes. Importantly, there is now a growing view that the English do not regard the Irish as 'foreigners'. For instance, a recent paper for the British Council stated that 'the great majority of the British feel more identity with the Irish than with other Europeans, and indeed most do not feel that the Irish are foreigners'.[35] Many continental Europeans also view Ireland as part of the 'British Isles', or more broadly as Anglo-Saxon.

Similarly, the Through Irish Eyes survey conducted for the British Council/British Embassy in Dublin revealed a change in the way Irish people regard Britain and the Anglo-Saxon world. Irish people felt most familiar with the UK and the US (75% and 71% respectively), compared to France (47%) and Germany (38%). According to the survey, most think that Anglo-Irish relations are good to excellent, and that they have improved in the last ten years. Almost none think that they have worsened.

When posed the 'Boston or Berlin' question, 73% said Ireland was closer to Boston, and only 16% said it was closer to Berlin. As regards the EU, 54% felt that Ireland is not influential in Europe, but do think it is more constructive in Europe than Britain is.

The Sellafield nuclear plant is apparently the most controversial issue between Ireland and England, with 72% feeling that there is a lot of room for improvement in relations regarding this issue. About 60% think that there is some room for improvement in matters relating to Northern Ireland. Almost 70% are in favour of a united Ireland, but only 36% think that it will happen at earliest in the next ten years.

In terms of culture, Irish people are most familiar with UK pop music, films and books and least familiar with classical music, artists and dance. In turn, Irish journalists, writers and entertainers are increasingly successful in Britain, more so than they are in either continental Europe or the US.

A follow-up study[36] to the Through Irish Eyes report in 2005 found that 60% of Irish people identify the UK as the country Ireland has most in common with, compared to 21% for the US, 4% for Australia and 3% for France.

Why is it important?
Whether Ireland is more influenced by the Anglo-Saxon or the European worlds is a central theme running through its experience of globalisation. The evidence supports the view that socially and culturally, even though there is an Irish exception in terms of its indigenous culture, it is increasingly influenced by the Anglo-Saxon world, especially as globalisation advances. Even if Ireland is European culturally, then it is best categorised as a 'New' rather than 'Old' European country. Given that the globalisation process is frequently criticised for emasculating indigenous cultures and spreading Anglo-Saxon values, the emergence of such a trend in Ireland confirms this critique.

If this is indeed the case, as most data, survey and anecdotal evidence would bear out, it is worrying from several perspectives. First, having achieved political independence from Britain through a number of manoeuvres, including EU membership, the irony is that Ireland now seems to be embracing it socially and culturally, and there is a strong case to be made that Ireland is only embracing the worst aspects of British life at that. While the cultural closeness of Ireland to England is pointed to by some as a sign of Irish self-confidence and a conscious effort on the part of English and Irish people to mend their previously difficult relationship, it nevertheless betrays the fact that culturally the Irish feel most at home in an Anglo-Saxon environment.

Secondly, there appears to be a very low level of awareness of the downside of Anglo-Saxon cultural and social norms, even though these are beginning to manifest themselves in a less fraternal and more unequal and ugly society. Thirdly, the lack of a serious debate on whether Ireland is more Anglo-Saxon or European underlines the lack of a vision as to the kind of society that is desired in the long term. What is its peer group of the future? Is Ireland happy to resemble a region of Great Britain, or does it have more ambitious designs on a new peer group. The need for such a debate is all the greater in the light of the great transformation ongoing in Irish society and public life.

Although the Anglo-Saxon nature of globalisation in Ireland contradicts its so far successful membership of the EU and the influence of Catholicism in Ireland, it has to date suited Ireland to have the best of Anglo-Saxon and European worlds. However, as the effects of globalisation become more pronounced, it may have to choose between one of these models. That Ireland's tilt towards the Anglo-Saxon world comes at a critical time for the European project is perhaps no coincidence. If in future Europe integrates on a deeper basis, then Ireland will face a difficult choice of whether to join the core countries that pursue further integration, or whether to remain in the political periphery of 'New European' countries.

Conclusion

Measuring globalisation is difficult, especially in the case of Ireland, where rapid social and economic change, as well as some data collection issues, makes it hard to get an overview of the progress of globalisation. However, most economic data and a number of surveys place Ireland at the head of the most globalised league table. Yet, the globalisation of Ireland is lop-sided, with the economic element well advanced and the social and developmental aspects falling behind. This broad trend is emblematic of other Anglo-Saxon economies.

Despite this, survey evidence suggests that Irish people are very well disposed towards globalisation as well as membership of the EU, most probably because they associate both factors with Ireland's strong economic performance. Yet, the economics literature on happiness suggests that the idea that globalisation will lead to better, happier lives for Irish people may well fall short of expectations, as issues like inequality and healthcare show few signs of improving.

Irish people's positive disposition towards globalisation betrays few of the worries that other Europeans and anti-globalisers have about it. One such concern is that globalisation erodes the identity of individual nations and communities. Ireland's delicate position balanced between the Anglo-Saxon and European worlds makes it an interesting case study of how globalisation affects identity. To date, most evidence suggests that it is becoming more Anglo-Saxon than European, to the extent that it could easily be described as Europe's leading 'New European' country.

Chapter Three

Views of unglobalised Ireland

'If instead of an expedition to Egypt, I had made one to Ireland, what would England be today?' Napoleon Bonaparte on St Helena[1]

In terms of its interaction with the rest of the world over the past century, Ireland has gone from being one of the most poor and isolated of countries to the most globalised nation. It is this speedy and dramatic change that makes the case of globalisation in Ireland a very interesting one. This chapter takes a brief detour away from globalisation in the twenty-first century to pass through nineteenth-century Ireland, the aim being to highlight how little it benefited during a century when international trade and commerce were flourishing. In turn the picture painted of Ireland in the nineteenth century makes its recent economic growth more remarkable.

Ireland's experience before and during the first period of globalisation was very different to the current one. During the first wave of globalisation, Ireland was politically isolated and had little means of enjoying the benefits of globalisation. For example, the ratio of Ireland's GDP per capita relative to that of Britain was 0.74 times in 1500, 0.63 in 1600, 0.57 in 1700 and 0.51 by 1850,[2] remaining at 0.56 times from 1870 to 1913. This ratio stayed close to 0.5 up until the 1970s, meaning that for most of the last three centuries Britain was twice as wealthy as Ireland on a per capita basis. Comparisons with other European countries reveal a similar, though slightly less unequal, picture over time. However, from 1974 the ratio of Irish output to that of Britain moved from a level of 0.74 to 1.15 by 2001.

The only way in which Ireland really figured in the first wave of globalisation was as a contributor to human flows. The scale of the change in its population during the nineteenth century was enormous. Consider that in 1500 Ireland had a larger population than each of the Nordic countries and a similar one to that of Greece and Portugal. Yet, by 1820 Ireland's population had increased seven times to 7.1 million, such that it had a population greater than the combined populations of the Netherlands, Greece and Portugal, almost three times the population of Sweden, close on twice the population of Brazil (4.5 million in 1820) and again greater than that of Iran (6 million). Ireland's population peaked at around 8.5 million in 1845, but dropped to 6.3 million by 1852 and then to 5 million by 1870. In 1921, there were only 3 million people living in Ireland.

There are a great many historical accounts that add colour to the above trends as they track Irish history in the nineteenth century and the subsequent drive towards independence. This chapter does not seek to repeat or reinterpret these accounts but to highlight some of the reasons for Ireland's economic and political isolation from the rest of the world by referring to four of the great thinkers whose work has influenced world history (Adam Smith, Alexis de Tocqueville, Friedrich Engels and Karl Marx) and still informs the debate on globalisation.

Left and right

Marx, Engels and Adam Smith are today viewed as coming from, if not having created, two ends of the intellectual spectrum in political economy. To this end, proponents of globalisation tend to call upon Smith to give credibility to their arguments, while anti-globalists are most likely to fall back upon Marx. As with many other cases where the views of historical figures are drawn upon to justify events that occur after their lives, Marx and Smith may not have been entirely comfortable with what currently passes for Marxism or free trade theory, respectively. However, on the question of Ireland it seems that they shared a case that validated their work, and towards which they felt much sympathy. Together with Tocqueville, these influential writers were largely sympathetic to the cause of Ireland, and their work helps to make the point that, in contrast to today, it suffered during the nineteenth century and before. The rest of this chapter follows the thoughts of these four thinkers as they take up the case of Ireland around the nineteenth century, starting with Adam Smith.

Adam Smith

At the end of the eighteenth century, England was faced with hostility from France, America and Spain and the fomentation of rebellion in Ireland. With the formation of the United Irishmen in 1791, Irish public life reached a certain level of maturity and became more singular in purpose. At this time, the Irish economy was weak, partly because of the array of restrictions placed upon it by London. The classic British mercantilism that grew out of the post-Westphalian political environment and the Industrial Revolution was strongly in favour of exports, but hostile to imports and foreigners. In the face of mounting pressure from within Ireland for the repeal of these trade restrictions, and furious opposition to this move from English merchants, the members of the Board of Trade decided to seek the opinion of Adam Smith (at this stage Smith's book *The Wealth of Nations* was well known and well regarded) on whether free trade with Ireland would necessarily hurt the fortunes of England.

Smith's replies are classic examples of his defence of free trade and echo many of the arguments on free trade that make up the wider debate on globalisation today. The letter that Smith wrote to Lord Carlisle, the President of the Board of Trade, outlines some of the trade restrictions placed on Ireland and acknowledges that the motivation for these barriers came from British merchants.[3]

> At present they (Irish) can export glass, tho' of their own manufacture, to no country whatever. Raw silk, a foreign commodity, is under the same restraint. Wool they can export only to Great Britain. Woollen manufactures they can export only from certain ports in Ireland to certain ports in Great Britain. The watchful jealousy of those gentlemen is alarmed lest the Irish, who have never been able to supply completely even their own market with glass or woollen manufactures, should be able to rival them in foreign markets.[4]

> The Irish probably mean to demand no more than this most just and reasonable freedom of exportation and importation; in restraining which we seem to me rather to have gratified the impertinence than to have promoted any solid interest of our merchants and manufacturers.[5]

Such inequitable terms of trade persist today, as underlined by Rodrik: 'the African Growth and Opportunity Act signed by US President Clinton in May 2000 provides increased access to the US market only if African apparel manufacturers use US produced fabric and yarns'.[6]

Smith then defends the principle of free trade as it applies to the Irish case, pointing out that free trade tends to increase both the level of trade and overall wealth, and is therefore beneficial to both parties.

> I cannot believe that the interest of Britain would be hurt by it. On the contrary, the competition of Irish goods in the British market might contribute to break down in part that monopoly which we have most absurdly granted to the greater part of our own workmen against ourselves. It would, however, be a long time before this competition could be very considerable. In the present state of Ireland centuries must pass away before the greater part of its manufactures could vie with those of England. Ireland has little coal, it is ill provided with wood: two articles essentially necessary to the progress of

great manufactures. It wants order, police, and a regular administration of justice, both . . . articles more essential to the progress of industry than both coal and wood put together.[7]

Smith's emphasis on the importance of legal and physical order is as relevant to this case as it was to the Russian and South-East Asian economies eight years ago.

In a letter to Henry Dundas, he also points to lobbying by English merchants as the main source of opposition to fair trade with Ireland, and underlines his preference for more open trade for Ireland:

> Whatever the Irish mean to demand in this way, in the present situation of our affairs I should think it madness not to grant it. Whatever they may demand, our manufacturers, unless the leading and principal men among them are properly dealt with beforehand, will probably oppose it.[8]

> Nothing, in my opinion, would be more highly advantageous to both countries than this mutual freedom of trade. It would help to break down that absurd monopoly which we have most absurdly established against ourselves in favour of almost all the different Classes of our own manufacturers.[9]

In this case the parallels with today's powerful industrial lobby groups in Washington are clear and have been reflected in the work of contemporary analysts of international trade.

Although Smith opined on the issue of free trade for Ireland some years before the Act of Union, he was in favour of union between Ireland and England, though the form of union he had in mind bore little relation to that imposed in 1801. The rationale for Smith's union was more like that of today's European Union. He believed that union would end the agitation between oppressed and oppressors and that free trade between them would increase the collective wealth. Smith's vision of the union was ambitious, stretching to a form that would encompass all of England's dependencies in a federal setting with home rule by local assemblies. He envisaged that members for America might sit in an imperial parliament and that, if the centre of power of the Empire moved towards America, then the parliament could move there too. As it has turned out, this is effectively what has happened to the Anglo-Saxon world, with the capital city of globalisation moving from London to New York.

Tocqueville

After Smith's pronouncements on Ireland and a little time before Marx and Engels addressed themselves to its problems, Alexis de Tocqueville passed through Ireland with Gustave de Beaumont in July and August 1835. Alexis de Tocqueville is best known for his work *Democracy in America*, a two-tome study of American social and public life whose analysis remains telling today. The two men had planned that Beaumont would write on Ireland, but Tocqueville also kept detailed notes of his interviews and observations, which have been translated and edited by Emmet Larkin of the University of Chicago.

The picture that Tocqueville paints of the desolation he found is striking and incisive. Larkin comments that the three themes to emerge from Tocqueville's writings on Ireland are: the poverty of the people, their hatred of the aristocracy and their faith in the clergy. All three are evident in this account of what faced Tocqueville on entering Cork:

> The entry into Cork is very fine. The merchants quarter is handsome. In the suburbs are squalid dwellings and a population more horrible still, such as one can find only in Ireland. The Catholic bishop lives in a little house in the middle of this quarter. The shepherd in the middle of his flock.[10]

Other remarks underline just how brutal life was. In a letter to his father he comments: 'what a complexity of miseries five centuries of oppression, civil disorders and religious hostility have piled up on this poor people'.[11] He describes a village in Carlow: 'most of the dwellings of the country very poor looking. A very large number of them wretched to the last degree. Walls of mud, roofs of thatch, one room. No chimney, smoke goes out the door. The pig lies in the middle of the house . . . the population looks very wretched.'[12] He comments that, unlike its neighbour England, the country had little or no means of production: 'In that part of Ireland there is no manufacturing, no industry, the people have only the land to live off, and, as they are accustomed at all times to live on the least that a man can subsist on, when a man has no land he really faces death.'[13]

Like the republicans who preceded him in America and France, Tocqueville was an advocate of democracy and strong institutions, as exemplified in the many voluntary associations growing up in America in the mid-nineteenth century, which he believed supported equality and fraternity. Tocqueville is also known for having invented the word 'individualism', which he took to mean excessive self-reliance and pursuit of private interests to the neglect of broad communitarian ones. In nineteenth-century Ireland, he observed this in practice, and is highly critical of the Irish aristocracy for their selfishness, poor leadership and contempt for the common people.

In the Ireland he visited there was a sharp divide between these two sections of society. His comparisons of the conditions in a Dublin work-house, 'the most hideous and disgusting aspect of destitution',[14] with those in Trinity College, and of the conditions that the people of Mitch-elstown had to contend with versus those of the estate of Lord Kingston, emphasise the gross difference in wealth between the classes. Inequality was largely a function of the prevailing system of ownership and distrib-ution of land, something that Marx would later point out. Most of the productive land was divided into large estates, and any land held or rented by small farmers was subject to crippling tariffs.

The main and perhaps only source of fraternity for the Irish was the Church, as represented by their local curate. Tocqueville observed that, unlike other European countries such as his own, the majority of Irish people were religious and in general moral. The priest, who usually lived amongst them, was their leader, spiritually and often materially. Liberty was in rare supply. In Tocqueville's words, 'there is no justice in Ireland. Nearly all the local magistrates are at open war with the populace.'[15]

Engels and Marx

Tocqueville's journey through Ireland was followed over twenty years later by one by Friedrich Engels, who visited Ireland again in 1869. Poverty, hostility from a series of European governments and poor health prevented Engels' collaborator Karl Marx from making a visit to Ireland. Despite this, Marx and Engels were very interested in the Irish case and an account of their letters, speeches and essays on Ireland was first pub-lished in Moscow in 1970.[16]

Around the time of Engels' first visit to Ireland, signs of economic globalisation were beginning to show around the world. Ireland, how-ever, had just emerged from the Famine. Whereas in 1820 its popula-tion was just below that of the US (7.1 million in Ireland versus 9.9 in America and 21 million in Britain), the population of Ireland only numbered over 6 million by 1850 (America and Britain had grown to 23 million and 27 million respectively). The social and economic devastation of Ireland drew a response from Marx and Engels, who with characteristic flair remarked, 'how often have the Irish set out to achieve something and each time been crushed, politically and indus-trially . . . Ireland has been stunted in her development by the English invasion and thrown centuries back'.[17]

The 'iron hand'

Engels had gathered together many detailed notes on Irish history. He shows a thorough understanding of early Irish history and describes the origins of the Irish in a manner that comes close to accounts offered by the likes of O'Rahilly (1971).

Marx and Engels' writings on Ireland centre on a period of time that marked the beginning of Ireland's emergence from wretchedness to modernity. Their work helps to make clear why Ireland did not part-icipate in the first wave of globalisation, and also why Ireland's example is relevant to many poorer countries today. Above all, the account that Engels and Marx give of post-Famine Ireland is of a country isolated from the positive influences of an enlightened and modernising world, with the 'iron hand visible in every nook and cranny, the government meddles in everything'.[18]

The detailed approach that Marx took towards analysing the Irish economy was not common at the time and his case study of Ireland in relation to England provided a sizeable part of the basis for his discourses on the means of production.[19] The irony is that his classification of an economic system into owners of production/capital and labour has shaped the history of many countries and continues to be a relevant frame of reference in most European political systems, but it has never really caught on in Ireland. Although socialism had flourished across continental Europe, in Ireland its development was impeded by the power of the Church, the agrarian nature of Irish society and the power of nationalism as the overriding political force.

The National Question

There is a strong nationalistic flavour to Marx and Engels' writings on Ireland. Their view of Ireland and the Irish was sympathetic, 'In addition he (the Irishman) bears the burden of five centuries of oppression with all its consequences . . . starving Ireland is writhing in the most terrible convulsions',[20] though at times unembellished: 'the Irishman is a care-free, cheerful, potato-eating child of nature'.[21]

Throughout their writings on Ireland both Marx and Engels show themselves to be what we would now call 'sound' on the National Question. In a letter to Engels regarding a public meeting about the Fenians, Marx wrote: 'our subject, Fenianism, was liable to inflame the passions to such heat that I would have been forced to hurl revolution-ary thunderbolts instead of soberly analysing the state of affairs and the movement as I had intended'.[22]

Engels spent some time chastising Daniel O'Connell, a 'cunning old lawyer', and in a reference to O'Connell's many followers said, 'one who has never seen Irishmen cannot know them. Give me two hundred thousand Irishmen and I will overthrow the entire British monarchy.'[23] He went on to say, 'how much could have been done if a sensible man possessed O'Connell's popularity or if O'Connell had a little more understanding and a little less egoism and vanity'.

Their understanding of Irish politicians is remarkably astute and has much to offer to analysts of contemporary Irish politics: 'one more thing should be thoroughly noted about Ireland: never praise a single Irishman – a politician – unreservedly, and never identify yourself with him before he is dead'.[24] In addition, Engels and Marx were also untiring in their exposure of the brutal manner in which Irish prisoners were treated in English jails, vividly describing the treatment of the likes of O'Donovan Rossa.[25]

The influence of the work of Marx and Engels on much of the world is still visible today, and remains relevant to the debate on globalisation. Their analysis of the Irish Question is no exception, providing us with universal truths such as 'there is something rotten in the very core of a social system which increases its wealth without diminishing its misery'.[26]

Another contribution of Marx and Engels is to internationalise the Irish Question, by setting events in Ireland in the context of international politics at the time. Two of the international events to touch the hearts and minds of the Irish were the French and American revolutions in the late eighteenth century, and these are drawn upon by Marx and Engels, acknowledging for instance that the fear that the English had of emerging republics in France and America led them to suppress the revolt in Ireland more fiercely.

Ireland and capitalism

The manner in which Marx presented a detailed, data-intensive analysis of the Irish Question served not only to aid his presentation of the struggle between the owners of capital and labour, but was unique for the way in which it studied the problems of the Irish. For Marx, the case of Ireland demonstrated the malign influence exerted by what was then the classic capitalist country, England, and provided him with the data from which he arrived at his theories on production. In his eyes, England was 'the metropolis of landlordism and capitalism all over the world'.[27]

In the emerging global economy of the second half of the nineteenth century, Marx saw that Ireland was forced to contribute cheap labour and capital to building up the productive capacity of Britain. Ireland was 'only an agricultural district of England, marked off by a wide channel from the country to which it yields corn, wool, cattle, industrial and military recruits'.[28]

Marx's data contributes to a scientific analysis of Irish history, especially the period around the Famine, and by presenting data in a scientific and rigorous manner he renders the problems that faced Ireland all the more starkly. For instance, Marx presents a detailed picture of emigration. He writes that in the period 1855–1866 '1,032,694 Irishmen were displaced by 996,877 head of cattle'.[29] Between 1847 and 1852, some 1.6 million people left England, Ireland, Scotland and Wales, but almost 80% of this exodus was comprised of Irish people. The sad reality is that this level of misery did not reflect itself in the overall wealth of the country, as a harsh article in *The Economist* pointed out:

> The departure of the redundant part of the population of Ireland and the Highlands of Scotland is an indispensable preliminary to every kind of improvement . . . The revenue of Ireland has not suffered in any degree from the famine of 1848–49, or the emigration that has taken place. On the contrary, her net revenue amounted in 1851 to £4.3m about 200k greater than in 1843.[30]

Marx took against this view, presenting a different perspective on the same phenomenon: 'the Irish famine killed more than 1m people, but it killed poor devils only. To the wealth of the country it did not the slightest damage.'[31] Much of what Marx believed about Ireland was at sharp variance with the views of some of the proponents of liberal economics, like David Ricardo. Marx criticised the views of Ricardo as they applied to Ireland: 'now I share neither the opinion of Ricardo who regards "Net Revenue" as the Moloch to whom entire populations must be sacrificed'.[32] These disagreements persist today, with modern-day debates on globalisation setting Marx against Ricardo and Adam Smith.

Marx was also sensitive to the effect of poverty on the mental health of the Irish and to levels of crime. He wrote that 'insanity has made such a terrific progress among them (the Irish)' and documents the rise in admissions to lunatic asylums of 2,584 people (roughly split equally between men and women) in 1851, 2,662 in 1852 and 2,870 in 1853.[33] The level of crime in Ireland, or at least the prosecution of crimes, rose and fell with poverty and population levels. In 1844 there were 19,448 people committed for trial, 38,552 in 1848, and 42,000 in 1849, dropping to 9,000 by 1855.

Marx identified the ownership of land as the crucial political issue. He wrote that 'in Ireland the land question has hitherto been the exclusive form of the social question because it is a question of existence, of life and death . . . inseparable from the national question'.[34] Judging by data highlighted by Marx it is not hard to see why this was so. In 1864 there were 176,000 farms of between 5 and 15 acres, 136,000 farms of between 15 and 30 acres and only 31,000 farms of a size greater than 100 acres. Thus, according to his figures, approximately 6% of all farms comprised some 30% of all land farmed.

Overall, Marx and Engels' analysis of Ireland in the middle of the nineteenth century helps to support the argument that it was economically impoverished and politically secluded, and that Ireland's only real contribution to globalisation was its massive human outflow, principally to the US. The Irish had little to no stake in the wave of globalisation that swept the world in the latter half of the nineteenth century. To put an end to Ireland's misery, Marx prescribed self-governance, independence from England, combined with an agrarian revolution and protective tariffs against England, many of the factors that would be put in place in the early years of the state in the context of a post-globalised protectionist world.

It is also interesting to note that, while in 1869 Marx called for the introduction of protective tariffs by Ireland on England, Smith's solution some eighty years earlier was to allow Ireland to enjoy free trade. Perhaps this difference of opinion is explained by the utter unwillingness of London to attend to the welfare of the Irish in the period between Smith's death and 1869. Yet, both Smith and Marx' analyses recognised that to be genuinely independent Ireland would have to be economically independent. For the free hand of the market to prevail, the 'iron hand' of occupation had first to be removed.

Conclusion

The brief accounts of Ireland by Smith, Tocqueville, Engels and Marx show how deprived and politically isolated Ireland was before and during the first period of globalisation. In the terms that we use to describe globalisation today, integration and interdependence, it is difficult to argue against the facts that Ireland was politically and economically dependent on Britain, enjoyed little benefit from the trade that flowed into its ports, and was not free to integrate itself with the social and political forces permeating Europe.

The accounts presented here also serve to emphasise the fact that Ireland in the nineteenth century resembled the state of numerous lesser developed countries today, many of which are correctly portrayed as victims of the globalisation process. Like many under-developed countries today, Ireland was politically powerless on the international stage, it suffered unfair terms of trade, capital was scarce to all but a few powerful merchants and in general the rules of the first world were set against it. Poverty was widespread, inequality was severe (ironically this was improved by the huge levels of emigration) and land ownership was the central political economic issue. By the same token, these accounts help to paint a background that makes the current turnaround in Ireland's fortunes all the more remarkable, not least because of the way in which Ireland's relative poverty persisted into the late 1980s.

Chapter Four

The Tiger

'The worst about the Irish is that they become corruptible as soon as they stop being peasants and turn bourgeois.'[1] Friedrich Engels

'We are neither prisoners of the left nor hostages of the right but pragmatists of the centre.' Charles Haughey

If Friedrich Engels seems to have had some foresight regarding the role that commerce would play in Irish political life, then so too it appears did Charles Haughey and some of his cohorts. However, there is little evidence to suggest that he or indeed any other Irish politician foresaw the extent of the growth in Ireland's economy that was manifest towards the end of the twentieth century (by 2003, the gross national product in real terms was five times the level it was at in 1960).[2] Very few commentators, politicians or external bodies are on record as forecasting that the Irish economy in the mid-1980s and 1990s would deliver continued above-average growth.

Forecasting and understanding the performance of the Irish economy has been made difficult by the fact that it has no single determining factor. Instead, the Irish boom is the result of a mixture, or system, of domestic and international factors. A consensus has emerged that identifies the main domestic factors in this mix as Ireland's education system, credit growth, the role of the IDA, Ireland's membership of the EU and its flexible labour market.

Yet most of these factors were in place during some of the bleakest years for the Irish economy, as well as the best. To a large degree they were triggered by outside factors, principally by the falling cost of capital, the trend towards the opening up of international markets and trade, diminished geo-political risk and the advent of new technologies – all of the ingredients of what are now taken to drive economic globalisation. The secret behind the Irish economic recovery of the 1990s, if there is one, lies in the confluence of domestic or endogenous factors with powerful secular external trends. It is this stew of variables that makes Ireland's case a fascinating one.

Crystal balls

Owing to this complexity, much of the language used to describe the economic globalisation of Ireland betrays the surprise of analysts outside and within Ireland. The fact that the word 'miracle'[3] is still used does not give sufficient credit to either globalisation or domestic policy-makers, although it does underline the sudden leap forward in Ireland's economic performance.

However, even a cursory understanding of financial markets and a brief look at the history of economics show that professional economists can rarely forecast economic booms and busts, and even when they do, they are usually so few in number or so at odds with consensus opinion that their advice is not acted upon. This is one reason that there is a well-known tendency for markets to overshoot their equilibrium levels, the sharp rise in equity prices in the late 1990s and their subsequent collapse being a good case in point.

Similarly, deep fault lines in economies can lie unseen by experts and markets, if the collapse of the Japanese economy in the early 1990s is anything to go by. Japan had become the model economy of the 1980s, with many western economists devoting themselves to discovering the secret of its success. Yet, as a study by economists at the US Federal Reserve argues,[4] relatively few western and Japanese policy-makers, as well as market participants, heralded the deflation of the Japanese economy in the 1990s and, even where they did recognise the weaknesses in the Japanese economic system, they denied that these would ever lead to such a painful correction.

Pre-globalisation

If, as in the cases of the Japanese economic collapse and the recent stock market boom, economists made their forecasts by extrapolating history into the future, then the long run of Irish economic history promised little to be excited about. As the previous chapter underlined, with help from prominent economists like Marx and Smith, Ireland's economy before and during the first wave of globalisation in the late nineteenth century was undeveloped and indeed remained 'pre-industrial' for much of the twentieth century. The north-east of the country was the only industrialised region. Independence, achieved soon after the first period of globalisation ended, came at a time when the international political economic environment was dominated by nationalism and protectionism and was beset by poor economic fundamentals.

As a result, although Ireland is now considered to be one of the world's most open economies, it was one of the more protected and isolated for significant parts of the last century. This trend was exacerbated by high tariffs and other protectionist policies from the 1930s to the 1960s. While the commentaries of both Adam Smith and Karl Marx on the crippling restrictions imposed on Ireland help us to understand the political motivation behind the drive towards self-sufficiency, it is generally accepted that the recognition by the Lemass government that the Irish economy needed to be internationalised was sensible. This was pursued through the Anglo-Irish Trade Agreement in 1965, entry to the EEC in 1973 and a more focused programme of national development.

Despite this, the Irish economy of the early 1980s, and indeed most of the twentieth century, offered little indication as to what would be achieved in the 1990s. The economic and social environment in 1980s Ireland was miserable. Unemployment peaked above 17% in 1985[5] and many foreign multinationals were leaving Ireland. Joe Lee's assessment of the country in the late 1980s makes for depressing reading: 'no other European country . . . has recorded so slow a rate of growth of national income in the twentieth century'.[6]

Some of the reasons Lee puts forward for how 'Ireland achieved and sustained this level of relative retardation'[7] relate to culture, politics and policy-making. He underlines the fact that, compared to other small European states, Ireland had few entrepreneurs and skilled managers and was poorly equipped to think its way out of under-development. According to him, one particular problem was the lack of educated and experienced policy-makers in the areas of economics and foreign policy.

Reversal of fortune
Looking back at this and other accounts of the Irish economy in the 1980s in the light of its current strength begs the question 'What has changed?', both at home and abroad. With this in mind, the first part of this chapter (Part I) outlines most of the domestic and international factors whose chemistry has driven the Irish economy, with a view to examining the extent to which Ireland's economic miracle has been determined by external globalising forces or by virtue of the quality of domestic factors and policy-making. In doing so, the aim is to demystify Ireland's economic growth and in most cases point out the illusions and contradictions that lie behind it. The intention is not to take away from Ireland's success but to remove the illusion of a miracle. This makes it easier for others to learn from the Irish case, and for Irish policy-makers to appraise the bases upon which success is built.

This process will also make it more straightforward to identify whether or not there is a discernible Irish model of economic growth, which if imported by other countries will deliver sustainable growth. Following on from this, the question of whether Ireland's economic boom is domestically or globally determined is very important for the future. If it is largely the result of external factors, then the long-term future of the Irish economy is on much less sound footing than if this growth is the result of good domestic policy-making. The middle part (Part II) of this chapter focuses on these issues by discussing whether there is an Irish economic model.

The next sections focus on the future (Parts III and IV), and in particular confront the limited and difficult policy options ahead. Steering a small globalised economy is a difficult task, made even more demanding when that country is at the mercy of powerful outside forces, and when many of the normal mechanisms used to marshal economic performance, such as monetary policy, are no longer available. The innovative use of microeconomic policy in a globalised economic environment may be one of the ways in which Irish policy-makers can distinguish themselves, particularly given the range of new challenges that are likely to face the Irish economy in the future, from asset bubbles to declining competitiveness.

Part I – The secrets behind the secrets of success

A detailed assessment of the performance of the Irish economy can lead in two potential directions. The first is to conclude that the outperformance of the Irish economy was long overdue, and that the welcome forces of globalisation have now merely delivered it to the level of wealth that it would have had if it had followed the trajectory of average European economic growth since the end of the Second World War. Indeed, O'Grada holds that the value of Irish output would be some 28% higher if it had had the same growth rate as Italy since 1950.[8] In this view, the only extraordinary element of the reversal in Ireland's fortunes is that it has taken so long to arrive.

A second, less critical, view, the tone of which is reflected in some texts,[9] is that the surprising performance of the Irish economy in the 1990s is largely the result of inspired Irish policy-making. This outlook errs towards the view that Irish 'genius', and much less events in the outside world, is the secret of Ireland's economic success.

The validity of the above views hinges on whether the successful globalisation of the Irish economy happened by design from Dublin or by default through the considerable influence of outside factors. The next section considers the system of domestic and international factors that are held to have contributed to the turnaround in the Irish economy, with an aim to demystifying their role in it. The domestic factors considered are Ireland's education system, its ability to attract foreign investment, its labour force, its institutional infrastructure, the expansion of credit and finally the role that its politicians have played.

Education

One of the most frequently cited reasons for the fact that foreign companies are drawn to Ireland is its well-educated workforce. Education is widely acknowledged by commentators and policy-makers[10] to be a driver of long-term economic performance. As regards the case of Ireland, there is some truth and a little illusion in this.

The key contributions from Irish education policy as regards economic performance have been a relative concentration on scientific and engineering qualifications and an opening up of access to higher education at university and vocational levels. The educational background of the Irish population has improved steadily over the past thirty years. For example, in 1960 an Irish citizen would spend an average of 6.5 years in school, but this rose to 7.6 by 1980 and 9 years in 1999.[11] In parallel, the percentage of people in the labour force with a third-level education increased from 11% in 1981 to 18% in 1991 (free access to third-level education was granted in 1987) and is now close to 35% (31% males, 38% females). The performance of Irish students in maths and science literacy tests is now close to the EU average, and reading literacy is above the European average.

However, wider access to education seems to have created an illusion of deeper and better education. Though the Irish education system and the skills it has imparted to the Irish labour force are almost always invoked to explain the attractiveness of Ireland as an investment location, Irish governments over the last thirty years have spent little more per capita on education than the European average. In fact, governments in the 1970s and 1980s spent more on education as a proportion of GDP than those in the 1990s, although it is likely that the benefits of spending on education in the 1980s were reaped in the 1990s. The NCC (National Competitiveness Council) reports of 2004 and 2005[12] underlined the fact that public and private investment in education was only 5.4% of GNP (or 4.5% relative to GDP), which ranks Ireland 9th out of fifteen peer countries. In addition, the 2005 OECD statistical profile of Ireland showed that spending on pre-primary, primary and secondary education in Ireland was low compared to OECD and European levels.

The EU's social situation study[13] also found that Ireland falls behind most developed EU countries in terms of the percentage of the population without upper secondary education. This problem is acute amongst older members of society, reaching a level of 60% in the 55–64 age group. Participation in lifelong learning is not impressive either, especially for males.

Only 7.7% of the adult population participates in education and training, compared to an EU 15 average of 8.5%, and rates of 16.6% in the Netherlands, 19% in Finland and 22% in the UK.

Maths

Like Ireland's economy, the quality of its education system has attained the level of the EU average. Yet, with an eye on the future, it looks vulnerable if demands for investment and restructuring are not fed. An indication of the potential enfeebling of the Irish education system and the way in which this exposes the exalted hopes of some policy-makers is the recent performance of secondary school students in maths- and science-based subjects and the general failure to foster anything more than an average level of research and development activity at third level.

Some commentators have made much of the fact that one of the reasons Ireland attracted large amounts of investment was that it is the only country in the euro-zone where English is the spoken language. As far as research is concerned, the ability to speak 'maths' rather than English is perhaps more important, and in this area Ireland is easily surpassed by the Nordic countries and many Eastern European and Asian ones. Without a healthy supply of maths-literate labour, foreign companies, which undertake two-thirds of commercial research and development in Ireland, may in future opt to relocate research activities to more maths-literate countries. Recent school-level exam results increase the possibility that this could happen. For instance, the 2004 and 2005 Leaving Certificate results drew comment on the high failure rates in maths and science subjects, with close to 5,000 students failing ordinary- and higher-level maths, while over 5,500 took foundation-level maths, which is not accepted by most third-level colleges. Failure rates were also high in ordinary-level science subjects – biology, physics and chemistry.

In the international context, a recent OECD survey[14] that examined a sample of over 250,000 students in 41 countries placed Irish students (the sample is based on fifteen-year-olds) in 17th place in terms of maths ability and 13th in the science ranking, though Ireland did rank 6th in terms of reading ability. In the maths rankings, Ireland fell behind the likes of Finland, South Korea, New Zealand, the Czech Republic, Iceland, Denmark and Austria.

The poor showing at secondary level will have implications for the number of students applying for science, medicine and maths-based third-level courses. As it stands, the number of maths and science PhDs per 1,000 of the population in Ireland is average by EU standards, and well below the likes of Sweden, Finland and Germany.

In addition, the Barro-Lee dataset[15] on international schooling years and schooling quality places Japan and the Asian Tiger economies of Singapore, Korea and Hong Kong well ahead of Ireland in terms of test scores in maths, while the 'new' European countries like Hungary and the Czech Republic, as well as Russia, also fare well. The picture is much the same in science, where pupils in Asian countries and in Eastern Europe perform above average, and in most cases considerably better than Irish students.

Ireland's relative competitive position in education also looks weaker when the intellectual heritage of some of the new accession states is accounted for. For instance, Hungary is well known for producing high-calibre scientists and philosophers; and during the 1950s many of the scientists that made up the US nuclear weapons research program were Hungarian. This is underlined by the following encounter:

> In the early 1950s the Scientific Advisory Board of the US Atomic Energy Commission convened in Washington DC. A first count of the members showed a minority absent, but still a quorum; another count enabled the chairman to ask his colleagues, in his faultless native Hungarian, 'Shall we conduct this meeting in the mother tongue?' Agreed and done.[16]

Universities

At the university level, the Shanghai Jiao Tong[17] ranking of the top 500 universities in the world, though not yet highly regarded, is nevertheless revealing. The top 20 universities are dominated by the large, well-known US universities of the east coast and California, and by Oxford and Cambridge. On the other hand, Africa has only seven universities in the top 500.

Irish universities fall well behind the second-tier UK universities, such as the Universities of Reading, Bristol and St Andrews. In fact, there are eleven UK universities in the top 100, but only one Irish university (TCD) makes it into the top 300, another (UCC) into the top 400 and three others into the top 400–500 bracket. By comparison to other small, developed European countries, especially Switzerland and Sweden, but also Norway, Denmark, Finland and Austria, Ireland's standing is un-impressive. New Zealand, Singapore and Hungary also rank above it, although Ireland does manage to come in ahead of India, Greece, Portugal and Poland.

In general the standard of Ireland's education system, though reaching the EU average, is beginning to fall behind the very high expectations that have been created for it. Partly in response to this there is a growing debate in Ireland as to the role of education, especially with regard to the structure and aims of the universities. A broad risk is that this debate slavishly follows economic rather than civic imperatives and consequently loses sight of the enormous civic role that education plays. Third-level, and to some extent second-level, education in Ireland has become overly focused on career-related specialisation and on an unquestioning emphasis on business-based subjects. Although in the past this focus has equipped young people for specialised jobs in new industries, it has robbed other areas of suitable graduates and potentially diminished the civic function of education. An appraisal of third-level education might take in an examination of the US third-level degree system, where undergraduates undertake wider-ranging degree courses, deferring specialisation till after their primary degrees.

Attracting foreign investment

If for most of the twentieth century the Irish population was reasonably well educated, then it was also under-employed. Unemployment was persistently high and the notion of the 'brain drain' was an accepted part of Irish life. In fact, it was only the arrival of foreign investment capital in Ireland that permitted the harnessing of human capital on a wide scale.

As a result, the correlation between the inflow of foreign investment and economic out-performance is high, though the causality of this relationship is hard to work out. Most of this investment initially came in what is called horizontal investment, which involves the duplication of production processes around the world by multinationals, but it has become more vertically based in recent years in that some corporations now base separate parts of their production and marketing processes in Ireland.

While the IDA had always sought to entice foreign corporate investment into Ireland, its real success came through targeting a number of high growth sectors such as pharmaceuticals and information technology in the 1990s. Conversely, the drive to attract foreign investment into Ireland came as a result of a failure to foster domestic industry and the country's inherent weakness following decades of protectionism.[18]

Ireland's success in attracting and sustaining foreign investment can be understood by briefly considering the example of the East German industrial sector. When the Iron Curtain fell, East German car and chemical companies were found to be uncompetitive and impoverished by lack of investment. Nevertheless, many foreign and West German companies found East Germany to be an attractive location for their production capabilities because of the large educated workforce, technical know-how and good infrastructure. However, the boom that many expected of Eastern Germany never materialised, for the opposite reasons that investment was drawn to the Irish economy: weak government and federal balance sheets, high taxes, a lack of dynamism in state agencies and relatively expensive labour (especially after the currency revaluation). As a Central Bank of Ireland report[19] shows, the reasons that foreign investors find Ireland an attractive investment location are consistency of economic policy, economic openness, and a focus on employment and enhancing productivity.

Despite the threat that these factors might be undercut by other countries, there is yet no sign of capital flight from Ireland. Direct investment flows (as a proportion of GDP) from foreign corporations into Ireland now continue to outstrip those into all other European countries (except Luxembourg). By 2002, foreign direct investment (FDI) had reached a level of one-fifth of GDP, to an aggregate level of 25 billion euro, having increased by well over the European average rate in the previous ten years. A report on international trends in FDI ranked Ireland behind only Canada, Britain and the Netherlands in terms of the amount of US manufacturing investment it received (FDI into Ireland from the US is two and a half times that into China). In some industries, like electronics, Ireland is the recipient of over 15% of all US foreign investment.[20]

Labour

Another reason why Ireland proved an attractive investment location is its labour force. The Irish labour market in the 1980s and 1990s was remarkable for the potential supply that it could offer, and for its relative quality. Demographics were for once kind to Ireland in that a growing and young population was available to meet demand for labour without significantly pushing its price up. In addition, the extended pool of relatively skilled Irish labour abroad added to the flexibility of the labour market.

A series of labour market changes were made in Ireland during the 1990s, but these were largely orthodox and did not significantly alter the structure of the labour market. Special employment and training schemes combined with lower disincentives to work will certainly have helped to ease unemployment, though in themselves they do not constitute a dramatic departure from those adopted across a range of other countries.

The combination of Irish labour and foreign production, brought together by the likes of FÁS and the IDA, led to the considerable political and economic achievement of bringing unemployment down from 17% to a sustained level below 5%.[21] While this is deserving of great credit, the praise that is heaped on the productivity of Irish labour is often misplaced.

The incredible rise in productivity that foreign companies have managed to produce in Ireland has attracted the interest of a number of analysts, notably De Freitas of the Portuguese Central Bank and a team at the European Investment Bank.[22] Both studies imply that the rise in productivity stemmed largely from the better utilisation of labour in Ireland. Better management practices, improving technology and foreign know-how will all have helped to drive efficiency in a previously under-utilised labour force.

However, it is odd that the highest rates of productivity in the Irish economy during the 1990s came in foreign-owned sectors like information technology, and in particular in pharmaceuticals and chemicals, while productivity in thriving domestic sectors such as construction is unremarkable. This contrast was underlined in a recent study of productivity in Ireland,[23] where the rise in productivity during the 1990s was ascribed to a small number of foreign-dominated high-tech sectors, and productivity growth in the traditional manufacturing and services sectors was shown to be more modest. Though there are few Irish companies with the manufacturing know-how and levels of research and development spending of Apple or Microsoft, there is still no convincing evidence that Irish business can match the levels of productivity achieved by foreign firms. This contention is supported by data from the NCC competitiveness report (2005),[24] which shows that private-sector productivity in Ireland ranks second last out of ten European countries, and that, specifically, productivity in the utilities and construction sectors in Ireland falls below international levels.

This disparity gives weight to the claim that the productivity miracle in the foreign-owned sector of the Irish economy is an illusion generated by creative accounting. Both O'Hearn[25] and Slevin[26] nod towards this explanation of the high level of productivity growth reported by foreign companies. The use of transfer pricing allows foreign multinationals to write up a large amount of value added to goods produced in Ireland and then to pay relatively low taxes on this output.[27] By exaggerating the value of output from their Irish production bases, they also exaggerate productivity.

If foreign companies, especially those in the technology sector, have been inflating the value that their Irish operations add,[28] this is not inconsistent with the corporate environment in the late 1990s and early 2000s, where a series of mainly US corporates overstated the profits they made and expected to make (Enron and Worldcom being the most notorious). The passing of the Sarbanes-Oxley Act in the summer of 2002 (it had been rejected some four months previously when the corporate governance scandals had not yet broken) is testament to the creative accounting frequently employed by many of the world's most admired companies.

Institutions

Neither was sound accounting the strong point of many senior Irish politicians during the 1980s and 1990s. Indeed, it is also safe to conclude that Irish politicians and policy-makers had not proved themselves in the realm of economic policy-making by the middle of the 1980s. Ireland's economic record until then was comparable to politically less stable states like Portugal, Spain and Greece, and to many second world countries.

However, Ireland was different from these countries in the relative stability of its domestic politics (most of the above Mediterranean countries were governed by military dictatorships up to the 1970s). Although some of Ireland's institutions were relatively young and inexperienced by then, compared for example to the institutional apparatus of Austria, Sweden and Denmark, political stability and the existence of a healthy democratic system meant that, politically, Ireland was at least a respectable member of the first world, even if it was dubbed the 'poorest of the rich'.[29]

The state's institutions were of sufficient quality to ensure that Ireland possessed the institutional prerequisites to be considered politically developed. In particular, the quality and general impartiality of Ireland's civil service ensured that it was able to do many of the things that new states find difficult, such as credibly engage foreign governments and corporations, or perform tasks such as collecting taxes (a severe problem in Russia in the 1990s was the inability of the government to collect taxes, which then led to an inability to pay government debt and a subsequent debt default). This view is supported by a paper from Alfaro[30] that discusses one of the paradoxes of international finance (the Lucas paradox, which holds that capital does not flow from rich to poor countries as much as theory prescribes). The authors hold that one of the determining factors in the ability of poor countries to attract foreign capital is institutional quality (e.g. political stability and an open society).

Politics

While many economists and commentators search for economic lessons in 1990s Ireland, the 1980s also hold some truths, the most depressing of which is that for things to get better they need to get very bad. Although this may seem self-evident, there are many countries and companies that seem intent on learning it the hard way (e.g. Brazil and Argentina). One outcome of the harsh experience of 1980s Ireland was that it led to a more focused and pragmatic approach to policy-making. For a political system that has until recently been dominated by nationalist ideology, modern Irish politicians have rarely let ideology get in the way of pragmatism and, when confronted with the economic disaster that was the 1980s, they acted accordingly.

To be fair, Ireland's politicians and policy-makers deserve credit for a number of decisions, namely a focus on reducing unemployment and an enthusiastic and professional approach to the project of EU economic integration. In practical terms, the pragmatism of Irish policy-makers and politicians manifested itself in the form of a more business-friendly attitude and little patience for labour market regulation. This was made possible by the lack of a strong social model of development in Ireland, the imperative of job creation and the relatively under-developed nature of regulation in Ireland. Yet, the success of this approach is more remarkable when compared to the performance of Ireland's economic peers of the 1980s on similar issues, like unemployment.

This was the key economic and political issue of the 1980s. Its importance as a policy issue in Ireland can be compared to the vigilance of German and US policy-makers over inflation in the 1970s. By 1987, Ireland was only fourteen years into its membership of the EC, a move that was beginning to reduce its economic dependence on Britain (even then, almost two-thirds of exports went to the UK) and open up its economy[31] and society. However, in common with other countries on the lower tier of the European economic ladder, like Greece, Spain and Portugal, unemployment in Ireland was well into double figures. This malaise did not hit some other small European countries as hard. Austria, Finland, Sweden and Norway had unemployment rates in the 1980s that were only a third of Ireland's.

The policies that led to the economic globalisation of Ireland probably did not have globalisation in mind, but simply the creation of new jobs. The political response to unemployment took various forms, although the overriding aim was to soak up domestic labour supply with foreign investment in production. Agencies like the IDA were tasked with importing employment, and they did so with a well-organised strategy of targeting high-growth industrial sectors with generous grant and taxation policies.

The domestic business climate improved as the state balance sheet was restructured and the national debt and budget deficits were reduced. The level of debt to output fell from over 100% in 1992 to close to 40% by 2002, with a 60% threshold being prescribed by the Maastricht criteria. Although the impetus for such fiscal reform has come from external factors like the need to reform government finances ahead of entry to the euro-zone, the performance of Ireland on this front has been exemplary. This improvement facilitated a sizeable domestic fiscal stimulus in the form of falling rates of income tax, which have now dropped to higher and lower limits of 20% and 42% respectively, as compared to 35% and 58% in 1988.

Admittedly, the process whereby public finances were brought into some kind of order, thus lowering the cost of capital, was as much a policy of last resort as an enlightened departure towards 'new economics'. Some commentators explained the effect that this had on the economy as an 'expansionary fiscal contraction', a phenomenon whereby domestic consumption rises in response to tighter fiscal policy as individuals expect future taxes to be lower. Although better state finances lowered the cost of capital, domestic consumption did not take off in the late 1980s (although 1989 was a good year). Instead, it was exports and investment by foreign companies that sparked the economic recovery. Foreign companies did much to improve the business climate in Ireland, which in turn has helped the domestic sector, though the decisive factor in the blossoming of the domestic economy has most probably been the ready provision of capital.

Money
One aspect of the economic globalisation of Ireland that has received relatively little attention from researchers is financial liberalisation. However, a recent paper from the Central Bank of Ireland[32] goes some way to remedying this. One of the important contributions of this paper is to highlight the role, difficult to quantify as it is, that credit growth has played in Ireland's economic boom. The authors outline the numerous measures that have been taken in Ireland since 1973 to abolish exchange controls, open up credit policy (especially to allow the increased provision of private-sector credit), develop domestic securities markets and change monetary policy.[33]

Largely as a result of these policies, and the combination of falling interest rates and improved financial stability internationally, credit growth in Ireland took off towards the end of 1995, fuelling growth in the domestic economy, particularly in small businesses, the housing market and the construction sector. Although there are numerous cases of credit expansion in other countries eventually leading to economic and financial market imbalances, the authors conclude that Ireland has so far avoided some of the pitfalls associated with a rapid expansion in credit, as lending has been reasonably well diversified and aimed at the fastest-growing sectors of the economy. Above all, in seeking to prioritise employment creation, facilitate the growth of domestic business and bring order to public finances, Irish politicians and policy-makers created the conditions by which globalisation could thrive in Ireland. In the wider world, globalisation itself was driven by a number of powerful economic forces, such as the secular fall in long-term interest rates, deregulation and the lowering of barriers to trade and financial flows.

External factors

By 1993, Ireland had repaired its balance sheet by steadily reducing government debt, was in a reasonably healthy fiscal state and price inflation was under control. In that context, the Exchange Rate Mechanism (ERM) currency crisis of 1993 was an embarrassing blow to Ireland's policy-makers and politicians who had done so much to turn the country into one of the better-behaved members of the ERM. Despite the fact that the Irish economy had become more integrated with that of continental Europe, its fortunes were still tied to sterling – if less so in trade terms, still so in the eyes of European policy-makers and currency traders (both of these parties were denounced by the Catholic Church in Ireland during the currency crisis). The ERM crisis marked one of the first episodes in recent decades when global financial markets were denounced as 'evil', an accusation that, like similar developments in the nineteenth century, marked the coming of age of the global financial system. The crises in the economies and financial markets of the Asian Tigers five years later would compound these views and lead to calls for the reining in of globalisation through measures such as the application of a (Tobin) tax on foreign-exchange transactions.

As sterling was edged to the outer limits of its permitted range in the ERM system, the punt was dragged with it. Irish interest rates were pushed up to try to make the currency more attractive, thus penalising Irish business and debt-holding households. Bernard Connolly's exciting chronicle of the events surrounding the collapse of the ERM shows that officials at the helm of the ERM system such as Hans Tietmayer and Jean-Claude Trichet (now President of the ECB) lost little sleep over the descent of the punt, leaving a humiliating devaluation inevitable.[34]

Although this squandered much of the hard work of Irish policy-makers in the early 1990s, the resulting drop in interest rates and competitive impetus from lower interest and exchange rates gave a considerable boost to the Irish economy. Still the breakdown of the ERM rudely demonstrated that external events can trump the best-laid plans of policy-makers.

Picking up the pieces – reconstructing the ERM

In a similar manner, the rethinking and reconstruction of the European monetary project that followed the crisis has had an even greater impact on the Irish economy. Still the formation of the euro-zone tightened the bolts on weak government finances around Europe. The principle benefit to Ireland from this was the effect of falling interest rates in Europe and also in the US.

The fiscal discipline of the first and second Clinton administrations (former Treasury Secretary Robert Rubin is granted most of the credit for this) combined with the Maastricht criteria to drive long-term interest rates in the US and Europe down from close to 9% in 1994 to below 5% now. In many parts of Europe (i.e. Italy) long-term rates were close to 20% during the late 1980s. This sharp drop in rates has had an immensely positive effect on debt-holders, and on the value of assets such as equities and property.

In recent years, the high rate of inflation in Ireland has meant that real rates were close to, and often below, zero. Real rates, as measured by the money market rate less consumer price inflation, averaged 0% from 1998 to 2001 and fell to close to −4% in 2000, having been as high as 10% in 1985 and 15% in the period around the first Gulf War. This 'free money' and the expansion in credit that allowed it to flow through the economy go a long way to explaining the boom in the domestic economy over the past ten years.

Notwithstanding the 1993 currency crisis, investing in Ireland was made less costly as the country's adherence to the Maastricht criteria removed much of the currency- and country-specific risk to outside investors. Domestically, consumers and Irish industry had cheaper costs of capital, as well as a less uncertain macroeconomic climate in which to undertake investment. The international cost of capital argument is especially relevant to the case of the Irish economy, as financial investment in it has been heavily financed from abroad over the last forty years. In particular, the very large current account deficits of the late 1970s and early 1980s and growing public debt were financed at a high cost to the Exchequer.

The result of a lower cost of capital internationally was the biggest boom in investment spending since perhaps the early twentieth century. Just as much of the investment spending in the pre-Depression era was directed towards building the factors that propelled the first wave of globalisation, such as transportation (e.g railways) and communications (radio and telegraph), the recent boom in spending occurred in areas such as telecommunications, biotechnology and computer chips, all parts of the modern-day globalisation story. In Ireland, each of these growth industries was also fortuitously targeted by bodies like the IDA.

Matchmaking
To sum up the interaction of the external and internal factors discussed above, the early stage of the recovery in the Irish economy has been built around the chemistry of Irish labour and foreign productive capacity, with the likes of the IDA acting as matchmaker. While this marriage of labour and capital has so far solved Ireland's unemployment problem, ignited its domestic economy and produced what appear to be fantastic rises in productivity, it is essentially a phenomenon of globalisation, and specifically one of the global corporation.

A sense of how globalised the Irish economy has become is gained by considering what would happen if the forces that are associated with modern-day globalisation, such as surging foreign direct investment and trade, the relatively low cost of capital, the breaking up of the production chain and the revolution in communications and technology, were reversed. If this happened, the Irish economy, domestic and outward-looking, would undoubtedly shrink, with painful effect.

What marks Ireland out as a classic example of globalisation is that it has sought to make itself attractive to globalising corporations by lowering set-up costs and providing skilled labour to drive production processes. To a significant extent the rest of the economy has then fed off of these global giants and the attractive business conditions they helped create.

Part II – Our success, or someone else's miracle

Ireland's role in the global business model
The leading management studies scholars Christopher Bartlett and Sumantra Ghoshal[35] have developed an organisational model that can take four different forms – multinational, global, international and transnational. The global and multinational types are common to Ireland. Under the multinational model, a decentralised network of operating units runs with some autonomy; control by headquarters is not rigid, although financial reporting demands are stringent. The global version is an extension of this, although control and strategic decision-making by the headquarters are much tighter.

The global business model states that, where cost, marketing or other advantages can be gained from locating any part of the production chain in another country, then these gains should be pursued. For much the same reasons that many large American corporations are now outsourcing tasks to countries like India, they found Ireland attractive because of the impact it had on net profitability (low taxes, relatively cheap quality labour) and the access that it granted to the European market. Thus, globalisation in Ireland is a particularly corporate phenomenon and a very American one at that. In this context, Ireland is a staging-post for foreign production, with Irish labour being used to transform inputs into high value-added outputs. The higher the value added the better, as the tax paid on this is far lower than in other countries.

That Ireland has become a production centre for foreign companies is clear in the national statistics. The single most important export destination[36] for Irish trade is now the US (most of this activity is US companies based in Ireland 'trading' with other units of the same company). The ratio of exports to GDP in Ireland is approximately 90%, a far higher rate than other European countries, while in 1985 it was 55%. In the thirty years from 1970 to 2000, exports from Ireland have grown by a factor of twenty times, and imports by eight times.[37] The aggregate result of this has been that Ireland is now considered the most open economy in the world, when not long ago it was one of the most protected.

Ireland's case is unusual in that the globalisation of its economy has not grown on the basis of its comparative advantage. That Ireland has effectively moved from a pre- to a post-industrial state in one step belies the fact that it really has no strong comparative advantage, and that its success is based more on the competitive advantage of the companies it has managed to attract to Ireland. This is reinforced by a Central Bank research paper[38] which analyses the determinants of Ireland's comparative advantage and holds that:

> Ireland has a strikingly high comparative advantage in predominantly foreign-owned sectors and principally in the broad chemicals sector. In contrast, the mainly indigenous sectors seem to be losing comparative advantage due presumably to declining competitiveness combined with wider and ongoing structural changes within the economy.

This is also the weakness of the Irish 'miracle' and the factor that makes it essentially a global story, in that somebody else (i.e. foreign multinationals and the European Central Bank) either owns or controls the levers of the Irish economy, which is not really a desirable outcome for a country that cherishes its independence. For instance, foreign investment has fuelled the Irish boom and the quid pro quo of this is that profits are taken out of Ireland with very little contribution to the Exchequer and very little serious investment in the country's infrastructure. In addition, the multiplier effect of investment in Ireland is vastly diminished when the lion's share of the returns from that investment leave the country.

There are a number of tell-tale signs of this phenomenon, the primary one being the large difference between gross domestic product (GDP) and gross national product (GNP). In straightforward terms, GDP refers to all output produced in Ireland while GNP denotes output produced by the Irish. For example, GNP (103.4 billion euro) in 2002 was some 20% lower than GDP (130 billion euro).[39] There is no other developed country where there is such a disparity between GDP and GNP. In Luxembourg, GNP is 90% of GDP, while the next smallest in terms of the GNP/GDP differential is Portugal at 97%. In Ireland in 1960 the opposite was the case, with GNP being higher than GDP because of inflows from Irish residents abroad.

It is no surprise then that measuring Ireland's wealth using GDP flatters to deceive. On the basis of GDP, Ireland's economy is a phenomenon in itself, rising to the top of the ranks of the world's most developed countries. On the basis of per capita GDP, Ireland is the second richest country in the EU after Luxembourg, but on the basis of GNP its wealth is merely average. As an aside, the fact that Ireland shares so many statistical honours and anomalies with Luxembourg, a tax haven, should itself be a cause for concern. Judging by the more honest measure of GNP, Ireland is still developing, and still a considerable distance behind the Scandinavian countries that should now form its peer group.

An analysis of the corporations operating within the Irish economy is more revealing of its two-speed nature. The 'miracle' part of the Irish economy seems to be driven by a relatively low number of high-technology multinationals (mostly American), while indigenous firms are pedestrian by comparison. The distinction that was coined in the late 1990s between the 'new' high-tech economy and the old 'bricks and mortar' economy is apt in the Irish case.

Based on the Enterprise Strategy Group report (2004),[40] agency-supported indigenous and foreign firms employ almost the same number of people (148,000 each) and spend roughly the same amount (e.g. raw materials, wages) within the economy (close to 17 billion euro each). However, the similarities end there.

There are 5.6 times as many indigenous agency-supported firms in Ireland as foreign ones, but foreign firms export 8.7 times as much as the domestic sector. Average annual wages and salary payments from foreign firms in 2002 were 14% higher than for indigenous ones, and foreign companies spent more on training and staff development. Foreign-sector firms are concentrated in high-technology sectors like pharmaceuticals and software, and 73% of the employment they create is in manufacturing and assembly roles. Foreign firms are also responsible for two-thirds of all business research and development in Ireland. In contrast, the majority of domestic companies operate in the 'old economy', mostly providing services. By comparison with foreign firms' high sales growth rates, the largest sector in the domestic economy, food, beverages and tobacco, has recorded no real increase in sales in the past decade.

Outside of agency-supported firms, the vast majority of businesses in Ireland are small and medium-sized enterprises. According to the ESG report, the Revenue Commissioners estimate that there are almost 250,000 such businesses in Ireland, with about 100,000 of these being single-person businesses (this helps to explain why Ireland has an apparently high rate of business start-ups and entrepreneurship). These firms are mostly involved in providing business services, distributive services and consumer services like hotels and catering.

Based on this snapshot, there is a stark difference in performance, research levels and export activity between the 'globalised' section of the Irish economy and the domestic sector. Although a great deal of the goods, profits and research produced in Ireland by multinationals are quickly transferred out of the country, multinationals have played a substantial role in contributing to the quantity and quality of the Irish workforce, and in providing the focal point for an emerging industrial structure. This base has provided the catalyst for broader growth in the domestic sector of the economy, which in turn has been spurred on by low interest rates. Despite this, there are very few signs that the indigenous economy has demonstrated a unique and distinctive approach to commerce.

Anglo-Saxon versus Rheinish capitalism

In addition to comparing foreign and indigenous firms, another means of analysing the Irish corporate sector is to fit it to one of the two broad categories of organisational and financial market structure. The first of these is the Anglo-Saxon model, based largely on American corporations (together with some British oil, pharmaceutical, banking and telecommunications firms) that are prominent amongst the globalised corporations of the world. The second is the Rheinish (German)/Japanese approach. Some commentators categorise the Anglo-Saxon approach as being right-wing or free-market and the German/Japanese one as left-wing and more liberal, although in many cases this is a misleading generalisation.

The Anglo-Saxon approach to capital markets is primarily equity-based, although the corporate debt market in the US plays a significant role too. Control of the Anglo-Saxon firm rests with its shareholders, who are the main source of finance. When control is contested, it is often through takeovers, hostile or friendly. Since the collapse of

Worldcom and Enron, shareholders, most of whom are fund managers, have shown themselves to be increasingly aggressive in disciplining errant management.

The executives of Anglo-Saxon firms are usually well 'incentivised' through share and stock option grants, although this does not always align their interests with those of the corporation. Non-executive directors are the chief internal means of disciplining executives, but very often they have too little time and inclination to do so in a meaningful fashion.

In theory, the capital markets that finance the Anglo-Saxon corporation should exist to channel public and private savings into sensible long-term investments, although they often give the impression of being a very exciting sideshow within themselves. They thrive on their efficiency and the ability of arbitrageurs to make sure that price differentials between similar assets should not exist for very long. The spirit of the Anglo-Saxon marketplace is very much fuelled by entrepreneurship, with other sources of capital, such as venture capital, available for new businesses that can later be taken to market.

Irish corporations essentially follow this model, with the Irish stock exchange being a legal cousin of its counterpart in London. Publicly quoted companies in Ireland effectively have the same formal and informal structures as those in the UK and the US. Since 1990, an increasing number of new Irish companies have been listed in the US. Two of the flag-bearers of the Irish boom, Elan and Baltimore, were quoted in the United States partly as a result of the under-developed state of Ireland's equity and venture capital markets in the early 1990s. However, they later over-represented their future success to the marketplace and collapsed, to the detriment of many small domestic shareholders.

The competing model to the Anglo-Saxon one is the Rheinish/Japanese approach, which, while popular in the 1980s, was held to be inefficient in the context of the 1990s equity market boom, although it is once again fashionable following the numerous corporate governance scandals in the US in 2002. The Rheinish and Japanese approaches to corporate governance and financial market systems have a common emphasis on the rights of many stakeholders, and not solely the shareholder. The notion of the stakeholder was appropriated by many of the intellectual acolytes of Tony Blair's Third Way political programme in the 1990s, although it still seems alien to many public and private bodies in the UK.

Stakeholders in the German/Japanese sense include other providers of capital such as banks, and long-term equity-holders like founding families, workers groups and unions. German companies have typically been funded by long-term loans from commercial and state/regional banks and normally have a dual board structure, with the Vorstand (management board) overseeing the running of the company and the Aufsichtsrat, which includes a sizeable proportion of worker representatives, supervising the executives. Although the take-off of new equity markets like the Neuer Markt in Germany fuelled moves towards Anglo-Saxon-style structures such as share options, most German companies remain resolutely long-term in their outlook, a factor that has enabled them to spend more on research and development than their English counterparts, for example.

The Japanese system is in many respects like that of Germany, one common feature being that both financial systems (including their central banks) were reconstructed by the Americans after the Second World War. Like that in Germany, the Japanese system is held to be long-term in perspective. Corporations are funded through long-term shareholders, with cross-shareholdings between companies and banks being commonplace. Like Germany, a premium is placed on research and development. Takeovers, particularly those of a hostile nature, are very rare. Business systems in other European countries have variations to the Rheinish model. France has perhaps more government involvement in big business, while Italian industry tends to be dominated by family-owned enterprises funded by a very small number of merchant banks.

Before the take-off in the US stock market in the 1990s, academics and business leaders in both Britain[41] and America expressed public fascination with and envy for the ability of German and Japanese companies to secure long-term funding in order to invest in research and development. Japanese manufacturing techniques were especially popular, and many leading business schools and universities set up courses and institutes in Japanese management studies and many Japanese management practices, like just in time (JIT) manufacturing, are still used in the Irish plants of large multinationals.

In most respects, Irish companies are unlike their German and Japanese counterparts. If they sought bank as opposed to equity financing, it was usually expensive, shorter-term and a poor reflection on the small size of Ireland's venture capital and equity markets. Neither has Irish industry put a premium on research and development in the same way that companies in the Rheinish region have. However, in one important respect, Ireland has borrowed something from the Rheinish model.

Although labour relations in 1970s and 1980s Ireland were not constructive, if the number of work days lost is anything to go by, the collective bargaining agreements[42] led by governments from 1988 onwards were positive. While similar types of collective bargaining had previously operated in the Netherlands, Norway and Austria, the success of partnership agreements is one of the few ways in which the economic boom in Ireland could be described as adhering to the 'European/Rheinish' model. Although most of the new jobs created in Ireland by foreign multinationals were not unionised, collective bargaining agreements contributed to the competitiveness of the Irish economy by keeping wage inflation under control. It also left the after-tax wage relatively high, and somewhat strengthened the role of unions in the state's economic policy-making process. At the same time the approach of the Irish authorities was sharply at variance with that of the Thatcher government's treatment of unions. If Thatcher succeeded in breaking the unions in Britain, the more continental approach taken by the Irish government won their co-operation.

The Irish exception – is there an Irish economic model?

Despite a lack of evidence, some popular accounts of the Irish economic 'miracle' seem to assume that a significant part of the strong performance of the Irish economy in the 1990s was due to some uniquely Irish approach to business. This is a mistake. If it were true, then we would not have had to wait so long for the 'Tiger' to arrive. In reality, there is no 'Irish' economic model to equal the Asian Tigers, or the differing Anglo-Saxon and Rheinish financial systems. Ireland does not have a world-class industrial system like Japan or Taiwan, nor does it have any world-beating innovative companies like Nokia and Ericsson.

At best, as the quote at the beginning of the chapter from Charles Haughey suggests, Ireland seems to have borrowed pragmatically from all codes, with the overall ethos and characteristics of the Irish economic 'miracle' being largely Anglo-Saxon with some aspects of the Rheinish model cleverly thrown into the mix.

A Tiger, a bull or a hare?

What makes Ireland interesting is that, while its economy now operates in the euro-zone monetary regime, domestic policy remains very Anglo-Saxon, to the extent that it owes much to the successful importation of the 'Washington consensus' policy mix. The concern for the future is that the weaknesses and problems of the Irish economy, such as inflation, high levels of private debt, a housing market bubble and falling competitiveness, are more commonly found in the Anglo-Saxon economies of the US and UK, but monetary policy for Ireland is set in Frankfurt. Conversely, the economic ailments that affect the larger European countries, such as the pensions/demographics shortfall, structurally inefficient labour markets and flagging growth are not major concerns for Ireland.

Savings in the continental European and Asian countries are much higher than in the Anglo-Saxon ones. At the same time consumers in the

Anglo-Saxon countries (i.e. the US, the UK, Ireland and Australia) have been borrowing heavily as spending exceeds income. Although this rise in borrowing has been offset by rising house prices in these countries, this combination of debt and high asset prices is potentially dangerous, as the recent equity market bubble showed.

Moreover, small government, typically a goal of the Anglo-Saxon right, is the norm in Ireland now. In fact, the role of the government in the Irish economy is one of the smallest in Europe. For example, total outlay by the Irish government is estimated at around 35% of GDP, the third lowest of sixteen peer countries (this figure is 43% on the basis of GNP, with the EU average being 47%).[43] Moreover, the tax wedge, or the contribution that employees and employers pay back to the state from wages earned, is one of the lowest amongst EU and OECD countries.[44] Reflecting this trend, the Heritage Foundation, a right-wing economics think-tank in the US, placed Ireland third in its Index of Economic Freedom,[45] after Luxembourg and Estonia.

In the sense that smaller government is more of an Anglo-Saxon trait than a European one, the image of a bull is a more fitting one for Ireland's economy than a tiger. If the Irish economy can be classified as largely Anglo-Saxon, it is a little surprising that the comparison with the Asian Tigers has stuck.[46] Denis O'Hearn's excellent comparison of the Irish economy with those of Singapore, South Korea, Taiwan and Indonesia reaches the conclusion that Ireland is not yet a 'Tiger' economy. There are several important differences, the main one being that the Asian Tigers have been growing at 'supernormal' rates of growth for over thirty years, while Ireland's boom is comparatively young. Growth rates amongst the Asian Tigers are also, on average, higher than those in Ireland.

Other structural differences exist. Similar to Japan, industrial and financial structures in countries like Taiwan and South Korea are based on networks that permit long-term financing and knowledge sharing. Good-quality physical infrastructure and high levels of research and development are also common amongst the Asian Tigers. State intervention is the norm in these economies, and the style of government in places like Singapore is authoritarian, with the state playing a strong role in labour policy and in ensuring plentiful investment capital through mandatory savings schemes. Ireland does not conform to these and indeed most other aspects of the Asian model.

One way in which Ireland may resemble the Asian Tigers is that many of its neighbours on the continent have had relatively less dynamic economies than Ireland's, in turn making Ireland a relatively more attractive investment destination. The same was true of the Asian Tigers. Lindert and Williamson state that:

> The original Four Tigers – Singapore, South Korea, Taiwan and Hong
> Kong – probably owe much of their export led success in the 1960s
> and 1970s to the protectionist and illiberal domestic policies of
> mainland China, North Korea, Vietnam, Burma, Bangladesh, India,
> and Pakistan. In the 1980s a newly-opened China began to catch up,
> perhaps partly because India and the others remained so anti-trade.[47]

The Asian Tigers have their European complement not in Ireland, but
most likely in the Nordic countries. Although economic growth rates in
the likes of Finland have not been as consistently high as those in Taiwan
or Singapore, the significant role of Scandinavian governments in their
economies and the ongoing emphasis on education, research and
development, and innovation in the Nordic region countries, allows parallels to be drawn between them and the Asian Tiger economies.

Having left its Mediterranean peer group of the 1980s (Spain,
Greece and Portugal) behind in terms of economic growth, Ireland
should focus its ambitions on the peer group that encompasses Denmark, Finland, Sweden and Norway. However, serious qualitative differences remain between Ireland and these countries. Firstly, most of
them – Denmark, Sweden and Norway – still exercise control over their
currencies and monetary policy. Secondly, levels of research and
development in these countries far outstrip the European average. For
example, although the per capita number of science and technology
PhDs in Ireland is close to the European average, it is well below the
level of the Nordic countries. Domestic expenditure on research and
development is only on a par with the likes of Greece, Slovenia and Portugal, while the number of patents submitted to the US patent office is
one quarter the level of Sweden and Finland. With regard to education,
Norway for example, has broadened access to education and attainment
levels to rates well above Ireland's.

The Irish model

For the moment, attaining the economic characteristics of the Nordic
countries must remain an aspiration, largely because of the shortcomings
of the domestic business sector. Although there is no definitive Irish
business model like that of the Asian Tigers and the Nordic region, there
seems to be emerging an Irish commercial ethos, one that is essentially
brash and showy. The public face of Irish business abroad is represented
by private airlines, the speculative activities of Irish oligarchs, the expansion of Irish property empires abroad and by the residue of the multiple
tribunals that are trying to explore the deep and intricate links between
commerce and politics in Ireland.

The idiom of Irish business is fast, aggressive and shiny, not unlike the newly monied classes of other emerging economies. Some Irish multi-millionaires have also begun to parody foreign multinationals that export their profits from Ireland at a low tax rate by themselves residing in tax havens, so that their personal profits do not pass through the hands of the Irish Exchequer. Ireland's main banks have acquiesced in this deception, with most of them involved in scandals over corruption, tax evasion and overcharging. If anything, Irish companies have only got poor corporate governance as a distinguishing characteristic.

The generally unremarkable quality of domestic corporations in Ireland increases the dependence on favourable external factors and this over-reliance goes to the heart of the economic aspect of its Global Question, which is how to maintain some independent control over the country's economic destiny.

Part III – Steering a small globalised economy

This question is made more difficult to answer because, through its accession to the euro-zone, Ireland has surrendered both its monetary policy[48] and control over its currency. In general, this has been a good move. The effect of membership of the euro-zone has been the lowering of government debt and the elimination of a habitually large budget deficit, both of which have so far been positive factors for the Irish economy.

It is usually desirable for policy-makers in small open economies like Ireland's to have a full arsenal of policy options (monetary policy, fiscal policy and currency) at their disposal, but Ireland does not. While neither does it have a distinctive approach to business and economic policy, the way in which Irish policy-makers can perform the trick of sustaining economic growth with only a limited set of policy options should provide grounds to justify a truly Irish model of economic management.

Ireland is now part of a larger trading block united under the euro, which at least theoretically is a more stable currency than most of the sovereign ones that went into its construction. It is less volatile than the punt was and certainly less vulnerable to financial market crises. The chief issue for Ireland as regards the euro is that, because monetary policy is controlled from Frankfurt (by the European Central Bank), the fortunes of the euro are effectively determined there as well. While Ireland is represented on the ECB council, the ECB considers economic factors across the entire euro-zone when deciding interest rates and, given that Irish GDP makes up about 3% of total output in the euro-zone, Ireland is little more than an interesting outlier to most euro-zone policy-makers. Therefore, it is easy for the level of interest rates in the euro-zone, as well as the level of the euro, to be at variance with the needs of the domestic Irish economy.[49] So far this has been to Ireland's benefit. First of all, the rising value of the euro against the dollar from 2002 to 2005 will have slowed the importation of inflation into Ireland. Secondly, during the late 1990s and early part of the twenty-first century, interest rates in Ireland were far lower than standard monetary policy models would recommend. It is very likely that a sovereign central bank would have acted to bring a booming economy with GDP growth of over 7% (an average over eight years) under control. Interest rates in Ireland during the period 1998–2002 would surely have been closer to 6% than the 3.25% they have averaged since the foundation of the ECB.

While prudent from the point of view of central bankers, such a policy would have sharply curbed the growth in the Irish economy, especially the domestic economy, although it would also have limited Irish inflation, which is amongst the highest in the euro-zone.

Goldilocks

If we consider the recent history of globalisation, not having the policy tools to either stoke growth or dampen inflation is highly problematic. In the late 1990s the US economy was characterised as a 'Goldilocks economy'. Essentially, economic growth was strong, but the side-effects that would normally be expected with this, such as high inflation, were not evident. Thus, like the porridge in the Goldilocks fable, the US economy was neither too hot nor too cold, and therefore not warranting a serious change in monetary policy. However, the 'Goldilocks' scenario very soon gave way to a falling equity market, a weakened corporate sector and a brief recession, the effects of which were soothed by aggressive loosening of monetary policy and a weakening dollar. The moral of this story is that even the biggest and often best economies need a full range of economic policy levers at their disposal.

Too hot

Ireland does not have independent control over mechanisms like monetary policy, so that if its economy is overheating (i.e. high inflation) it must rely on other measures. This is especially the case when the performance of the euro-zone economy differs from Ireland's. If for example the Irish economy is growing at a rate of 4% and the euro-zone economy is growing at a rate below 1%, then euro-zone interest rates may fall to boost growth. The effect of this on the Irish economy is to effectively raise growth well above desired levels, which can lead to overheating rather than stability. For an economy with high growth and rising inflation, falling real interest rates are the monetary equivalent of pouring petrol on a raging fire, and 'inappropriate' from a policy point of view. The American economist Martin Feldstein makes this problem clear: 'the experience of Ireland is an example of how countries and regions may experience unacceptably high inflation without any reaction from the ECB and of course without any spontaneous automatic rise in the country's interest rate'.[50]

Or too cold
The opposite of an overheating economy is one where growth is stagnant or declining. With interest rates in the US now rising from recent lows, the danger for Ireland is that real interest rates will rise, the euro remains strong and the domestic economy slows (perhaps through loss of competitiveness or some shock, such as a correction in the housing market). Once again, Feldstein emphasises that 'if the Irish economy were to experience a substantial economic recession, there would be no countervailing effect from Irish interest rates or from the exchange rate to help the economy recover'.[51]

The scenario of rising interest rates in the US and Europe seems a likely one over the medium term as economic growth recovers and the government bond market rally (of almost ten years) is unwound. The raising of interest rates by 2.5% by the US Federal Reserve between February and November 1994 following the 1990–1991 recession led to a sell-off in the bond market, which saw long-term rates move from 5% to 8%. A similar scenario today could be disastrous for the Irish economy. Rising rates would slow investment from abroad, undermine the housing market, make the huge levels of consumer debt in Ireland very painful to bear and significantly curtail consumption. Fiscal stimulus would be the only means of counteracting this, assuming that euro-zone interest rates were to rise too.

The extremes of 'too hot' or 'too cold' demonstrate the fact that euro-zone monetary policy and the level of the euro can easily remain at levels that are unsuited to the needs of the domestic Irish economy for considerable periods of time. One of the side-effects of 'inappropriate' monetary policy is significant shifts in price levels (either inflation or, less frequently, deflation). In Ireland's case, asset prices, especially the property market, bear all the signs of this.

Bubble trouble
The scramble for land and housing in Ireland today suggests that house ownership, and the high rents that are now paid for housing, continue to be significant factors in the Irish economy. The large amount of private debt that has been built up in recent years and the high level of house

prices have arguably made the Irish economy more sensitive to interest rate changes, though again it is the ECB not the Central Bank of Ireland that has power over rates. Although opting out of the euro-zone so as to recover control over monetary policy is not and to a large degree should not be an option, the domestic housing market is at the mercy of outside forces, a fact that has been acknowledged by the Central Bank of Ireland:

> It is apparent that households and recent newly mortgaged households in particular, are heavily exposed to the potential for short-term market interest rates to rise rapidly, and unexpectedly, for reasons that are unrelated to the state of the Irish economy . . . the cause for concern is greater now in the context of Ireland's membership of the monetary union. This is because any rescue operation might be more difficult than in the past because of Ireland's membership of monetary union.[52]

The dilemma for Irish policy-makers is highlighted by the case of a central bank that has stayed outside the euro-zone, the Bank of England. Since it was granted independence in 1997, the Bank of England's Monetary Policy Committee (MPC) is widely recognised as having acted in a consistently sensible manner, such that the success of the MPC is considered to be a significant factor in the Treasury's unstated aversion to joining the euro-zone. Over the course of 2004, the Bank of England, in contrast to the ECB, aggressively raised rates to a level of 4.75%, compared to 2% in the euro-zone, although consumer price inflation in both monetary jurisdictions was rising.

In raising rates quickly, the MPC was responding to the high rate of growth in the British housing market and consumer demand for credit. Their actions are telling, because conditions in the UK housing and credit markets are mirrored by those in Ireland (which, like England, has a housing market where over 75% of dwellings are owner-occupied). Debt levels relative to disposable income in Ireland are at similar levels to those in the UK. In Ireland in late 2005, household debt as a percentage of disposable income reached 132% (in the UK this figure was close to 140%), from a level of 48% in 1995. In the US, similar indicators, like the debt payments to disposable income ratio and total consumer debt to GDP, are close to their highest levels in at least thirty years. In contrast, household debt levels in most other European countries are far lower than those in Ireland, Britain or the US.

Most household debt in Ireland is mortgage-related (80%), with the remainder going to direct consumption. Between 1994 and 2002, the value of the average mortgage trebled, from 44,400 euro to

136,500 euro, driven by falling rates (mortgage rates fell from 7% in 1999 to 4.93% in 2002), demographics and the upward pursuit of house prices.

The growth in credit has understandably fed through to rising house prices. They have grown at an average rate of 17% in the period 2000–2004, comparable to the rate of growth in the UK. Over a slightly longer period of time, from 1997 to 2004, the percentage change in Irish property prices was 181%, as measured by the *Economist*,[53] with the next highest being South Africa (168%), the UK (132%), Spain (125%) and Australia (110%). In contrast, the change in German house prices over that period was –3%, France had an increase of 68% and Italy of 62%. In addition, Irish house price levels relative to incomes are now widely recognised to have risen far beyond what would be deemed a fair multiple. At the end of 2004, the ratio of average house prices to average income was over 50% higher than its long-term average.[54] Reflecting these trends, the Central Bank of Ireland's *Financial Stability Report* stressed that the primary risk to the economy is credit growth and the high level of indebtedness.

There has also been a significant expansion in credit card debt, which has risen threefold in over four years. As a proportion of disposable income, credit card debt was 0.9% in 1995 but 2.5% by 2004.[55] A new data series on credit card debt from the Central Bank's Statistics Department shows that, in 2003 and most of 2004, it grew at an average rate of over 25% per month.

Under normal circumstances, high property prices, consumer debt and inflation would be tempered by an independent central bank, as the MPC is now doing in the UK. Yet, as Ireland makes up only 3% of the euro-zone economy, bubbles in its economy are only boils when viewed from the ECB headquarters in Frankfurt.

Price stability
The rise in property prices and credit reflects a wider inflationary trend, leading the Central Bank to comment that it is the 'euro-zone country with the highest inflation rate, a record that the country has had since the inception of the euro at the beginning of 1999'.[56]

Consumer price inflation has consistently been at approximately 2% above the European average in the early part of this century. Inflation has been stoked in recent years by low interest rates and an expansionary budget in 2000. Factors like higher indirect taxes, domestic price shocks and strong growth have also played a strong role, according to O'Rourke and Thom.[57]

Reflecting this, the NCC's statement on prices and costs in September 2004 underlined in stark terms that Ireland's consumer price inflation has exceeded the euro-zone and wider EU 15 average for the past seven years.[58] It is now the most expensive country in the euro-zone for consumer goods and services. Most of this inflation is generated in Ireland, with 68% of inflation occurring in non-traded sectors (i.e. restaurants and pubs, alcohol and tobacco and housing and fuel costs). Business costs are rising too; only London and Paris are more expensive than Dublin in terms of the cost of office space.

The general picture of the domestic sector in Ireland is of one that is prone to overheating, where lack of competition in the services sector does not whittle prices downward and where there are bubble-type conditions in the housing and credit markets. Normally these conditions require harsh monetary medicine to control them. Even the recent experience of the Federal Reserve has demonstrated that bubbles in asset prices are hard to identify and harder still to manage. Given that conventional macroeconomic policy measures are effectively not available to Irish policy-makers, focused microeconomic adjustments within the housing, banking and construction sectors are perhaps the only way to achieve a balanced economy and prevent stresses in the consumer sector from feeding back into public finances. The remaining policy option, fiscal policy, needs to become more innovative in the future. In this respect, Ireland is beginning to show itself as an inventive policy-maker.

Innovations
The likely challenge for policy-makers will be to try to use fiscal policy to stimulate or rein in economic activity when monetary policy is not obliging. To borrow a military term, fiscal policy will have to be used to target surgical strikes on specific areas of the Irish economy. There are already a number of emerging examples.

One of these relates to the setting up of the National Pension Reserve Fund. Compared to most other European countries, demographics in Ireland are favourable. The bulk of the population is currently young[59] and in employment, while the average profile elsewhere in Europe is of a much older workforce, leading to a scenario in twenty years time where a large part of the population of, say, Italy is retired and dependent on a small workforce to generate the tax revenues to pay the state pensions of retirees.

The fact that the pensions 'time bomb'[60] facing Ireland is not as bad as in other countries is no reason to ignore it, which thankfully is what policy-makers have not done. The setting up of the National Pension Reserve Fund (run by the National Treasury Management Authority – NTMA) establishes an investment fund that is financed through the receipt of 1% of GNP each year, as well as some other revenues, such as proceeds from the sale of state assets.

Similar funds have been set up in other countries, principally to invest the oil revenues of Abu Dhabi and Norway,[61] and to tackle the pensions deficit in France. Still, this is a relatively new type of project and several issues present themselves. For example, how aggressively will the fund invest its capital in equities, or will it opt more for government bonds? Should it not invest in Irish firms in order to avoid conflicts of interest, how will it behave in contests of ownership (i.e. takeovers), should it only undertake ethical investments and how will its officers be appointed and remunerated? Some of these questions have already been answered, but others are likely to persist. Despite this, the Irish National Pension Reserve Fund remains an exception amongst its European neighbours, and stands as an example of a sensible way of dealing with a structural economic problem.

A second example is the scheme set up by the government in 2001 to encourage saving, the Special Savings Incentive Account (SSIA). The scheme is not unlike those employed in other countries, such as ISAs in the UK and some of the savings schemes operated in the Asian Tiger countries. The SSIA is a savings account where an individual deposits a regular amount each month, to which the government adds 25% of that amount. The deposits cannot be withdrawn for five years, with interest accruing at the normal medium-term rate. The benefit of such accounts is that they encourage savings, and theoretically at least help to reduce consumption-fuelled inflation. It is estimated that, in 2001 and the early half of 2002, 12 billion euro went into SSIAs, which in turn should boost consumption in 2006 when the five-year limit on accounts set up in 2001 runs out.

Although theoretically appealing, there are a number of problems with such accounts. Firstly, they decrease the fiscal flexibility of the government in the future. Secondly, consumers often merely substitute the SSIAs for other forms of savings. With relatively high inflation in Ireland, a considerable premium over long-term EU rates is required to induce savings. Thirdly, the release of SSIA-based savings can arrive at an inconvenient time, such as a period when the economy is strong and is in less need of liquidity.

Part IV – Staying competitive and lucky

A pensions reserve fund and special savings accounts are just two innovative means of structuring the Irish economy so that imbalances are avoided in the medium and long term. A more difficult problem to deal with is maintaining Ireland's competitiveness in relation to other small open economies.

Most available evidence suggests that Ireland is becoming less competitive. Since the beginning of this century, the consequences of economic success have begun to erode Ireland's competitiveness, such that the price of doing business in or with Ireland is becoming prohibitive. At the same time its advantage as an English-speaking source of skilled labour is increasingly being challenged by countries as far away as India and the factors that make Ireland attractive to global corporations, such as low taxes, are being copied by its fellow EU Member States in Eastern Europe. This trend is made clearer by the *World Competitiveness Report*, published by the IMD,[62] in which the US ranked as the world's most competitive economy, with Ireland moving from 5th place in 2000 to 10th in 2004.

The report underlines the fact that Ireland has become a staging-post for globalisation, taking in foreign investment capital and exporting profits and manufactured goods like no other country. In terms of the factors that concern foreign investment, Ireland ranked highly for economic performance, especially for investments. Similarly government efficiency warranted a high ranking for indicators like corporate taxes (1), investment incentives (1), political stability and a lack of discrimination against foreign companies.

However, with regard to issues that concern the domestic economy and workplace, such as inflation, the cost of living, resilience of the economy to global economic cycles, discrimination, harassment, gender, export credits and corruption,[63] Ireland fared poorly. The report also pointed a finger at under-developed physical and distribution infrastructure, internet access, maintenance of infrastructure, alcohol and drug abuse and urbanisation of cities. Amongst the worst results for Ireland were factors like (out of 29): discrimination (29), consumer prices (25), industrial disputes (26), distributional infrastructure (29), internet access (29), maintenance of infrastructure (28), alcohol and drug abuse (27) and bribery and corruption (19).

Another Swiss-based study, the World Economic Forum's Global Competitiveness Index,[64] ranked Ireland in 26th place out of 117 countries. Finland and the US topped this ranking, and Ireland fell behind most other small growing and developed economies.

The results of the IMD and World Economic Forum surveys are supported by the National Competitiveness Council's (NCC) extensive Annual Competitiveness Survey, which benchmarks Ireland against a sample of fifteen countries on the basis of 128 competitiveness-related indicators. The National Competitiveness Council reports in 2003, 2004 and 2005 identified the weak links in Irish industry as innovation, creativity and technological infrastructure. The overall quality of physical infrastructure is on a par with Hungary and Poland and the efficiency of the distribution infrastructure is no better than in Poland, Hungary and New Zealand. Motorway efficiency, the quality of ports and the speed of business deliveries are all of poor relative quality. Business costs, such as energy, insurance and office rents, are high too.

Although the rate of government investment is picking up, this reflects the continuing catch-up of the Irish economy with others such as Hong Kong and Singapore, where technological and physical infrastructures are first class. Government spending on infrastructure (through the National Development Plan 2000–2006) is climbing, but the cumulative level over the past twenty years is very low because public spending on capital stock has not kept pace with economic growth. The fact that government spending on capital stock is now growing as quickly as many of the accession states (i.e. Hungary) shows that Ireland is still in catch-up mode.

Similarly, compared to countries like Denmark and Korea, the proportion of households and companies using broadband is tiny, as is collaboration amongst business clusters relative to the likes of Finland and Japan. The intensity of local competition is low (Ireland ranks joint 13th out of 15), although at the same time the burden of regulation on businesses is also low. Also, the total number of researchers (per 1,000 employees) and patent applications is low when judged against leading innovators such as the US, Japan, Sweden, Finland and France. Finally, in the 2005 NCC report Ireland scored badly on the basis of competitive advantage (13th out of 15), a fact that should focus attention on the need to move away from cost competitiveness towards innovation and knowledge-based activities.[65]

Despite over ten years of growth under the influence of the world's most prominent high-tech companies, Ireland is still well behind its European and global peers in terms of capital invested in research. Ireland's business expenditure on research and development is only 73% of the EU average and 57% of the OECD average, while gross expenditure on research and development at 1.39% of GNP is below the EU average (1.7%) and that of the US (2.7%). On most measures of research intensity, Ireland is below the levels of the EU average, the Nordic countries and the US.

While EU governments have set a target ratio of research and development to GDP of 3% by 2010 – which would be a doubling of Ireland's rate – it is very difficult to see this being achieved by Ireland. In fact, Slovenia currently has a more intensive research rate than Ireland, with the Czech Republic coming close. Singapore has a research and development rate that is almost twice Ireland's.

The cause of research and development in Ireland is further weakened when we consider the findings of a thorough evaluation of business research and development in Ireland.[66] In general, Ireland is still below average levels of research and development in the OECD and EU 25. The comparison with other states is starker when we consider that Finland, Sweden and Denmark all spend at least twice as much as Ireland does on research and development.

At the industry level, in Ireland business research and development is concentrated in the electronics (20%), software (35%) and pharmaceuticals (18%) industries. However, most business research and development in Ireland is carried out by foreign firms, which undertake 95% of business research and development in the pharmaceuticals industry and 80% of that in electronics. Overall, less than one-third (28%) of research and development spending in Ireland is attributable to domestic firms (about 40% of this is in software).

Government funding for research and development (33 million euro in 2003) is dwarfed by that spent by foreign corporations (775 million euro in 2003) and Ireland ranks as one of the lowest amongst the OECD countries for the proportion of business sector research and development that is government funded (3% in 2003), ranking 21st out of 25 countries.

Research and development activity in Ireland is revealing of the nature of economic globalisation in Ireland. It is largely driven by foreign corporations in a small number of industries, with reasonably few spin-off effects on the domestic economy. For one of the most globalised economies in the world, the domestic Irish economy is low-tech and compared to some of its European peers eschews research and development as a core business activity. In the face of deteriorating competitiveness and rising competition from the new EU entrants, the implication is that domestic industry needs to invest more in research and, analogously, become more high-tech. Yet, most of the available evidence suggests that this analysis has not yet been accepted by domestic business in Ireland.

In this context, the Irish economic miracle faces three broad challenges in at least the next five years. The first is that most of the magic ingredients that have propelled its economy over the last ten years have run their course. The second relates to the challenge of managing a globalised open economy with a relatively meagre set of policy tools. The third issue is that many of the factors that made it an attractive investment location are being mimicked by the Eastern European countries and others further away, like India. These three issues are outlined in the following paragraphs.

Factors that have driven globalisation are fading

The Irish experience of economic globalisation has been hugely success-ful, with the greatest prize being the reduction in unemployment, from 17% to under 5%, as the country moved from an under-developed Euro-pean nation to one whose gross national product is now at the EU aver-age. However, most of the factors that have driven the performance of the Irish economy appear to have run their course. US and European inter-est rates are beginning to rise, while corporation and personal taxes in Ireland seem to have little room to fall further. Moreover, in the near future Ireland will become a net contributor to the EU's coffers as opposed to a net recipient of funding. Also, the level of investment in the US high-tech sector that was seen in the late 1990s is unlikely to be repeated in the near future, and the US economy itself is subject to a number of imbalances, such as the very high level of government debt, a weak fiscal situation and the combination of low savings with high con-sumer debt. The dangers these trends pose to the US economy and their relation to the euro-zone have been highlighted by the former Chairman of the Board of Governors of the US Federal Reserve, Alan Greenspan,[67] amongst many others.

The social partnership agreements that have managed to contain wage inflation in the past ten years are also part of this trend. A very broad view of these agreements sees them as exchanging tax cuts from the government for wage growth moderation on the part of employees. This axis is now likely to be undermined from a number of quarters. Firstly, the ability of the government to deliver further tax cuts is limited. Secondly, rising house and consumer prices increase the pressure on workers to break with wage-setting agreements. Thirdly, income distrib-ution, which unlike other European countries has not figured prom-inently in Irish collective bargaining agreements, remains an issue in Irish society and may become a more pressing political issue in the future. Finally, the wage agreements hammered out in recent partner-ships are dependent on competitiveness and productivity, both of which, in the domestic sector at least, are uninspiring.

New problems

The exuberant growth of the Irish economy in the 1990s created wealth and prosperity, and for a while seemed to have few of the side-effects that critics of globalisation would have expected. However, the social and eco-nomic consequences of this great transformation are beginning to show themselves. One which has already been referred to is that the economy is still bloated by inflation in house prices, consumer prices and high debt levels, all of which are making life difficult for the consumer.

An assessment of inflation in Ireland by the Central Bank of Ireland[68] expresses serious concern about inflation, particularly service sector inflation, stating that 'there is still some way to go before it could be said that the economy has "bought in" to a culture of price stability'. In turn, inflation is hurting competitiveness and, according to the Central Bank, 'as previous Bulletins have reported, Ireland's competitiveness has worsened significantly over the past two years. The Bank's Real Trade Weighted Competitiveness Index (RTWCI), which measures changes in competitiveness arising from differing rates of inflation and exchange rate fluctuations, shows that, since joining EMU in 1999, Ireland's competitiveness has dis-improved by about 15 per cent.'

A common thread between service price inflation and the competitiveness of the economy internationally is the level of competition in the domestic economy. A number of reports have highlighted the absence of serious competition in certain areas of the economy, such as telecommunications, transport and the professions, and international surveys such as the World Competitiveness Report give Ireland a very low ranking in terms of the intensity of domestic competition. Lack of competition can leave Irish companies unprepared to match their international peers, either at home or abroad. This much is already clear in the contrast between foreign companies operating in Ireland and domestic businesses, and in turn makes it imperative that, if Ireland is to become a truly globalised economy and not merely a staging-post for global corporations, then indigenous firms need to become more competitive.

Competition policy is one area where policy-makers can be active, and the recent Competition Act of 2002 has helped to make inroads into this issue. However, the Competition Authority in Ireland is not sufficiently resourced, nor does it seem to have adequate political backing. The incentive on the part of Irish business to protect uncompetitive segments of the economy is high and may lead to intensive lobbying of politicians. Ironically, the threat of competition may drive domestic business people in Ireland to revolt against globalisation.

On a broader scale, policy-makers are beginning to address some of the weak points in the Irish economy. The recent Enterprise Strategy Group (ESG) study and the Department of Enterprise's *Building Ireland's Knowledge Economy* are the most significant attempts to take stock of the Irish economy since the Culliton Report in 1992. They perform the valuable research function of providing detailed accounts of the state of Ireland's industrial and services sectors. The ESG report unsurprisingly concludes that 'the enterprise model that worked for us in the past, and that delivered unprecedented growth will have to be modified considerably if we are to continue to grow and develop'.[69]

This report recognises that, in order to sustain a high level of economic growth, the country must have a comparative advantage relative to other nations, or indeed its companies must have a competitive advantage. Apart from the food and beverage, and construction sectors, and perhaps a small number of technology firms, not many Irish companies possess a distinct competitive advantage in the fields in which they operate. Neither do low corporate taxes and a reasonably well-educated workforce constitute a comparative advantage, as they are already being copied by plenty of emerging European economies.

So, if Ireland is to acquire expertise in certain areas (the ESG report lists several potential ones), it must do so by investment in research (supported of course by increased spending on infrastructure). However, it is at this point that the aspirations of policy-makers and the fact that Ireland can hardly be described as a leading research nation diverge. Calls to increase the number of sales and marketing personnel in Irish companies and demands that the level of research must be increased ignore the fact that domestic companies export very little compared to foreign companies because they focus on local service markets, are in low research and development industries like catering and construction, and operate in uncompetitive environments.

Part of the growing-up process of the Irish economy is the related growth in institutions such as the NCC and the ESG that inform the debate on the Irish economy. Yet, the problem remains that, even if the level of policy debate on globalisation is picking up from low levels, it still does not guarantee that this change in attitude is passed on to indigenous businesses.

New competitors
The third problem for policy-makers and politicians in Ireland lies in maintaining and developing Ireland's attractiveness as a destination for foreign investment capital, and in so doing proving that the economic boom of the late 1990s occurred more by design than chance. To a large extent Ireland has become too fond of and familiar with the steady flow of investment capital from abroad, principally from the US. As a result, both the public and policy-makers may not yet be fully attuned to the fact that the flow of capital is unsentimental and will just as easily find other Tiger economies to incubate.

Specifically, the challenge is to ensure that the policies and factors that drew foreign investment into Ireland in the first place are not quickly superceded by other countries. The Irish economic miracle will have been built on weak foundations if comparatively decent educational systems in Hungary and Poland, low corporation taxes in the Baltic states (for example, Estonia now has a zero % rate of corporation tax), relatively good physical infrastructure (e.g. Poland), low wages[70] and generally cheap labour in the new EU Member States begin to sap Ireland of its foreign investment. The fact that the EU's new entrants are already copying Ireland's economic policies is clear from the fact that the likes of Poland, Hungary and Latvia have all cut corporation taxes to low levels.

The low personal and corporate tax rates in some of the accession states have spurred a debate on 'flat taxes'. Flat taxes have worked in these countries because they are straightforward and, in the context of emerging democracies that did not have the institutional structures to administer and collect taxes, helped bring in more revenue than more complex systems. Russia is an excellent case in point. Its government finances collapsed in the late 1990s because of a huge shortfall in government revenue. However, a flat personal tax of 13% introduced in 2001 saw many more households pay taxes and government finances improve thereafter. However, the simplicity of the flat tax can be misleading. The fact that it has proved useful and popular in several emerging nations does not mean that it is equally attractive for developed countries. Low flat taxes can be difficult to reverse, and do not place a premium on fairness. Moreover, they further diminish the flexibility of fiscal policy, which in Ireland's case will be very important in the future.

In the medium term, however, liberal economic policies like the flat tax are likely to be popular with Ireland's emerging economic competitors in Eastern Europe as they seek to replicate its high economic growth. In turn, because many of the factors that led to high economic growth in Ireland are easily mimicked, the danger of Ireland being undercut by the likes of Slovakia and Hungary is very high.

New goals, new peers
It is because this threat is serious that economic policy in Ireland needs to focus on new goals and a new peer group. The economic goal of creating jobs has now been achieved and Ireland has left its old peer group of Spain, Greece and Portugal behind. Yet, by comparison with the other small developed economies of Europe (i.e. the Nordic countries), Ireland is not yet fully developed. Infrastructure is generally weak and research and development are low, to mention but two structural differences. While preserving most of the factors that have led to its recent success, economic policy in Ireland must focus on a new peer group with the specific aim of qualitatively improving the structure of its domestic economy.

Part of the reason for this is that Ireland is too dependent on overseas multinationals for jobs and investment, and also on secular trends in global financial markets, such as the fall in long-term interest rates over the past ten years. The fact that the Irish economy has come through the recent downturn in the global economy relatively unshaken says much for the new-found growth in domestic sectors and for the relative strength of government finances. Yet this should not fuel complacency. During the nineteenth century era of globalisation, Argentina was one of the richest countries in the world, with highly developed financial markets, yet it never recovered from a series of financial market shocks and the era of protectionism that followed the Great Depression.

A reflection of this problem lies in the challenge for Irish policy-makers to bridge the gap between growth in gross domestic and gross national product, which over the past few years has typically been 4% and reached as high as 7% in 2002. This trend is also reflected in the disparity between foreign and domestic levels of funding for research and development. Well over half of business-based research and development in Ireland is undertaken by foreign companies. This means that many of the benefits of investment do not stay in Ireland nor do they accord with national development objectives.

This is one example that underlines the point that globalisation can take as well as give. Ireland is remarkable in that it has so far been a substantial net beneficiary of economic globalisation. Keeping Ireland lucky[71] will take some doing. Its fortunes are now firmly hitched to globalisation, leaving it exposed to the risk that economic globalisation could fluctuate or fade. Thankfully at the moment, despite a healthy supply of scare stories, there are not many signs that globalisation is about to grind to a halt, although the level of noise generated by debates on issues like immigration, outsourcing and protectionism is rising, as these topics become political issues on both sides of the Atlantic.

Outsourcing is now a major political issue in the industrialised countries of the world, with politicians in large countries like Germany and France calling for an end to it. The contention that globalisation leads to wage pressures in developing countries is underlined in a recent World Bank report that states that 'it has put real pressure on less skilled workers in rich countries, and this competitive pressure is a key reason why the growing integration is controversial in the industrial countries'.[72] Despite this, a study published by Wei and Amiti showed that, overall, large developed countries are net gainers from the outsourcing process.[73]

As one of the most globalised countries in the world, Ireland should be worried about the general health of the global economy and the rise of economic nationalism and protectionism. These forces stifled the wave of globalisation that stretched from 1870 to 1913 and created a difficult international economic climate into which the Irish state was born. As

then, wars, profound structural financial imbalances and rising protectionism are now threatening open societies and economies.

Conclusion

An analysis of the turnaround in the Irish economy yields few secrets and
little evidence of an exceptional Irish economic model. What is clear is
that a combination, or system, of pragmatic, business-friendly policy-
making, supported by a healthy supply of labour, the framework of
European economic convergence and positive global trends in investment and interest rates, drove economic growth in Ireland. In future, it
is unlikely that powerful external forces such as falling interest rates and
helpful domestic factors (e.g. a plentiful supply of labour) will be as kind
to Ireland.

Although it would be more attention-grabbing to write about the
impending collapse of the Irish economy, the most likely progression of
its economy in the future is that, once imbalances are resolved, it will take
up a path of growth that is closer to the EU average. In turn, this implies
a dilution in expectations of growth from their current high levels.

This is just the kind of phase that France and Germany are going
through at present, though in a moribund fashion. Following their economic miracles, or 'trentes glorieuses', in the two decades up to the
1980s, their economies, especially Germany's, are close to stagnation and
beset by structural problems. In both of these countries tension is emerging between the desire to safeguard the high standard of living and social
cohesion that have been built up over the past forty years and the need
to invigorate their economies.

Over the coming years, Ireland will have to face the same dilemma
but from the opposite point of view, namely from a growing need to prove
that growth can be sustained and also translated into an improved level of
human development, better infrastructure (financial and physical)[74] and
less inequality. The means by which this debate can be resolved is primarily through fiscal policy and this will present a number of challenges.

The first of these is not so much to sustain growth but to derive it
from new sources and to minimise the downside risks to the current dri-
vers of economic performance. High relative levels of inflation, debt and
expectations will have to be carefully managed if they are not to trip up
the economy, while the domestic industrial sector needs to be persuaded
and helped to produce higher long-term average earnings growth before
it finds itself exposed by foreign competitors.

The second broad challenge is to spread the benefits of growth in a
more far-sighted manner. Should the debate on globalisation in Ireland
swing in favour of more 'social' policies and a greater role for the state,

then one implication will be higher taxes. Granted that Ireland's economic success has been based partly on a foundation of low and falling taxes, raising them is likely to be controversial. However, there is scope to change tax policy in several sectors of the economy. Higher taxes on very high earners, capital gains on property (especially commercial property) and a further clampdown on tax evasion are all potential means of stewarding both economy and society. In addition, spending on infrastructure will need to be increased, but at the same time made much more efficient than it currently is.

Underlying the above challenges is the fact that policy-makers in Ireland operate with a limited policy arsenal. In this regard, innovations in policy will be precious and will offer Irish policy-makers the opportunity to truly distinguish themselves and to show that there is a discernible Irish model of economic management.

Chapter Five

The Republic

'We will not borrow liberty from America nor from France, but we will manufacture it ourselves and work it up with those materials which the hearts of Irishmen furnish them with at home.'[1]
United Irishmen

This chapter deals with the challenge posed by globalisation to society, public life and institutions in Ireland. The central argument is that, like the economy and foreign policy, globalisation has brought about a great transformation in Irish society and that, in turn, politics and government institutions will have to adapt to the changes wrought by globalisation, and to the reassessment of political and social values that must follow in the wake of its path through Ireland.

These changes can be seen from at least two perspectives – those outside the state or at the macro and supra-national levels, and those within the state at the micro or local levels. Although Irish society is nowhere near as globalised as its economy, the side-effects of globalisation are manifesting themselves, notably at the local/micro level. On the other hand, supra-national bodies like the EU are playing an increasing role in Ireland's affairs.

The first part of this chapter focuses on the micro level and specifically on the effects of globalisation on Irish society, or at very least the dramatic changes that have coincided with it, from wealth creation to multiculturalism to reduced solidarity.

Part I – Globalisation and the Republic

In the analysis of globalisation in Ireland presented so far in this book, a number of trends will already have become clear. One is that, before the current wave of globalisation, be it during the nineteenth century or in the period up to the end of the 1980s, Ireland was economically bleak by comparison with other European states. For most of this period ideology had a firm grip on politics, largely in the form of constitutional republicanism commingled with nationalism. This has now changed and ideology has been swapped for pragmatism. Though this change in mindset has been an enabling factor in Ireland's economic success, it has blurred prior ideological distinctions between the main political parties in Ireland, and has diminished the sense that there is a broader framework or objective guiding policy-making.

Political pragmatism has drawn Ireland closer to the neo-liberal model in respect of economic and social policies and as a result has meant that when compared to other small developed states Ireland is something of an outlier. Though highly globalised, the role of government is small (particularly in the areas of spending, taxation, social welfare and insurance provision) and the level of human development is comparatively low, whereas in other countries, like Denmark, the opposite is the case. In general, small open economies need to have, and in most cases do have, a greater role for government to insulate society against the effects and risks of the outside world.

This trend suggests that economic globalisation in Ireland has proceeded with little thought for its effects on society and the broad risks that economic openness poses. It also suggests that the triumph of pragmatism over ideology may have run too far, and that a political framework is needed that will restore some balance to what has so far been a very lop-sided globalisation process.

In this respect, the key role that the political idea of republicanism has played in the state, and the modern conception of it as 'freedom as non-domination', suggest that it is the appropriate reference point to use in tracking the impact of globalisation on Irish society. Indeed, in other European republics, notably Germany and France, there is a widespread and strengthening view that the state ought to insulate its citizens from the side-effects of globalisation.

The first part of this chapter uses the context of republicanism to examine the dramatic changes that globalisation has wrought in Ireland by very briefly outlining the meaning and background of republicanism and then assessing how its components are changing in the context of the transformation of Irish society and public life over the last ten or so years.

What does republicanism mean?

The struggle for independence from Britain has been the holy grail of Irish politics, a quest that in some people's eyes is not yet complete but in the minds of others has been drawn to a close with the Good Friday Agreement. As has been mentioned previously in this book, this drive for independence, combined with Ireland's economic, intellectual and political seclusion from most of the developed world over the course of the past four centuries, has meant that it largely missed out on enormously influential events in European history, from the Renaissance to the two world wars.

Despite this, a universal political idea, republicanism, found its way to Ireland and took root, profoundly influencing its politics and history. As the formative political force acting on Ireland, the way in which republicanism is understood and practised is important, more so in light of the challenge posed to it by globalisation and the manner in which the meanings of republicanism and nationalism in Ireland have become conflated.

Republicanism refers to a system of government that fosters the common rather than the individual good and promotes freedom and equality. One of the leading scholars of republicanism defines it simply as 'freedom as non-domination', by which he means 'not being subject to the arbitrary sway of another or being subject to the potentially capricious will or the potentially idiosyncratic judgement of another'.[2] This definition is particularly relevant to the case of a globalised society, because the social and political aspects of the Global Question centre on whether globalisation emasculates, taking away the power of sovereign states and citizens and leaving them in thrall to powerful market forces. The popular view of globalisation promoted by anti-globalists is one where nations are powerless when pitted against the force of financial markets, where consumers are the dupes of mega brands and where élite cabals run the world. Even this pessimistic view of a world dominated by globalisation speaks to the above definition of republicanism.

The common good

Many countries in the developed world now possess republican constitutions, varying in form from Germany's Federal Republic to Iran's Islamic Republic. In ancient times, Plato represented republican values as supporting a just, egalitarian form of government existing for the benefit of all of its citizens, underpinned by a consideration for the less advantaged. On a similar basis, the Roman version of republicanism consisted of strong institutional forms, a society governed by the notion that its citizens were free from domination by others (citizens, unlike slaves, had no masters) and that acted for the *res publica* or the common good.

The ideal of the republic fell dormant until it was resurrected over a thousand years later by Machiavelli in his *Discourses*.[3] He emphasised the fact that the republic and its rulers existed for the purpose of virtu, the common good. Freedom rested on the non-domination of citizens, who in turn contributed to the republic through active involvement in civic life. From this point, the sense that the republic was built for the welfare of its citizens survived to the revolutions of the eighteenth century that overthrew colonial and monarchical regimes in America and France. The revolutions in America and France[4] in 1775 and 1789 are commonly seen as crucial factors in the life of modern republicanism. For instance, the republican spirit is evident in the American Declaration of Independence that brought the War of Independence (1775–1783) to a close and in the later Gettysburg Address (1863), where Lincoln spoke of a 'new nation, conceived in liberty, and dedicated to the proposition that all men are created equal'.

The development of the modern republican system took place against a geopolitical background where the three Atlantic powers (America, Britain and France) traded ideologies, goods and labour. In terms of ideas, America received the Enlightenment from Europe, whose revolutionaries soon came to regard America as the republican Utopia. America also received military and financial support from the government of Louis XVI, and in turn it provided France with a blueprint constitution, as well as a real-world example of what a republic could look like, with roving intellectuals like Benjamin Franklin to promote it.

Franklin in particular was influential, acting as a lynchpin between the intellectual republican movements in the three countries, and co-opting the energy of the likes of Thomas Paine. In turn, Paine, together with other writers like Montesquieu and Rousseau, contributed to the intellectual framework behind the first French Republic. The spread of their ideas provided an attractive outline to movements in other countries that were dedicated to ideal forms of government.

Republicanism in Ireland

In the context of Ireland's seclusion from the rest of the world up to the end of the eighteenth century, the American and French revolutions were the first international events (outside Britain) to have a major impact on public life in Ireland. At this point in time and for a considerable period afterwards, Ireland was a desolate and depressing place, a fact emphasised by Benjamin Franklin after his tour of Ireland in 1771 (his descriptions are very like Tocqueville's observations some fifty years later):

> I have lately made a Tour thro' Ireland and Scotland. In these Countries a small Part of the Society are Landlords, great Noblemen and Gentlemen, extreamly [sic] opulent, living in the highest Affluence and Magnificence: The Bulk of the People Tenants, extreamly poor, living in the most sordid Wretchedness in dirty Hovels of Mud and Straw, and cloathed [sic] only in Rags.[5]

The republican model inspired one of the first explicit attempts to imagine and construct a model of what an independent Irish state might look like, a project taken up by the United Irishmen. The foundation of the United Irishmen in October 1791, 'For the purpose of forwarding a brotherhood of affection, a communion of rights and a union of power among Irishmen of every religious persuasion, and thereby to obtain a complete reform in the legislature founded on the principles of civil, political and religious liberty'[6] marks an important event in the history of ideas in Ireland, and one that is directly relevant to the debate on globalisation today.

First of all, it marks the incorporation of the republican principles of liberty, equality and fraternity into Irish public life. The notion of a political system rooted in secular, democratic politics and based upon universal ideas of equality and justice remains the espoused form of government in most developed countries today, and these values have been incorporated into the recent UN Millennium Declaration. In Ireland, the power of this secular and egalitarian outlook was evident in that specific causes like the Catholic Question and the Land Question were later rendered subservient to the greater issue of establishing independence, the Irish Question.

Secondly, the spirit of the United Irishmen's endeavour was decidedly internationalist, and marks a decisive point in Ireland's intellectual engagement with the rest of the world. The United Irishmen clearly wanted to be part of the broader democratic movement taking hold in the New and Old worlds. The flipside of the internationalisation of domestic events in Ireland was that the strategic threat that the rebellion of its American colonies posed to Britain, coupled with the political threat from the overthrow of the French monarchy, made London all the more resolved to crush any rebellion in Ireland.

Revolution
Little mercy was therefore shown to the likes of Theobald Wolfe Tone, who was captured in October 1798 as a member of a French expeditionary force to Ireland.[7] Wolfe Tone helped build the intellectual bridge between the French revolutionaries and the United Irishmen. Through his pamphleteering he was the main interpreter of the French Revolution for the United Irishmen. For example, he wrote that:

> 'In a little time the French Revolution became a test of every man's political creed, and the nation was fairly divided into two great parties, the Aristocrats and the Democrats . . . it is needless to say I was a Democrat from the beginning.'[8]

Wolfe Tone remains one of the inspirations, or 'morning stars', as he put it himself, for Irish republicans. His example, amongst others, has given the Irish republican ideal and the unsuccessful 1798 rebellion the heroic status that has endured through the past two centuries. After the 1798 rebellion and the Act of Union that followed, the flame of republicanism flared again in the late 1840s with the Young Irelanders, whose version of republicanism espoused the same republican principles of secularism (this inspired the Irish tricolour), separation from Britain and equality.

By the time the first wave of globalisation was breaking across Europe, there was little prospect that Ireland would be free, or that it would participate fully in globalisation. Though Irish output rose during this period, it grew by far less than that of Britain and most other industrialised countries. With the exception of Belfast, the country remained unindustrialised and, even by the beginning of the twentieth century, there was very little by way of a developed industrial base in Ireland.

The end of the first period of globalisation was marked by the rise of nationalism and huge political change across Europe, culminating in the First World War. The emergence of a militant and aggressive unionist block in Northern Ireland, the deterioration in the Irish economy with consequent harsh social and labour conditions, and Britain's engagement in the Great War provided the backdrop for the 1916 Rising. Although the objective of this revolution was separatist, leaders of the rebellion such as Pearse and Connolly had already framed a vision of a free Irish society. This was reflected in the Proclamation of the Republic, which, true to the legacy of the United Irishmen, avowed that:

> The Republic guarantees religious and civil liberty, equal rights and equal opportunities to all its citizens, and declares its resolve to pursue the happiness and prosperity of the whole nation and all of its parts, cherishing all of the children of the nation equally and oblivious of the differences carefully fostered by an alien government, which have divided a minority from the majority in the past.

Like the 1798 rebellion, the bloody outcome of the Easter Rising dramatised and crystallised the principles of republicanism in Ireland, but also made the independence of the island from Britain an imperative. This was partially gained some five years later. Faithful to the traditions established by the American and French republicans, Irish revolutions were usually followed by 'Terrors', normally prosecuted by the British but carried out with deadly effect by the Irish themselves during the Civil War.[9]

Civil war left its mark on Irish politics, and with the partition of the six northern counties provided the legal and political foundations for the growth of nationalism. Although it is present at varying times in the politics of almost every state, nationalism has been a powerful force in Irish politics, sufficiently so that it has eclipsed other ideas such as fascism and socialism.[10] It has also been influential enough for many people in and outside Ireland to see republicanism and nationalism as standing for the same thing, the independence of Ireland from Britain and the ending of partition. Although both of these ideas are easily grouped together under the umbrella of the 'National Question', there is a significant difference between them, especially where the Global Question is concerned.

Nationalism

A 'nation' refers to a community of people that usually possess common characteristics, like geography, history, language and customs, which form the basis for its existence. For example, Joseph Stalin defined a nation as 'primarily a community, a definite community of people, with a common language, a common territory, a common cohesive economic life, a common psychological make up'.[11]

Similarly, nationality is a derivative of the nation, denoting people's origins and the characteristics that enable them to belong to a nation and derive identity from it, while nationalism is the manner and extent to which these are expressed. Nationalism can be simply put as love or celebration of the nation. A good example of a patriotic view of the nation comes from Sean Lemass: 'patriotism as I understand it is a love of country, pride in its history, traditions and culture, and a determination to add to its prestige and achievements'.[12]

The key difference between nationalism and republicanism is that nationalism is the expression of the characteristics of the nation, whereas republicanism is a political idea that proposes a model of governing a society/nation. More than republicanism, nationalism dictates a consistent relationship between the characteristics of a nation and the political institutions and arrangements of the nation state. In Ireland, as in other countries, the concept of the nation has incorporated a sense of national territory, with most nationalists believing that the territory of the nation and the state should be one and the same. In particular, the unfinished business of partition has meant that many people regard republicanism and nationalism in Ireland as representing the same thing – the end of the partition of the island of Ireland. The opportunistic and superficial way in which some Irish politicians have employed these terms has not helped to make them any clearer.

To be specific, nationalists should desire the end of partition because its existence deprives the nation of part of its territory, and therefore separates the community that makes up the nation. Strictly speaking, republicans should find partition objectionable because the partitioned section of the nation is administered in a way that is contrary to all the values of republicanism. In Northern Ireland, the rise of aggressive republicanism during the Troubles was triggered by widespread civil rights abuses, and high levels of inequality and racism.[13]

Globalisation is changing the way in which nationalism in Ireland is expressed and may provide the means to disentangle it from republicanism. One danger is that Irish nationalism turns both complacent and foolish in that the so far successful globalisation of the Irish economy leads to an exuberant celebration of Ireland's success and the mistaken notion that there is something intrinsically exceptional in the way globalisation has been adopted in Ireland. In such an environment, nationalism provides a nursery bed for misplaced confidence and the growth of expectations that will later be confounded.

In addition to playing a significant role in the political life of the Irish state, nationalism also has an important place in the debate on globalisation. Nationalism and economic isolationism played a major role in drawing down the curtain on the first wave of globalisation, and were in turn exacerbated by its collapse.

The re-emergence of nationalistic conflicts in the former Yugoslavia, Rwanda, Sudan and Asia in recent decades has demonstrated that nationalism is very difficult to control once unleashed. In turn, this has bred new life into the question of whether globalisation transcends differences in nationality or exacerbates them. Though the increasing openness of borders, especially in European countries, together with the project of European integration, suggests that Europeans live in greater harmony now than before, recent trends also support the view that, rather than dampening down nationalism in favour of world-citizenship, globalisation can exacerbate its negative side. Immigration, for instance, is becoming a key electoral issue in many countries, and many of the reasons for the rejection of the EU Constitution in countries like the Netherlands and France can be traced to nationalism and economic isolationism.

Democracy
This chapter does not explicitly deal with democracy. Though republicanism, nationalism and democracy are all intrinsically linked, they also have separate roles. Republics do not have to be democratic, though the best ones are. Similarly, many of the world's democracies are not republics.

In general terms, the current wave of globalisation is different from the nineteenth-century version, in that there has been a growing number of communities seeking and gaining nationhood since the end of the

Second World War and the Cold War. The second wave of globalisation has flourished partly because democracies have been receptive to it, and in some cases it has helped to create them. Democracies usually have the legal, political and public infrastructures with which to import globalisation. There is, however, no strong evidence to suggest that democracy automatically begets development. Ireland is a prime example of a country that had a healthy democracy for much of the twentieth century but was none the wealthier as a result of it. If anything, the globalisation of Ireland has coincided with the deterioration of public life, as signalled by numerous financial and political scandals.

On the other hand, the Asian model of globalisation suggests that the spread of globalisation does not necessarily have to rely on democratic foundations. The Sinatra doctrine ('do it my way') of highly globalised Asian states like Hong Kong and Singapore has been built on authoritarian regimes whose democratic credentials are questionable. The example of the wider Asian region also shows that the existence of a functioning democracy is not always a guarantee of liberty, as there remain a relatively large number of countries that are democratic in name but that are in fact illiberal in nature. In his book *The Future of Freedom,* Fareed Zakaria refers to these as 'illiberal democracies'. His central argument is that, in a significant number of countries, such as Ghana, Venezuela or Kazakhstan, democracy is flourishing but liberty is not, in that 'across the globe democratically elected regimes, often ones that have been re-elected or reaffirmed through referenda, are routinely ignoring constitutional limits on their power and depriving their citizens of basic rights'.[14]

An investigation of a country's democratic credentials does not alone provide a good framework for analysing the effects of globalisation on society and public life, partly because the link between democracy and development is unclear, and also because it is possible to have democratic systems that permit very low levels of equality, liberty and civic virtue. Viewing the nation as a republic is better suited to this.[15]

The primary contention of this chapter is that the stresses that globalisation places on forms of government and society will, at least in Ireland's case, necessitate the reinforcing of the republican political system. In a world where external pressures on societies are increasing, the role of the state becomes more important. Globalisation can lead to situations where, to use Pettit's definition of republicanism, people, societies and economies are not free from domination by markets, corporations, consumer trends and other facets of globalisation, like global organised crime.

The great transformation

A theme that is prominent in many of the major works of political economy is the great change that societies undergo following significant changes to their long-term wealth.[16] When great political and economic upheavals take place, the most recent European cases being Georgia[17] and the Ukraine, revolutions follow in society and public life. Ireland is an excellent case study in this regard. Amongst the changes taking place following its bout of high economic growth are a rise in crime, particularly of the violent and organised kind, a fall in support for the Church, the unravelling of numerous financial and political scandals, the proliferation of consumerism, and the liberation of women in Irish society.

In examining social and political change in Ireland today, it is tempting to first evoke a picture of the Ireland of old as poor but happy and to balance it against the current scenario of Ireland as rich but malcontent. But, as surveys and plain economic evidence show, the attitude of Irish people to globalisation is positive. Wealth and low unemployment are infinitely preferable to glorious poverty. However, there can be little doubt that the economic success of Ireland in the past ten years has been accompanied by an eruption of social change.

To be both rigorous and fair to globalisation, many of the problems that continue to beset Irish society pre-date globalisation. Some of these are now apparent because they are being reported for the first time, like the various tribunals and investigations that are leeching Ireland of the ills of its recent past. In cases of financial and political corruption, globalisation has simply provided a deeper trough for the greedy to feed in.

Yet, there is already a growing body of thought that holds that Irish society is suffering the ill-effects of globalisation, and that the state is not adequately prepared to manage the way in which globalisation impacts upon Ireland. For example, in his book *The Celtic Tiger in Distress,* Peadar Kirby underlines how the emergence of 'values such as individualism, materialism, intolerance of dissent, lack of concern for the environment and a failure to value caring are identified as characterising life under the Celtic Tiger'.[18]

The next section of this chapter examines these arguments by analysing the ways in which the common good in Ireland is, and is not, served by globalisation, and where globalisation has not been harnessed to the benefit of the common good.

Equality

The key issue that highlights the way in which tension is growing between the republican view that underpins Irish history and the challenges posed to society by globalisation is inequality. There are a number of ways of examining inequality, from levels of poverty to differences in income and wealth. Differences in income and wellbeing can either be compared across countries, or within them. Inequalities between countries, such as first versus Third World countries, can provide stark results, such as comparing life expectancies in Northern Europe with those in sub-Saharan Africa, but comparisons within similar populations are also shocking, such as the fact that African-Americans are far more likely than the average American to die early, suffer poverty or be imprisoned.

Inequality is a very important issue for a range of reasons. First of all, inequalities at the lower end of income distributions are the root cause of serious issues like poverty and social disadvantage, problems which if they persist in turn lead to crime, weakened civic life and increased demands on public services like healthcare. Robert Wade suggests that in this sense even neo-liberals should find inequality problematic because, 'aside from the moral case against it, inequality above a moderate level creates a kind of society that even crusty conservatives hate to live in, unsafe and unpleasant'.[19]

Second, in many European countries, Ireland included, equality is an established political credo, though one that more often than not is paid little real service by politicians. Given Ireland's relative poverty historically, one would think that equality of income, wealth and opportunity would be a political priority in Ireland today, especially as strong economic growth provides the conduit with which to arrive at this. In the context of the globalisation of Ireland, it would be a great pity if Ireland's leap forward economically did not reduce inequality, or in fact exacerbate it. In this respect it is worth considering that similar spurts of growth in the UK (1980s) and the US (1990s) actually led to increased inequality[20] and that economic growth Anglo-Saxon style seems to be particularly associated with inequality.[21]

Unequal Ireland
On balance, the evidence suggests that significant inequalities persist in globalised Ireland, especially when compared to other small, developed European countries. This section details various aspects of inequality in Ireland, from disparities in income and wealth to gender inequality, levels of poverty and human development, meritocracy and the increasing preference for privatised public goods.

Starting with income inequality, Nolan and Maitre state that 'Ireland is still shown as having a relatively high Gini coefficient, but it is now rather lower than Portugal, and similar to a group that includes the UK, Spain and Greece',[22] and that, while inequality fell slightly from 1973 to 1987, it rose again from 1987 to 1998. Their work highlights the fact that over the past twenty years the richest 10% of the population consistently reaped 25% of disposable income, while the bottom 10% had only 3% of total disposable income.

Their findings are supported by other work, such as a paper by Nolan and Smeeding (2004). Using similar data they state that 'Ireland remains an outlier among rich European nations in its high degree of income inequality' and they specifically find that:

> The share (of total disposable income) of the top 1% rose from 4.8% in 1990 to 8% in 2000 – almost all of the growth in the top 10% was concentrated in the top 1%, this meant that by the end of the 1990s the share of the top 1% was more than twice the level prevailing through the 1970s and 1980s.[23]

These authors also find that government policy measures like taxation and transfers have done little to reduce income inequality and relative poverty. They conclude on a depressing note that, 'overall, lower income Irish are worse off than the low-income persons in all other nations, save Britain'.[24]

Comparing Ireland to its European peers, the EU Social Situation in Europe (2004)[25] report showed that income inequality (as measured by the Gini coefficient) in Ireland is higher than the EU average, although it has declined slightly in recent years.[26] As measured by the ratio of the income of the highest income quintile (top 20%) to the lowest quintile (bottom 20%), in Ireland the top 20% earned 4.4 times more than the bottom 20%, as compared to 3.1 times in Denmark, 3.7 in the Czech Republic, 3.6 in Germany and 4.9 in the UK.

Inequality is often difficult to measure because of a lack of available data (i.e. tax evasion creates problems). A study by O'Neill and Sweetman[27] tries to overcome some of these problems by examining data on both income and consumption patterns (using household budget surveys). Their findings support the view that there has not been much change in inequality in Ireland over time.

One aspect of inequality that income-based measures do not pick up is wealth inequality. The structural rise in asset prices, mostly property, as well as public and private equity, has fuelled a huge increase in private wealth in Ireland. Although a significant premium was demanded to hold Irish assets prior to the late 1980s, the surge in property and equity valuations has widened the gap in wealth between those who held these assets or had the borrowing power to leverage their holdings and those that did not. If anything, wealth more than income has been concentrated in the hands of a few. This is important, not just for the way in which it multiplies through the rest of the economy, but also for its social impact.

Moreover, the ability and desire of some in Ireland to evade tax in recent years has in effect widened the gap in income and wealth inequalities. The numerous tax evasion scandals involving the major banking groups, politicians and the entrepreneur class suggest that, until recently, many income streams and capital gains incurred little tax, thus stretching the post tax gap in incomes between tax avoiders and tax payers.

The social situation

The continuing presence of serious income and wealth inequalities in Ireland and the emergence of a class of new rich is all the more striking when compared to the high levels of poverty in the country. The EU Social Situation study shows that Ireland has the highest proportion, 21%, of its population living in relative poverty of the 25 EU countries (the EU average is 15%).[28] Excluding social transfers does little to alter this picture, as the Irish rate of 30% of the population at risk of poverty compares unfavourably with the EU average of 24%. It also has one of the highest 'at persistent risk of poverty'[29] rates, at 13%, with only Portugal and Greece being worse off. Further, real improvements in incomes in Ireland also seem to have had little impact on poverty, especially in rural areas.[30]

An ESRI study, which refers to some of the same data as the EU Social Situation report, holds that:

> Ireland is consistently among a group of countries with relative income poverty rates considerably above the European Union average (though not as high as the USA). This has not changed over the course of Ireland's recent economic boom, since our relative income poverty rates themselves have not fallen, indeed they have generally risen over that period.[31]

Both the ESRI and EU studies highlight the fact that spending on social protection per capita is low in Ireland, even when compared to other countries with similar levels of unemployment.[32] In terms of both social service provision and cash transfers, Ireland ranks below most other European countries. In 2001, on a per capita basis, spending on social protection in Ireland was half that in the Netherlands. Again, in countries like Denmark and UK where the breakdown in social protection receipts is similar to that in Ireland, Irish spending on social protection remains comparatively low.

In common with other Anglo-Saxon countries, marginalisation has persisted during Ireland's experience of globalisation. Even though recent social partnerships have tried to give marginalised sections of society a say in public policy, recent accounts suggest that these groups do not feel that their views are incorporated into policy recommendations and that as a result inequalities persist. This is supported by the views of Community Platform, a network of 26 anti-poverty and pro-equality organisations set up in 1996, which has often highlighted the way in which minorities and marginalised sections of Irish society are left out of the political process.

Persistent human under-development
In terms of measures of social inequality like life expectancy and literacy, the 2004 and 2005 UN Human Development Reports (UNHDR) do not flatter Ireland either. The fact that so many Irish people fall below internationally recognised development thresholds is worrying, and does little to support the case that equality is thriving in Ireland.

Relative to its peer group of seventeen high-income OECD countries, Ireland ranks only 16th on the basis of human poverty, with Sweden being the best performer. Some of the indicators that contribute to this low ranking are embarrassing for a country with such a high level of wealth. In Ireland, 8.7% of the population are not expected to survive to the age of 60 and over 22.6% of adults lack functional literacy skills (ranking 14th out of 18 countries). According to the UNHDR, Ireland comes 20th out of 28 countries in terms of the proportion of its population living below the poverty line.

With respect to Ireland's contribution to the elimination of inequalities in less developed countries, the 2005 UNHDR report shows an improvement in official development assistance from Ireland, which has risen from $19 per capita in 1990 to $103 in 2003, well ahead of Australia, Canada and the US in per capita terms. Yet, Ireland is still eclipsed by other small European countries like Switzerland, Sweden, Denmark and Norway (which gives over three times the Irish per capita amount).

Women and men
Although there have been substantial advances in gender equality in Ireland over the last twenty years, inequality is still a major issue, according to the UN figures. In terms of overall gender development, Ireland ranks 11th, below many of its European peers. The UNHDR also tracks whether women take an active part in economic and political life.[33] As far as Ireland is concerned, the figures are not impressive. It ranks in the bottom half of countries in terms of the proportion of seats in parliament held by women, and performs poorly on the basis of female administrators and managers as a proportion of the total managerial class, and in terms of the proportion of female professional and technical workers.

It ranks higher, 19th place, on estimated female earned income, although this is still much lower than the male equivalent.

A study by the CSO entitled 'Women and Men in Ireland 2004', published in December 2004,[34] highlighted some sharp differences between the sexes in terms of income and welfare. Adjusting for hours worked, women's income was 82% of men's. The proportion of women at risk of poverty, after pensions and social transfers, was 23%, the highest rate in the EU 25. With regard to social issues, the proportion of lone-parent families with children under the age of 20 headed by women has increased from 87% in 1994 to 91% in 2004. On a related basis, Irish women make up 17.2% of all criminal convictions, the second highest in the EU after the UK, with most offences being classed as 'offences against property without violence'. In addition, the rate at which Irish women were undergoing a range of preventative medical examinations in 2002 was considerably lower than the rate for women in the other EU Member States.

The CSO study also shows stark differences in women's representation in positions of power relative to men. Only 13.3% of TDs in Dáil Éireann were women. Women are also poorly represented on the boards of state-sponsored bodies, local and regional authorities, An Seanad and as government ministers. Also, around 59% of women in the Civil Service were clerical officers, compared to only 10% of assistant secretaries, while 86% of primary school teachers were women but only 51% of primary school management were. On the plus side, women live longer than men in Ireland (by five years) and are increasingly better educated.

Overall, the picture that emerges of equality in Ireland is of a society that closely resembles the Anglo-Saxon countries, or at times its old economic peer group of the Mediterranean nations. In most cases, Ireland falls well behind the 'model' societies of the Nordic region and the larger European nations like Germany and France. Globalisation has made Ireland much better off, but it has not been harnessed in a way that has spread wealth to the parts of society that need it most.

Meritocracy

This much is also evident in the structure of Irish society, and the degree to which it can be described as a meritocracy. Until recently, many professions in Ireland – banking, law, medicine and academia – were not perceived as being 'meritocratic' and entry to them and progress up their hierarchies was to an extent dependent on education and social background. To some extent, and perhaps more in terms of gender than class inequality, the arrival of multinationals appears to have levelled some playing fields by operating on a skills not contacts system, which has contributed to better management practices.

However, a study[35] of social mobility in Ireland from the period 1973 to 2000 shows that, though there have been dramatic structural changes to Irish society (for example, the proportion of workers in the professional/managerial class rose from 13% to 23% between 1973 and 2000), these have done little to make Ireland a more meritocratic society. The authors state that:

> Ireland has experienced a great deal of social mobility in the last 30 years, but almost all of this mobility (96%) is due to the changing occupational structure and the sheer number of higher class positions available, rather than being due to increasing openness in the way that higher class positions are allocated.[36]

By this they mean that the absolute level of mobility has improved across society but relative mobility has changed very little. In other words, if the rising tide has lifted all boats, it has not changed the number of yachts relative to rowboats. In addition, they hold that 'class differentials are being preserved intact . . . no evidence of a general trend towards increased meritocracy' and 'throughout the course of the boom Ireland has remained a highly unequal society in terms of the distribution of income'.[37] On the basis of this evidence, globalisation and the way in which it has been managed again seems to have failed to break up inequalities in the structure of Irish society.

The privatisation of public goods
An emerging source of inequality relates to the privatisation of public goods in Ireland and the under-funding of them by the government. Education is a case in point. Although it is frequently invoked as one of the reasons for the strong performance of the Irish economy, government spending on it is not high, and the competitive nature of the education system is leading to a drift towards privately run colleges. In this way, Irish society is following Anglo-Saxon countries like Britain, Canada and the US,[38] where the attraction of privately financed schools relative to public ones is pronounced.

The growing popularity of 'grind' schools and private schools[39] specialising in Leaving Certificate courses exacerbates income inequalities, and in turn undermines the principle of equal access to third-level education. For instance, although the proportion of Irish people with a third-level education is above the OECD average, the proportion without a secondary-level education is below the OECD average. A more shocking example is quoted in the NESC report on the Developmental Welfare State: 'similar proportions of Irish and Swiss 25–64-year-olds had a third level attainment in 2002, but the proportion of Irish 25–64-year-olds with less than a completed secondary education was 2.7 times greater in Ireland than in Switzerland (40% v. 15%)'.[40]

Indicators in other fields, such as the rise of private medical clinics, the time that hospital consultants spend on private rather than public health provision and excess demand for good-quality local authority housing, help to build a picture of a growing trend towards the privatisation of public goods, the catch being that quality services are available only to those who can pay for them.

Ireland's culture of contentment

The above evidence underlines the danger that the economic success that stems from globalisation can breed contentment and a self-satisfaction that dulls the critical faculty of policy-makers when facing real and persistent social problems, and shows that over-confident celebration of the 'Celtic Tiger' rings hollow in the light of low levels of human development and equality.

The prevailing ethos of Irish society increasingly mirrors J. K. Galbraith's critique of America's culture of contentment, where he warns of the dangers that prosperity bring to a society, notably a complacent attitude towards the weak and poor, who are often left out of mainstream political discussion:

> What is new in the so-called capitalist countries – and this is a vital point – is that the controlling contentment and resulting belief is now that of the many, not just of the few. It operates under the compelling cover of democracy, albeit a democracy not of all citizens but of those who, in defense of their social and economic advantage, actually go to the polls. The result is government that is accommodated not to reality or common need but to the beliefs of the contented, who are the majority of those who vote.[41]

His assessment of the link between wealth and political participation still holds true with respect to the US, where the latest census showed that 40 million Americans live below the poverty line, many of whom do not or are not registered to vote. At the other end of the spectrum, aggressive lobbying by corporations often produces laws and regulations that appear irrational in economic terms and impose high social costs on the public.

The changes taking place in Irish society have not escaped domestic commentators either. In *Reinventing Ireland,* a group of social scientists take aim at the 'new culture' of modern Ireland – 'the precondition of Ireland's economic success, namely subservient integration into a radical free market or Anglo-American informational capitalism has itself shaped values, attitudes and forms of cultural expression'.[42]

Their reference to Anglo-American capitalism picks up on the distinction between the broad Anglo-Saxon and European models of society,[43] which is one of the key threads running through the globalisation of Ireland. The tension between the republican view of the world and the Anglo-Saxon model of globalisation presents a dilemma for Irish policy-makers. The emerging culture of contentment in Ireland is part of this dilemma. It expresses itself in a number of ways, from denial that Ireland's economic boom will falter, to a lack of political courage to decisively remedy institutional failure, to the erosion of fraternity. Irish society has long enjoyed a solid civic fabric, with institutions like the GAA and the localised nature of political party organisation being some of the factors that bred a sense of responsibility and involvement.[44] However, fraternity is deteriorating and there is an unmistakable feeling that Ireland has become a more materialistic and consumerist society, two trends that are readily associated with globalisation. The transition of Irish society from frugal to consumerist has been a sudden and in parts an inelegant one, with ugly social changes like an increase in homicide,[45] violent crime, anti-social behaviour and alcohol[46] and drug abuse[47] taking place along the way.

There are also increasing signs that the changes in Ireland's social and economic climate are being mapped onto the political landscape. Election turn-outs have been falling and cynicism about public life has been rising, indicating that Irish citizens are less engaged by public life. This is not surprising, given that both the state and the Catholic Church have had their credibility severely damaged by scandals involving corruption and sexual abuse.

Liberty

Another element of globalisation is the influx of immigrants into Ireland, and the associated rise in racist attitudes towards foreigners. As Irish society has become more integrated with the rest of the world, more foreigners have come to work and live in Ireland, but their liberty has been threatened from several quarters. These encroachments are discouraging, given that one feature of Irish political life has been a growing concern for the liberty of people in foreign countries (e.g. South Africa and East Timor) and a willingness to come to their aid, as manifested in the activities of the relatively large number of Irish NGOs and the actions of Irish individuals, be they public or private figures. However, concern for the liberty of foreigners in their own countries does not seem to have translated into respect for their liberty in Ireland.

The 'New Irish'[48] are an increasing though still small section of Irish society. The last census showed that, of the over 4 million people living in Ireland, 3.5 million were born there, and approximately 400,000 were born outside Ireland. Of these, 280,000 were born in the EU, with a further 30,000 born in the Americas.[49] This leaves approximately 90,000 residents of Ireland that were born in Asia, Eastern Europe and Africa, or just 2.3% of the total population. Add to this figure the relatively large influx of 85,000 Eastern Europeans who came to Ireland after the accession of the new EU states in May 2004[50] and the figure is just 4%.

To put matters in perspective, the city of Singapore, which comes ahead of Ireland in the AT Kearney/*Foreign Policy* globalisation rankings, has a population of which over 33% were not born in Singapore. By contrast, even if every foreign-born person in Ireland lived in Dublin, then the ratio of foreigners to natives would be just above 25%. In addition, the NCC Competitiveness report highlighted the fact that the stock of foreign workers as a percentage of the total labour force in Ireland is only 6.5% (though this represents a jump from a level of 3.7% in the 2004 report), as compared to 9% in Germany and 19% in Switzerland.

These figures help to make an important point about the nature of globalisation in Ireland. The first wave of globalisation in the nineteenth century distinguishes itself from the current one by the extent of international labour flows, with this trend having been led by the likes of the Irish and the Swedes. In the current period of globalisation there is now net migration into Ireland, with the Irish population unusual amongst its European peers in that it is expected to grow by up to 1% annually for the next ten years, and to rise to 5 million by 2020.[51] However, ironically there is plenty of evidence, culminating in the result of a mean-spirited referendum on citizenship in 2004, to show that the Irish are far less welcoming of labour inflows than they are of investment flows.

There are plenty of instances of racism in Ireland. The National Consultative Committee on Racism and Interculturalism (NCCRI) pointed out that by the end of April 2004 there had been an increase in the number of racist incidents reported in the weeks surrounding the referendum on citizenship. In addition, the Equality Tribunal[52] has seen an almost 100% jump in the number of complaints from workers who felt they were discriminated against at work because of their race. As the Irish have shown in many other countries, immigrants have an important role to play in Irish public life, offering a supply of labour,[53] diversity and ideas.

Owing to its seclusion from the rest of the world for a long period of time, and the resulting homogeneity of the population, Irish society has only recently been tested by issues such as immigration, but a striking phenomenon of modern-day Ireland is that the Irish no longer seem ready to be kind to those who are in the same situation that many Irish were over the past three centuries.

Free, but still dominated

In summary, the Irish experience of globalisation is true to the theory that large-scale economic change in turn drives great transformations in society. On balance, the evidence indicates that inequality persists in Ireland and, despite the overall rise in the country's wealth, social structure has not changed much. In social terms, Ireland still has much more in common with the Anglo-Saxon countries, or even its old peer group of Greece, Portugal and Spain, than it does the 'model' Nordic societies.

In addition, fraternity, or civic participation, which has for long been valued in Ireland, is showing signs of withering. This is manifest in increased levels of suicide, homicide, violence and materialism. The prevailing ethos in Irish society could be better described as a culture of contentment than as a culture of caring. Complacency over economic success and its origins is one way in which nationalism is being foolishly expressed. Another is hostility to immigrants, who should in time be an important facet of a globalised Irish economy and society.

These trends represent ways in which Ireland, though a healthy democracy, is becoming less free from the domination of the economic and social side-effects of globalisation, and suggest that not enough is being done by the state to mediate the effects of globalisation on Irish society.

Part II – Globalisation, international politics and institutional change

The second part of this chapter relates to institutional change in Ireland, of which there has been much in the last ten years. This has come about largely through Ireland's increasing interaction with 'world' institutions, changes to the notion of sovereignty in Ireland, and internal institutional change.

The integration of Ireland with the rest of the world is now more complex and deeper than ever before, a process that has left it acknowledged as one of the most globalised countries in the world. However, it is this openness that presents new challenges to both sovereignty and independence. In the context of international politics, one of the major effects of globalisation has been the way it has changed the traditional understanding of sovereignty, and how sovereignty is bartered for membership of international institutions and institutional change.

The meaning of sovereignty is changing

The convention in international relations has been to see the sovereignty of the nation state as deriving from the principles set out by the Treaty of Westphalia in 1648, though in Ireland the absence of both sovereignty and independence up until the early twentieth century meant that it never really felt the effects of Westphalia. Indeed, just after the Treaty of Westphalia, Ireland was brutally ransacked by Oliver Cromwell.

A key assumption behind the Westphalian system was that national frontiers were absolute barriers to outside interference. In effect, the treaty set up fundamental rules for sovereignty and statehood, asserting that a king or state ruler had primacy within his own realm, including the power to choose the official religion of the state. Importantly, Westphalia established the system of the balance of power, where powerful and aggressive states were reined in by coalitions of other nations. The balance of power was a competitive inter-nation state affair, something that has changed with the advent of globalisation. Now states, or developed states at least, tend to co-operate rather than compete. Where they do compete, it is a relatively civilised game, underwritten by international rules, and one that very rarely extends to war. More than ever before, this competition is intermediated by supra-national institutions, close economic interdependence and financial markets.

Sovereignty is now much less defined along the lines of territory, as was traditionally the case. Many states exchange a degree of sovereignty for membership of supra-national bodies (the EU being the obvious example), and some countries are increasingly governed at the sub-state level, to the extent that commentators on globalisation now refer to the 'end of sovereignty'.[54]

The Irish Question

This trend is very much evident in Ireland's case, and there are at least two broad examples to highlight this, one being Ireland's role in supra-national institutions like the EU and the other relating to Northern Ireland and the Good Friday Agreement.

The thread running through at least the last three hundred years of Irish history has been the struggle to achieve independence and sovereignty. Both of these goals, as well as the ideas that drove them, republicanism and nationalism, have been strongly associated with territory. However, the ending of the Republic's territorial claim to the six counties of Northern Ireland has changed this outlook and, together with the complicated arrangement over the sovereignty of Northern Ireland, is beginning to represent a more flexible view of sovereignty. In turn, this has led to substantial institution building, like the North–South ministerial body and Council of the Isles.

A great deal of the debate on globalisation focuses on the problems of the unglobalised world and how it is disadvantaged by the corporations and institutions that make up the global world order. Ireland of the nineteenth century and before would easily fit into this category. Now, as one of the world's most globalised countries, Ireland has a different but perhaps more interesting contribution to make to the literature on globalisation. One of the issues that makes global-isation in Ireland an appealing subject is that the distinction between globalised and non-globalised countries comfortably fits the divide between the twenty-six (Republic) and six (Northern Ireland) counties.

North–South divide

Having been the only part of Ireland to be industrialised during the 1870–1913 wave of globalisation,[55] Northern Ireland has now fallen behind the Republic and the south of England in terms of job creation, labour productivity, inward investment and foreign trade. The contrast between the north and the south provides an interesting case study of what happens when globalised and non-globalised regions meet, and where globalisation may eventually take them.

Politically, socially and economically, Northern Ireland has not inte-grated with the outside world to the same extent as the Republic. There remains a sharp cultural and religious divide in Northern Irish society[56] and its economy is heavily dependent on spending by the British state, a fact that barely masks serious structural problems, such as the low level of skills of the workforce, especially amongst the unemployed. Though Britain has declared that it has no selfish strategic or economic interest in Northern Ireland, the North's social and economic problems would be greatly exacerbated if London removed its financial support. In addition, the reality of the accession of ten new member countries to the EU is that foreign investment is more likely to be attracted eastward than it is to regions like Northern Ireland.

While Northern Ireland has experienced fewer of the benefits of globalisation than the Republic, it is nevertheless subject to many of the pressures of globalisation. Many traditional industries in Northern Ireland are being undercut by cheaper competition from abroad. Sophis-ticated criminal gangs in the North are now linking up with other criminal networks in Europe and immigration is proving hard to digest for the North's homogenous population, with increasing numbers of attacks on Asians, especially by loyalists.

The low level of globalisation of Northern Ireland has many causes, not least of which is the Troubles, as well as a reliance on government spending and the militarisation of society. An additional factor is that peripheral regions in large centralised countries tend to be relatively unglobalised. Many parts of mid- and northern England, Scotland and Wales are unglobalised, a trend that reflects the relatively low level of globalisation of Britain's economy and society. This tallies with the fact that, in the AT Kearney/*Foreign Policy* globalisation ranking, the UK came 20th in terms of economic rankings but 12th overall (it made up ground by ranking 7th in the political rankings and 11th in the technological rankings).

Cross-border trade

Consistent with the fact that Northern Ireland is less globalised than the Republic is the view that economic integration between the two regions is not as good as it should be. The notion that cross-border trade and peace in Northern Ireland should be linked is a longstanding one. For example, in 1959 the Minister for Industry and Commerce in the Republic, Sean Lemass, stated that 'Ireland is too small a country not to be seriously handicapped in its economic development by its division into two areas separated by a customs barrier'.[57] Despite this, cross-border trade today is muted by the standards of the Republic's trade activity with the outside world, and is largely restricted to goods in the food and beverages industries.

There are a number of reasons as to why this is the case. Politicians on both sides of the border tend to regard the issue of Northern Ireland in almost entirely political terms, and attempts to promote economic integration are likely to be viewed suspiciously, in much the same way that euro-sceptic politicians view efforts towards deeper integration of the EU's nation states. Other impediments include a lack of trust and communication between the two communities, poor physical infrastructure, different monetary and fiscal regimes and the physical barrier of the border, all of which have conspired to lessen the amount of cross-border trade.

Another difference between the two economies is industrial structure. The Republic has a more high-tech economy, while the North's economy remains focused on traditional industries. This contrast drew Esmond Birnie, one of the authors of *Can the Celtic Tiger Cross the Irish Border?*, to conclude that 'the great idea of an "island economy" may be a nice marketing concept, but in substantive terms it can only make a comparatively minor contribution to increased economic competitiveness'.[58]

The potential for integration

There clearly remain substantial differences between the Republic and the six counties in terms of their relative levels of globalisation and attendant wealth, though it may yet be too soon to judge if globalisation can bring them closer together or not. After all, other examples of dramatic political change, such as the unification of Germany or the end of apartheid in South Africa, have not gone smoothly either. On the other hand, new European states like Slovenia, Slovakia and the Czech Republic have not done badly since gaining their independence. Given time, globalisation may complement the Good Friday Agreement by bringing northern and southern Ireland closer together economically and socially.

For instance, there is potential for increased economic activity in the area between Derry and Donegal, the central region of Armagh, Fermanagh, Sligo, Monaghan, Leitrim and Cavan, as well as the eastern corridor from Down to Louth. While economic co-operation between authorities on both sides of the border is currently limited to issues like inland waterways, food safety and special EU programmes, in recent years Enterprise Ireland and the tourism bodies on both sides of the border have worked more closely together. The fact that the Irish economy is operating at a far higher speed than that of the North may mean that in the course of time the tight Irish labour market looks north for its supply of labour, or, as is already happening, foreign multinationals will locate near the border, gaining tax breaks in the Republic and labour from the North.

Globalisation is also changing perceptions, or misconceptions. The massive changes brought about in the Republic by globalisation make the stereotypical case that Ireland is an impoverished, backward, papist state very difficult to make. By most standards, it is now wealthier and more progressive than Northern Ireland. In the broader international context, one encouraging trend has been the spread of ideas and experiences resulting from the Good Friday Agreement. This is now being used as a template in the resolution of other conflicts, while other arrangements such as the Truth and Reconciliation Committee in South Africa are being discussed in the North.

International governance and globalisation
If the slowly improving political situation in Northern Ireland is changing the way in which the sovereignty of Ireland is interpreted, then so too is Ireland's close involvement in a number of supra-national and transnational institutions. The chief example is the creation of the EU, which, as the case of Ireland demonstrates, involves a dilution in sovereignty in exchange for the benefits of membership. Many aspects of life in Ireland are now governed on a dual constitutional basis, with laws and directives made in Brussels often taking precedence over those emanating from Dublin.

The core motivation in joining such international bodies is that it gives small countries like Ireland a voice in international affairs and helps to shelter them from international economic risks. Countries like Ireland have little hope of directly altering the course that globalisation takes and, in some cases, they are dwarfed by large corporations and international bodies, and rendered insignificant by cross-border flows in finance, trade and information. In this way, the sacrifice of some sovereignty for increased power on the international stage is consistent with Pettit's definition of republicanism, in that small republics should act to avoid domination by larger countries, markets and corporations.

Big business

The rise in the power and number of transnational institutions is partly a response to global commerce and the rise of global corporations. Most of these can now easily escape national regulations and jurisdictions, meaning that global regulations and standards are required to rein them in. Critics of globalisation and plain anti-globalists frequently raise the spectre of large corporations like Microsoft, Wal-Mart, Shell and Citigroup dominating medium and small-sized countries. As the cases of the East India Company and the Rockefeller empire showed, large corporations that have the power to overwhelm states are not a new phenomenon. The modern-day battle for power between the Kremlin and oligarchs in Russia shows that developing states may be most at risk from big business interests, or perhaps vice versa. In the globalised world, nation states and transnational bodies like the EU that shield them face a number of challenges from the globalised corporate world.

The first is regulation, where jurisdiction is a serious problem. The global nature of many corporations allows them to site their legal headquarters in a location that offers the least punitive taxation or regulatory environment, or in other cases a location that is permissive in terms of labour and environmental standards. Prosecution of corporations by nation states is made all the more difficult by the evasiveness that globalisation permits.

A further issue is that, while international bodies, treaties, national and transnational regulatory systems are in general controlled and staffed by sovereign nations, they face a barrage of lobbying from large business interests, often at the expense of the public interest. The practice of lobbying in the US political system is now virtually institutionalised, and is also widely recognised as operating to the disadvantage of the public interest.[59] A well-known example is the tobacco lobby in the US, which illustrates the fact that large corporations have sufficient wealth to direct at research projects and other means of influencing policy-making that public groups cannot compete with.

A second problem occurs when corporations come to dominate governments and bring pressure to bear upon them to change policy in favour of corporate interests. Although this has always been a reality of the interaction between business interests and politics, the globalisation of industry now means that a threat made by a large corporation to withdraw from a country is a credible one.

Similarly, in their eagerness to attract large corporations some governments may sacrifice broader social and economic policy and enter into what economists call a 'race to the bottom', where tax rates, environmental and labour standards are lowered to socially sub-optimal levels.

The fact that outsourcing and relocation have become key electoral issues in many developed countries suggests that multinationals will take full advantage of such practices. UNCTAD[60] estimates that one-third of all cross-border transactions in goods and services take place between units of the same corporation, as multinationals recycle revenue and cost flows through low tax locations in order to minimise their tax liabilities. As far as corporate taxation is concerned, Ireland has led the way in the European race to cut tax to the 'bottom' (EU regulation has in recent years pushed up Ireland's corporate tax rate), with the Baltic States and other new EU entrants following downwards in competitive spirit.

The dangers of allowing large corporations to dominate government strategy are manifold. One major risk is that paying homage to the corporate world can skew government policy towards the right, and disrupt attempts to pursue more 'social' and egalitarian forms of government. In Ireland, the mantra of 'jobs, jobs, jobs' has, to date, sufficed to deflect criticism that governments cower before large companies, but as the domestic economy develops, unemployment stabilises below 5% and the contribution of large companies to the Irish economy becomes more transparent, this policy may need a rethink.

The response of other European governments to the rise in the power of corporations has been interesting. First, the project of vertical European integration is seen by some of its proponents as a bulwark against the Anglo-Saxon form of globalisation and a means of protecting the European way of life, though critics of the EU's horizontal expansion use the opposite argument. Second, many European governments, France and Germany in particular, are actively debating the promotion of national champion companies, a move that many economists deem to be uncompetitive and unprofitable.

Techno-politics

By clubbing together, countries can produce a broad and powerful response to the rise of non-state actors like global corporations and organised criminals. The emergence of supra- and transnational institutions such as the European Union and World Bank represents a key difference between the current wave of globalisation and the one that swept the world in the nineteenth and early twentieth centuries. The growth of these 'world institutions' serves a number of purposes in the globalised world. They represent the reality that few nation states can now act alone against the powerful forces that globalisation unleashes, such as financial flows and large corporations. They are an efficient means for small countries to tap into international policy-making. By pooling financial and political resources, they allow small countries access to policy research at a relatively low cost and offer the chance to build coalitions that move for or against certain policy recommendations. These relatively new bodies have institutionalised co-operation and dialogue between nation states.

The growth of transnational institutions has driven the rise of techno-politics, where a mixture of diplomats and policy-makers populate organisations like the UN and the WTO. As a result, unelected officials make an increasing number of significant policy decisions, though these officials are very often experts within certain policy fields. Inevitably this has led to the charge that transnational bodies suffer from a democratic deficit, in that policy is made by unelected bureaucrats, and that large developed countries have proportionately greater sway over policy outcomes than less developed ones.

To some extent this is a fair accusation, though the imbalance in power is reflected in informal rather than formal influence. In formal terms some organisations, like the World Bank, manage to appear democratic by having a one nation, one vote policy. The problem of informal influence arises in that smaller and developing countries cannot field large bands of highly educated professional technocrats to compete with those that are bred on the east coast of America or in the French *grandes écoles* and are less able to plug into, influence and argue against the orthodoxy of international institutions like the IMF.

Faced with these powerful but sometimes opaque institutions, Ireland should have little to complain about. The inequalities inherent in techno-politics suit it well, as Irish civil servants have been amongst the finest practitioners of the art of institutional politics in recent years. The very high praise that greeted the successful Irish Presidency of the EU in the first half of 2004 is proof of the ability of its technocrats to operate at the highest level, though in the future Ireland will need to cultivate the technocratic skills of its diplomats more, with particular emphasis on the technical aspect of the role. This will involve a more intense effort to sharpen the international relations and scientific, economic and linguistic skills of incumbent civil servants, while also allowing specialists in areas such as defence, science and economics exposure to the policy-making process.

Domestic institutional changes

The rise of transnational bodies like the IMF has been paralleled by the rapid growth in domestic Irish institutions, of both the governmental and non-governmental varieties. Non-governmental organisations (NGOs) operate predominantly to cater for the many roles and functions that governments cannot, or fail to, undertake, and to alleviate many of the problems that result from globalisation. The number of Irish NGOs has grown noticeably in the last decade. Many of these are well known, particularly where aid and poverty are concerned. These organisations group together under the umbrella organisation Dochas,[61] which enables them to co-ordinate their activities and frequently to speak with a single voice.

In addition, changes to Irish society and its economy have prompted the creation of a relatively large number of institutions that contribute to and govern Ireland's economic success – from the new universities at DCU and Limerick, to the Competition Authority, Forfas and others, like the National Criminal Intelligence Agency.[62] However, although Irish society has changed greatly during its engagement with globalisation and the institutions that make up Irish public life are also going through enormous flux, there remain institutional blockages.

One problem is that local politics in Ireland is ill-equipped to deal with the array of changes that globalisation presents to it, such as the integration of immigrants into urban and rural areas, and the huge amount of physical infrastructure that is required to be built around the country. Local administration in Ireland is dominated by a very centralised national administration, and local politics has in the recent past been shown to be riddled with corruption, incompetence and inefficiencies. In brief, local politics in Ireland needs both more power, and more scrutiny. Based on other examples around the world,[63] a potential solution to the above problems is to elevate local government to the regional or provincial level, with four provincial assemblies in Munster, Leinster, Connaught and Ulster executing local administration issues such as planning, development and public services.

There are already two regional assemblies in Ireland. The Border, Midland and Western Regional Assembly and the Southern and Eastern

Regional Assembly were set up in 1999 to manage the regional operational programme under the National Development Plan (2000–2006), and to monitor the impact of EU programmes and public services within their respective regions. Restructuring these assemblies on a provincial basis and widening their scope and powers would allow local politicians to address local issues in a more strategic and dynamic manner.

This formula has a number of attractions. It may offer an antidote to the proposed decentralisation of the Civil Service, which would involve the movement of up to 10,000 civil servants to locations in 25 counties. This has so far proved unpopular and underlines the need to decentralise politics, not administration. In economic terms it may help to alleviate the growing disparity between the regions of Ireland. By virtue of having assemblies in the four provinces, it would allow Connaught and the three/nine counties of Ulster to claim regional aid from the EU in a more focused way and perhaps to draw preferential fiscal treatment from Dublin that would promote a better redistribution of state resources.

An obvious problem is Northern Ireland, where the sovereignty of six of the nine counties of Ulster crops up. On one hand, the creation of regional assemblies in Ireland is consistent with similar moves across the UK and with the Belfast assembly. Yet, an Ulster assembly for just the three Ulster counties in the Republic would most likely not achieve much more than their local councils do, and for practical purposes they could sit with the Connaught assembly. A more ambitious proposal might be to follow the spirit of institutional change in the Good Friday Agreement and group the nine Ulster counties together to work on shared local government issues.

Overall, though new institutions are being created in Ireland at a rapid pace, the fact that political structures have not changed reflects both the lop-sided nature of globalisation in Ireland and the very quick spread of its effects. In the future, it is increasingly likely that local and national political structures will have to adapt to the effects of globalisation in Ireland.

Conclusion

Combined with the post-Communism countries in Eastern Europe and the modernising Asian economies, Ireland is a case in point that significant economic change leads to great transformations of society.

Much has changed in Irish society in parallel with the globalisation of its economy. Some of these changes are direct effects of globalisation, while others, like corruption, pre-date it. Overall, while it is not yet clear that Irish society is anything as globalised as its economy, it is most certainly feeling the side-effects of globalisation. It is also questionable whether the state has a framework for dealing with the effect of globalisation on Irish society, especially at the micro level. When judged from the point of view of republicanism, the dominant political idea in Ireland, society is not free from domination by globalisation.

As it stands, Irish society seems more in need of such a framework than in previous decades. The cohesion of a previously fraternal society is breaking down as trust in institutions withers and as levels of crime and anti-social behaviour rise. Despite the wealth created by Ireland's economic boom, its distribution has changed little in thirty years. Serious inequalities remain and the level of human development in Ireland is more comparable to some of the poorer Mediterranean states than the 'model' Nordic countries. Liberty is being tested in new ways, most acutely in the case of the treatment of foreigners working and living in Ireland. Nationalism, which for long has been a positive force in Irish life, is increasingly expressed as racism, or in a complacent celebration of the successes of Ireland's experience with globalisation. In turn, this is feeding a growing culture of contentment, where the overall glow of economic success seems to be blinding politicians to the many social problems and considerable risks to the sustainability of Ireland's so far successful engagement with globalisation.

Globalisation offers a unique opportunity to make long-lasting improvements to society and public life, because it provides the necessary environment and wealth with which to do so. In this respect several challenges present themselves. One is to tackle longstanding problems like inequality and poverty. Another more ambitious one is to restructure domestic political institutions to fit a more responsive role in a globalised world. Related to this is the project of domestic institution-building, so that buffers can be constructed to the effects of globalisation. Finally, globalisation is creating new problems, like the relatively large inflow of emigrants to Ireland, and these need to be managed in an open-minded manner.

Chapter Six

Neutrality in a new world

British Prime Minister Lloyd George complained that arguing with de Valera was like 'trying to pick up mercury with a fork', to which de Valera responded, 'why doesn't he try a spoon?'[1]

The previous two chapters have examined the changes and challenges that globalisation has brought to Ireland's economy and society, respectively. This chapter examines the way in which globalisation will test Irish foreign policy, and tracks this through the defining policy of Irish foreign affairs, neutrality.

The challenge of globalisation comes as the geo-political landscape is changing and as the long-term projects of Irish foreign policy are maturing. In particular, the great endeavour of Irish foreign affairs for the last sixty years, establishing and emphasising its independence from Britain, is drawing to a close with the achievement of the Good Friday Agreement and the improvement in relations with Britain. As far as Irish foreign policy is now concerned, the issues of Northern Ireland and relations with Britain remain crucial but are no longer the driving forces behind policy-making. Similarly, with Ireland now well established as a European success story, there are signs that public appetite in Ireland for deeper EU integration is waning.

The wider world is changing too. As the previous chapter outlined, concepts like sovereignty that have ordered international relations are in flux. Physical borders and sovereign jurisdictions are being compromised in new ways by issues such as internet security, flows of immigrants and asylum-seekers, non-state actors such as international criminal organisations and private military companies, and the standardisation of international commercial law and business practice, to name but a few examples of modern-day globalisation.

Also, globalisation is beginning to throw up new and challenging issues, such as America's unipolar role in geo-politics,[2] Russia's demise and potential rise again, the proliferation of drugs and weapons of mass destruction, environmental threats, the rise of both China and India as potential superpowers, the increased importance of Islam, and the plague of Aids in Africa. Because globalisation means that Ireland is less isolated geo-politically, these issues have become more relevant to it.

Globalisation and neutrality

Most neutral countries are good barometers of how many of the above changes affect foreign policy because they are moving from relatively isolated to more interdependent and integrated roles in the community of nations. Ireland is a case in point. During the first wave of globalisation, and indeed for much of the last century, it was a geo-politically unimportant and secluded nation, thanks in large part to its geographic location. In fact, Ireland has been unimportant enough strategically for Irish neutrality to have been allowed to develop untested by the major powers over the last fifty years.

However, Ireland is now widely regarded as one of the most globalised countries, its isolation[3] from the rest of the world having been brought to a speedy end by the process of globalisation. But, although it is less of a geo-strategic backwater now, Ireland is far less globalised politically and in terms of foreign policy than it is economically. Some reasons for this are its low strategic status (e.g. it has no oil like Norway or crucial geographic setting like Greece) and the fact that it has relatively meagre diplomatic resources, in addition to a short tradition in diplomacy, unlike new EU entrants such as Hungary and Poland.

The challenge that globalisation poses to Irish neutrality is all the more interesting for the threadbare way in which neutrality is practised in Ireland. As with other policy areas, neutrality is implemented in a pragmatic manner and bears a weak resemblance to the policy employed by Ireland's peer neutrals across Europe. In truth, Irish neutrality now effectively extends only as far as non-membership of military alliances.[4] Despite this, neutrality is cherished in Ireland and the popular and positive appreciation that is afforded to it by the public suggests that their understanding of what neutrality means for Ireland is more ambitious than that of the politicians who practise it. In future, this tension between the practice and perception of neutrality is likely to be further exposed by globalisation.

This chapter examines the ways in which this may occur in the future. It is divided into four parts, starting with a brief outline of Ireland's policy of neutrality, as well as considering how it compares to other European neutrals. Part II examines the ways in which traditional notions of defence and security have been changed by globalisation, while Part III highlights some of the European responses to these threats and the difficulty presented to neutrality by Ireland's special relationship with the US. Finally, Part IV highlights several potential strategies that could be used to reinvigorate and bring focus to a policy of neutrality in a globalised world.

Part I – Neutrality

The development of Ireland's policy of neutrality was a manifestation of its desire for independence from Britain and of the need to carve out a separate international identity. In its early stages, neutrality was something of a bargaining chip. It was employed in order to gain the release of Ireland's strategic ports, which had remained in British hands since the Anglo-Irish Treaty of 1922, and ultimately to win Ireland's sovereignty. The crafting of the 1938 Anglo-Irish Agreement with Britain and subsequent discussions on partition during the Second World War reflected the intrinsic link between neutrality and partition.[5] One compromise proposed by de Valera was that the six counties of Northern Ireland would join the twenty-six of the South to form a united Ireland which would then be neutralised by all sides in the war (at this stage Hitler and Mussolini had already invaded eight neutral states).

Rather than following earlier and established templates of neutrality like those of Belgium or Switzerland, the expression of Ireland's neutrality was a relative one, based on its relationship with Britain. Irish neutrality is not defined in Irish statutes and is more of a policy than a legal framework, although, as a neutral state, Ireland fell under international laws governing the treatment of neutral states.[6]

Ultimately, the formation of Ireland's policy of neutrality was allowed to pass and was not physically contested by either the Allies or the Axis powers during the war. Extensive intelligence co-operation,[7] combined with an agreement not to allow Ireland to be used as a base for an attack against Britain, meant that Britain's interests were served by a neutral Ireland.

Like some of the terms that have characterised Irish political life over the last century, such as republicanism, and indeed the concept of globalisation itself, Irish neutrality has taken on a meaning that is far broader than its original conception intended. Much like the popular view of republicanism, Irish neutrality still stands for exception to Britain, but is also more generally thought of in terms of involvement in UN peace-keeping and non-involvement in both wars and military alliances. More broadly, the commitment in the Constitution (Article 29.1) that the state 'affirms its devotion to the ideal of peace and friendly co-operation amongst nations founded on international justice and morality' is projected onto the popular view of neutrality. However, this exalted view of neutrality, or, as one historian states, the 'public mythology which now portrays Ireland as the moral conscience of an otherwise depraved, cynical and egotistical developed world',[8] is very different to the way in which it is practised.

Pragmatic neutrality

The reality of Ireland's policy of neutrality is that politicians interpret it widely enough to accommodate the pursuit of pragmatic economic and foreign policies, and resist the need to re-evaluate it. The commentary of Irish politicians on neutrality over the years suggests that Ireland's neutrality is bounded by the recognition that in moments of need its place lies amongst the westernised, and more likely Anglo-Saxon, countries. A former Minister for Foreign Affairs, Sean MacBride, commented that there is 'no nation [US] in the world with whom we have closer links'.[9] Sean Lemass, Taoiseach in the 1960s, held that, were an international crisis to arise, 'there would not be a moment's doubt as to the side on which our interests and sympathies would lie'.[10] Similarly, de Valera suggested that, were Ireland and Britain both independent nations, they could be 'the closest possible allies in a moment of real national danger to either'.[11]

De Valera's pragmatism on neutrality was widely acknowledged and supported in Ireland.[12] According to John Bowman, during the Second World War de Valera, with an eye on the emerging threat from Germany, 'knew well that no policy other than neutrality was politically possible: politicians, diplomats, the press, the churches, ex-unionists, Irish writers – and the voters when consulted – all approved'.[13]

Others were more critical. Ireland's isolation found little favour with commentators like Sean O'Faolain, who felt that 'Ireland had been snoring gently behind a Green curtain that we have been rigging up for the last thirty years – thought proof, world proof, life proof'.[14] In addition, Lee holds that 'Ireland was not therefore a neutral of Swedish or Swiss vintage. They both pursued a policy of armed neutrality. Ireland pursued at most, a policy of half-armed neutrality.'[15]

Neutrality and the European Question

After the Second World War, neither the West nor the East tried hard to tempt Ireland away from its policy of neutrality, largely because neither of them needed to.[16] The attraction of membership of the European Community (EC) in the early 1970s provided the next challenge to Ireland's interpretation of neutrality. Membership of the EC granted it a place amongst Europe's leading nations, in addition to providing it with economic aid and a diplomatic platform apart from Britain. To this extent, EC membership enhanced Ireland's identity as an independent nation and made it less dependent on Britain, two criteria that had originally driven the formulation of the policy of neutrality. In this sense, joining the EC was compatible with the end goal inherent in the policy of neutrality, although it did require it to be interpreted flexibly.

However, on Ireland's entry to the Community the three other European neutrals, Finland, Sweden and Austria, had yet to commit to joining the EC, feeling that, amongst other issues, their neutrality would be compromised. It seems the Irish political class was sufficiently realistic to understand that the economic and political benefits of joining the EC would outweigh the discomfort involved in fitting Ireland's neutrality into the strictures of a pan-European body. Following this line of thought, and reflecting the changing nature of the world, Austria, Finland and Sweden joined the EU in 1995.

Europe's other neutrals

The five neutral European countries rank amongst the top eleven most globalised countries in the world.[17] They are joined in this group by Denmark and Norway, two small countries with active foreign policies. Although the causality of the relationship between globalisation and foreign policy is hard to gauge, it does seem that having a small open economy facilitates, and also necessitates, active engagement with the outside world. Yet, when compared to the Swiss and other EU neutrals (new EU members Cyprus and Malta also follow a policy of non-alignment), the rigour of Ireland's policy of neutrality is laid bare.

The requirements of a policy of neutrality are generally thought to encompass a credible military deterrent against infringement of neutrality, non-participation in military alliances, and a constructive foreign policy. By these standards, Ireland's policy of neutrality has gradually weakened over the last forty years. It is incapable of defending itself militarily, although this is perhaps a reflection of the small threat of direct invasion. The White Paper on Defence states that 'Ireland enjoys a very benign external security environment' and 'Ireland faces virtually no risk of external military attack on its territory from another State and there is at present virtually no risk of externally instigated conflict in our immediate region'.[18] In addition, the Good Friday Agreement has reduced the risk of political violence.[19]

In contrast, in the cases of Finland, Austria, Sweden and Switzerland,[20] neutrality is supported by a credible military force that has in the past been mobilised to defend the doctrine of neutrality (i.e. Finland against Russia in the Second World War). Furthermore, unlike the Swiss or the Austrians, Ireland's neutrality is merely a policy, and is not explicitly formulated in law.

Today, the critical element of Ireland's policy of military neutrality is non-membership of military alliances, especially NATO. In addition, Ireland's active participation in UN peacekeeping missions, together with other facets of its foreign policy such as aid to the under-developed world and active association with NGOs, is warmly associated with neutrality by many Irish people, though at the same time there is a perception that Ireland's close ties to the US render its neutrality obsolete.[21]

However, there are similarities between Europe's neutral states. Neutrality is a popular policy in the European countries that employ it, and not many political parties have ventured proposals to fundamentally change or do away with neutrality. In most cases, neutrality is regarded as a clever formula that has enhanced security, fostered prestige and kept its adherents out of harm's way. Balanced against this, there is a sense that some EU neutrals are drifting towards a policy of non-alignment, rather than one of pure neutrality (non-alignment is only one of a number of requirements of a policy of neutrality). In addition, there are several cases where the prime motivation of non-alignment has been the presence of a larger hostile neighbour, such as Russia in the Finnish case or Britain's role in Irish politics. In most instances, Europe's smaller states now live in greater harmony with former foes than ever before, prompting the question as to whether neutrality is relevant any more, or at least whether it needs to be overhauled to reflect the changing geo-political climate. Above all, however, what Europe's neutral states most have in common are the new threats to their security and the challenges posed to their policies of neutrality by efforts to integrate EU foreign and security policies in response to these threats.

Part II – Challenges to defence and security

European history over the last fifty years is remarkable when compared to the previous five hundred years in that there have been no wars between developed European nations (save the Balkans, of course). Russia, the prime threat to the West, is now part of the globalising world and is closer in political and practical terms to NATO than was thought possible ten years ago. Conventional warfare between developed nations, or even large-scale nuclear war between them, is now a remote possibility.

Yet, against this improving geo-political backdrop, the direct threats to the security and defence of nation states are changing. Where previously the security risk came from super-states like the old Soviet Union, weak and failed states (e.g. North Korea, Iraq and Afghanistan) now represent significant threats. Specifically, the recent UN Secretary General's High Level Panel on Threats, Challenges and Change[22] underlined the dangers posed by the interlinking security threats of poverty, crime and terrorism. These threats are just as relevant to Ireland as to other countries. In response to the UN report, the Minister for Foreign Affairs stated that 'we live in an increasingly interlinked and interdependent world where none of us is isolated from the threat of terrorism, the proliferation of weapons of mass destruction, and of course the consequences of war, as well as famine and the scourge of poverty'.[23]

The emergence of new threats can be captured in the way the distinction between defence and security is changing. In a broad sense, for most developed nations traditional defence (in the sense of hostility from another nation) is of lesser importance, while security (i.e. threats from organised crime and terrorism) has become more important. This trend is central to the way in which neutrality is interpreted, as in its traditional form it has been configured around defence in the context of wars between states. Following from this, the rise in prominence of the non-state actor is perhaps the crucial change to the way that security and defence are conceived. Non-state actors can range from terrorist groups, pirates[24] and organised criminals to private military companies. Each represents a threat to the nation state in its own right.

Global terrorism

The rise of global terrorism holds particular terror and the fight against it takes up huge financial, political and military resources. The dramatic impact of the Al-Qaeda[25] attacks over the past six years means that Islamic terrorism will always assume a large presence in western news agendas, and will often feed public fear and scaremongering by politicians. In fact, the ways in which that Al Qaeda-related operations are crafted to have a high media impact, and the global media's portrayal of Al-Qaeda, are two of the factors that make this network a global[26] rather than an international or national organisation.

Most terrorist groups have by definition been devoted to nation-specific struggles and there are few examples of terrorist organisations that have prosecuted global campaigns. Al Qaeda is considered different in this respect. It began life as a militant body with a nationalist aim of 'regime change' in Saudi Arabia. The sanctuary that was afforded it in Afghanistan allowed it to flourish, as did growing links to combatants in other conflicts (notably Chechnya and the former Yugoslavia). Although it also eschewed many aspects of globalisation,[27] it did not become a 'global' network until after some of its internationally based attacks brought it both notoriety and support. It is global in that the template for its actions has been formulated in one region, for use around the world, and maintained by sophisticated communications and financial networks. Attacks in Turkey, for example, have been launched by foreigners with local help, directed from afar, following a prescribed style (i.e. multiple attacks without warnings against public targets), aimed ultimately at western society. Its actions mirror some of the basic definitions of globalisation, such as the manner in which they transcend national jurisdictions.

Unfortunately, the 11 September attack by the Al-Qaeda network demonstrated the negative consequences of a borderless world and led some to herald the death of globalisation (though globalisation continues to thrive, the thesis of John Gray[28] is being proved correct in some aspects, such as the sharp drop in foreign students studying in the US). In turn, the presence of Al-Qaeda has given a degree of legitimacy to the doctrine of pre-emption, a policy that transcends borders and disregards sovereignty.

With respect to Ireland, it is unlikely but not impossible that it will be the target of an Islamist-inspired terrorist attack. Although global, chiefly Islamic, terrorism is likely to feature high in public consciousness, the likelihood of a direct attack on Ireland in the manner of the March 2004 bombings in Spain and the July 2005 attack in London is low. However, as host to a number of potential targets, such as large US corporations or the thousands of American tourists that visit Ireland each year, Ireland offers a potential base for an attack against US or western interests.

Ireland as a terrorist target would serve the same role as Kenya and Tanzania did in 1998 when the US embassy in each country was bombed by Al-Qaeda on 7 August with the loss of many African lives. The frequency with which drugs and small-scale armaments are smuggled into and out of Ireland, and indeed the ease with which domestic criminals appear to be able to acquire weaponry, suggest that the logistics of mounting an attack in Ireland would not be difficult. Of course, another way in which global terrorism may impinge upon Ireland is money laundering and the financing of terrorist operations through the use of facilities linked to the International Financial Services Centre (IFSC) in Dublin.

However, while global terrorism deserves to be taken very seriously, there is a strong argument to be made that it is not the most likely or significant security threat that globalisation poses to countries like Ireland. In this respect, global terrorism is superseded by global organised crime, both of which are often intertwined, though it is likely that the impact of organised crime is more costly in financial and human terms. Afghanistan is a case in point. Although it served as the training base for units of Al-Qaeda fighters,[29] it also produces huge quantities of drugs that find their way onto the streets of European cities with massive social and economic impact.

Global organised crime

Non-state actors in the form of organised criminal gangs are perhaps the greatest security threat to emerge from globalisation. They live off the flows of finance, trade and information-based transactions that pass around the globe with a degree of sophistication that leaves many governments helpless. International organised criminals are increasingly forming networks that allow them to source weaponry, drugs and labour and in turn to launder cash flows. Criminal gangs originating in Turkey, China, Jamaica, Colombia, Nigeria and Russia are now actively operating across the EU. Increasing sophistication in telecommunications, weaponry and finance makes it harder to track down and prosecute these gangs, while criminal law in Europe and internationally has yet to adapt to this situation, meaning that they can easily evade national jurisdictions.

There is an increasing number of foreign criminal gangs of Chinese, African and Russian origin in particular operating in Ireland. However, most organised crime in Ireland is still largely domestically generated, either by well-known criminal families or by former paramilitaries. A recent report from the Northern Ireland Organised Crime Taskforce identified 150 local/regional gangs and a further 85 international gangs operating in and around Northern Ireland, a large number of whom were former paramilitaries, although there is also an increasing trend of South African nationals working in cannabis-related crime. The report noted that 70% of extortion-related activity was pursued by loyalists (in 81% of total cases the police could not pursue any action as the victim requested them not to), while up to 70% of republican and 60% of loyalist gangs are involved in the illegal tobacco trade. One side-effect of the peace process, like the ending of similar conflicts in Africa and the former Yugoslavia, has been the proliferation of huge amounts of small arms.

The malign effect of organised crime is most visible in social problems like drug abuse. The Drug Prevalence Survey in Ireland showed some of the side-effects of the flood of drugs coming into Ireland[30] by highlighting the large proportion of young people who had used drugs and the health problems that are associated with abuse. Unfortunately, drug abuse has blighted Irish society (especially Dublin city) for at least the last twenty-five years. This makes the specific effects of globalisation on crime hard to untangle, though there are a number of unambiguous trends, such as the rapid rise in homicides in Ireland.[31] The direct effect of globalisation on countries where drug abuse and crime have gone from low to very high levels is underlined in a study by the European Monitoring Centre for Drugs and Drug Addiction (EMCDDA) of drug abuse in the EU accession states.[32]

The EMCDDA found that the neo-liberal orthodoxy that has

replaced Communism in many parts of Eastern Europe has, like other parts of the world, seen the role of the state peeled back to leave society open to the activities of criminal networks. In addition, the authors note a change in attitude in the accession countries, where collectivism has waned and attitudes have shifted towards greater individualism. Large-scale changes to social welfare programmes have given rise to increased poverty, while the privatisation of state pharmaceutical companies has led to the manufacture of more lifestyle drugs and to looser control over supply and research.

Private military organisations

Globalisation is also spreading to the world of the military, with a sharp increase evident in the number of private military companies being set up over the past five years.[33] Some of these are now large and sophisticated, allied to commercial ventures like mining companies, possessing their own training centres and intelligence networks, and in some cases more powerful militarily than many small countries, including Ireland. While the threat to nation states from private military companies has yet to fully manifest itself, their direct focus on profits and their utter lack of accountability should cause unease.

There are large numbers of private military organisations operating in Iraq. The main role of these companies is to provide security, although some of them are effectively replacing official military personnel in tasks like prison maintenance, interrogation and intelligence work (there are an estimated 200 former Royal Ulster Constabulary/Northern Ireland Prison Service officers working in Iraq, in addition to hundreds of former special forces soldiers). The troubling issue is that many of the duties that private companies are hired to perform are normally carried out by official military personnel who operate within strict guidelines, are generally accountable to their chain of command and have the benefit of legal authority. Private military companies have scant legitimacy and legal authority. On a number of occasions they have been hired to overthrow governments in small mineral-rich states (e.g. Equatorial Guinea).

Although the exploits of these dogs of war can make interesting reading, the privatisation of military expertise represents one of the more dangerous outcomes of globalisation. Like organised criminal gangs, these companies flourish in a world where financial flows are plentiful and hard to track, control over the supply of weapons is loose, and where governments struggle to monitor their activities. Although the stated motive of the governments that outsource security work to them is cost efficiency, the activities of private security firms are often far more costly than is envisaged in financial, political and human terms.[34]

The expansion of this industry mirrors that of the hedge fund industry in finance, where generally successful and experienced professionals leave large organisations to set up private entrepreneurial ventures. In both cases, profit is the motivating force, accountability is low and in some instances the sovereignty of individual states and the welfare of their citizens are threatened.

The potential dangers of blurring the thin line between states and private military organisations are underlined by a series of inquiries that are beginning to bring to the attention of the wider public the effects of collusion between bodies like the RUC, the LVF (Loyalist Volunteer Force), the UVF (Ulster Volunteer Force) and British military intelligence. In Northern Ireland, there have been over 200 cases of murder where such collusion is suspected.[35] In the Republic, in the worst incident of the Troubles, 33 people were killed and over 250 injured in bombings in Dublin and Monaghan on 17 May 1974. Recent inquiries, such as that by Justice Barron, point to likely collusion between loyalist terrorists and elements within the British security forces. These incidents show the frightening way in which undisciplined state and private military units can act, with little structure, accountability or moral sense, and it is therefore worrying to see the expansion of the privatisation of military power.

Part III – Mars and Venus

The emergence of non-state actors presents threats to all countries, but the manner in which these threats are dealt with has highlighted a sharp divergence in policy between the US and Europe, to the extent that one author has commented that 'Americans are from Mars and Europeans from Venus'.[36] In this respect, Ireland is unusual in that it straddles both worlds, and the ways in which these two regions respond to new security threats will in turn present challenges to Ireland's neutrality. This section first of all examines the way in which the building of a common EU foreign and security policy could potentially compromise Ireland's neutrality, and secondly it highlights the danger that Ireland's special relationship with the US threatens to do the same, if it has not done so already.

Mars – Europe's common security and foreign policies
The new security threats that have emerged from under the blanket of globalisation now lie at the heart of EU foreign policy. This was made very clear by Javier Solana in a key speech to EU heads of state in Thessaloniki in June 2003.[37] Solana painted a picture of security in the context of a globalising world: 'the post Cold War environment is one of increasingly

open borders. Flows of trade and investment, the development of technology and the spread of democracy have brought growing freedom and prosperity to many people.' He underlined the key threats to EU security as: the use of strategic terrorism, the proliferation of weapons of mass destruction, regional conflicts, state failure and organised crime.[38]

His comments highlight the way globalisation is providing the means by which warfare is changing. As Dominique de Villepin, the former French foreign minister, pointed out in an address to the UN Security Council,[39] warfare is now asymmetric, where communications, transport, open borders and prosperous western societies provide the means, motive and targets for attacks by the weak upon the strong. A further example is referred to by Donahue and Nye, who mention a report in the *Washington Post*[40] that reflected how the Chinese military establishment was thinking of alternative means of attacking the US: 'in devising a strategy to stand up to the US, some Chinese officers are proposing terrorism, drug trafficking, environmental degradation, and computer virus propagation . . . they argue that the more complicated the combination – for example, terrorism plus a media war plus a financial war – the better the results'. The globalisation of warfare is chilling in many respects. It means that attacks like that on the US on 11 September 2001 can be devised in one country (Afghanistan), prepared in another (Germany) and then launched against a western target.

Muddling through

The strategic reality that none of Europe's nation states can meet the new threats to security alone is driving the development of the EU's common foreign and security policy strategy. Collective action offers a means of optimising hard and soft power. For the time being, however, this collective project is likely to remain an inter-governmental rather than a federal affair. It is hard to imagine old colonial powers (i.e. the UK and France), with significant overseas interests and large armies of diplomats, civil servants and military personnel, relinquishing control of foreign policy or sharing sensitive intelligence across the 25 EU states.

The process by which common foreign and security policy is driven in the EU seems particularly crisis-led. In much the same way as the 1993 currency crisis helped to firm the resolve of European politicians to ultimately bring their currencies together, the bombings in London and Madrid, as well as the diplomatic crisis between Europe and the US over Iraq, have concentrated the minds of European foreign policy makers like never before and has resulted in an acceleration in policy development.

The introduction of the euro has already demonstrated that Europe possesses the latent power to compete with the US economically, and to place itself in a position to ensure that the globalised world is not a unipolar one in economic terms. However, the case of the euro also demonstrates that considerable compromise and periodic crises are the price to be paid for deeper integration. Whether by design or not, attempts to build a Common Foreign and Security Policy do not look dissimilar and in fact in some areas, such as trade, foreign and economic policy, are increasingly linked.

The foundations of the current drive towards a common foreign policy were put in place in 1993 with the Maastricht Treaty, where the pillars of the euro-zone system were also set in place. Several changes were made to the common foreign policy framework in 1999 with the Amsterdam Treaty and the recent Nice Treaty (2003). In the same way in which a small group of countries formed the core of the European monetary system, the three largest countries now seem to be forming what is termed a 'directoire', to speed the development of a common European foreign policy.[41] Unlike the common monetary policy project, the UK is part of this group.

Reflecting the driving influence of the large states, Europe's Common Foreign and Security Policy (CFSP)[42] has five broad objectives,[43] though, as with all well-meaning EU policy initiatives, fulfilling these objectives in practice is proving difficult. One obstacle is a lack of military hardware in Europe, as highlighted by the imbalance between European and American military capabilities. With its emphasis on 'full spectrum dominance', the US has the most impressive military force ever assembled. The EU countries, on the other hand, together spend a meagre $220 billion on defence annually, compared to America's $400 billion,[44] and have much less hardware like aircraft carrier groups and heavy lifting aircraft. The EU military budget is still huge compared to that of other regions, but the overriding problem is that it is spent in an inefficient manner. However, it is acknowledged that some EU countries have excellent national intelligence services and special operations units and are skilled in peace-keeping and nation-building. If anything, the war in Iraq has proved the value of these capabilities.

The broad choice for Europe then is either to try to match the US in terms of military hardware, or to focus on more specialised counter-insurgency and peace-keeping capabilities. The path that the EU takes will in turn affect Ireland's policy of neutrality.

Ireland and European security

The dilemma for small neutral countries like Ireland lies in reconciling the need for a greater pan-European security effort with the policy of neutrality. Few governments can ignore the fact that the growing integration of societies, especially in Europe, breeds common threats that increasingly must be dealt with on a common basis. On the issue of security, small countries must by necessity seek the close co-operation of other states.

An example of the growing dilemma posed by emerging security threats to Ireland's policy of neutrality came with the admission by former Minister for Defence Michael Smith[45] that Ireland was not adequately equipped to deal with a large terrorist attack, and may in the event of such an attack have to call upon Britain for military aid. The fact is that Ireland's security infrastructure is just not equipped to deal with sophisticated organised crime or even foreign terror groups. In the past, the focus of the army and the gardaí has been almost exclusively on security threats arising from domestic 'subversives'.

Like other European nations, Ireland is trying to get to grips with the changing security environment. For example, as part of its response to the rise in organised crime in Europe, the address of the Irish government to the Action against Organised Crime conference focused on the need to improve judicial and police co-operation between European nations, a necessity underlined by the Madrid bombings in March 2004. Under the Dublin Declaration a range of measures was proposed, such as the view that 'EU member states review their criminal intelligence systems and procedures with a view to rendering them mutually compatible with common minimum standards',[46] and that they combat organised crime using tactics like the asset seizures practised by the Criminal Assets Bureau (CAB).

Ireland is also a member of a number of pan-European security networks like the Trevi Group and international ones like Interpol, and is involved in an increasing number of bilateral relationships, in particular with UK police forces. In contrast to the strong opposition in Ireland to military alliances, few objections have been raised to the impact that security-based co-operative arrangements and the increasing Europeanisation of law enforcement have on neutrality. In particular, the very close co-operation between Irish and British security forces is not widely debated publicly.[47]

NATO

The real political quandary presented to Irish neutrality is that a more integrated EU security and defence policy is based on the structures and apparatus of NATO. Given the convenience of existing NATO structures, such as its headquarters in Brussels and the fact that the vanguard of Europe's military nations (Germany, France and the UK) are all NATO members, the likelihood that an EU army or security and intelligence service might be built on NATO structures is high.[48] An EU defence structure that merely adds a veneer to the existing NATO one would make non-alignment more difficult for countries like Ireland.

Ireland currently commits resources to EU military operations carried out under the ESDP (European Security and Defence Policy) and the range of its military activities is bounded by the Petersberg tasks. The Petersberg tasks encompass humanitarian, rescue and peace-keeping responsibilities, the aim being that the EU is self-sufficient in its ability to carry out these tasks without recourse to US assistance. Under the Seville Treaty, Ireland's participation in activities that come under the ESDP umbrella is subject to its sovereign decision[49] rather than a directive from the EU. In this way Ireland has so far balanced its sovereignty with maintaining a contribution to EU security and defence operations.

Similar to its experience of UN peace-keeping, the Petersberg tasks are popular with the Irish army as they allow it to benchmark itself against other armies and to undertake reasonably sophisticated exercises. The Seville/Petersberg formula should continue to allow Ireland to contribute to an EU military force, but should the distinction between an EU defence force and NATO become blurred then this would present a serious formal threat to Ireland's stated policy of neutrality. Even if assurances like that granted in Seville could be gained, the perception that neutrality would be rendered null and void is too hard to avoid.

Overall, it looks likely that the future development and probable integration of EU security and defence policy will present difficulties for Ireland and the other EU neutrals. Not only is Ireland's perceived neutrality very popular domestically, but there does not appear to be much appetite amongst Irish people relative to other Europeans to be part of a common defence umbrella, despite the fact that the EU is increasingly taking the lead in a number of worthwhile peace-keeping and humanitarian missions. In general, although surveys show that only Luxemburg is more pro-European than the Irish, there is relatively little appetite amongst Irish people for a common EU defence policy.[50] This tension between public opinion and the requirements of EU policy suggests that political pragmatism may continue to rule over Irish neutrality.

This attitude is also manifest in Ireland's relationship with the US. Like their European counterparts, most Irish people were averse to the invasion of Iraq, and concern is often voiced over the dominance of US economic and military power. However, it is also acknowledged that Ireland's closeness to America has provided the bounties of US involvement in the peace process, and heavy financial investment in Ireland that allowed it to ride on the coat tails of the longest US economic boom in at least fifty years.

Venus – the special relationship

Ireland's special relationship with the US has contributed significantly to the ending of its economic, if not political, seclusion and its hearty participation in the current wave of globalisation. This relationship is unique in that no other neutral country possesses a special relationship with the US, although non-aligned countries like Japan are close to it. Similarly, Irish neutrality has not been formally challenged by the Americans because Ireland has long been an implicit ally of the US and neutrality has its roots in the partition of Ireland, a sensitive issue amongst Irish-Americans. Nevertheless, the economic dependence of Ireland on the US and the failure of Irish politicians to strictly interpret and enforce the policy of neutrality have reinforced the image that it is not at all neutral when American interests are at issue. The dominant role of the US in the globalisation process can only exacerbate this perception.

The origin of the term 'special relationship' is found in the close wartime relationship between Britain and the US, as exemplified by the personal relationship between Churchill and Franklin Roosevelt.[51] A special relationship could be defined as a durable cultural, social and economic bond between a given country and America that allows that country the power to draw upon the political, economic and military resources of the US, and vice versa.

A special relationship is, and indeed should be, different to a strategic relationship. For example, the US and Russia both continue to have an overwhelming strategic interest in each other's fortunes, but little evidence can be garnered to build a case for a special relationship based on common understandings, experiences and cultures. Conversely, Ireland is and has been of meagre strategic interest to the US but can be said to have a special relationship with America, given their long-lasting cultural, political and social ties. Britain, it seems, is both of strategic interest to the US and enjoys a special relationship with it.

The joint case of Ireland and Britain is interesting in outlining how a special relationship is formed and mobilised. As mentioned above, both countries enjoy special relationships with the US, but the manner in which these relations have been formed and later invoked is very different. More importantly, the joint example of the individual relationships of Britain and Ireland to the US is especially compelling, as they have both sought to use American political resources against each other.

Building a special relationship

Their interaction with the US highlights at least four lessons for countries with ambitions for a special relationship. The first is that the relationship and the way in which it can be subsequently mobilised are dependent on its origins. Conquest, adventure and forced migration served as the vehicles to carry millions of Britons and Irish to the US over the last three centuries, to the extent that few other countries have left such long-lasting imprints on American life. However, the roots of Irish and British influence on American life became institutionalised in very different ways. As we now know it, Ireland's legacy to the US is primarily people-based, whereas the British presence is more obvious in the techno-structure of American life. Americans speak the English language, go to work and live in a society framed by Anglo-Saxon laws, religion, customs and working practices. However, while the trappings of American society derive in large part from Britain, many Americans happily claim Ireland as the home of their forebears (according to the 2003 census[52] there are over 33 million Irish-Americans plus 5.2 million Scots-Irish).

The second lesson to be garnered here is that the material success of the special relationship is a clear function of its aims and how these are mobilised. In this respect, the objective of the British approach has been clear. As architects of the concept, they used the special relationship to place themselves at the high table of world decision-making, to the extent that they played an important role in the setting up and running of bodies such as NATO and the Bretton Woods system. The *modus operandi* was just as focused, relying upon frequent access to the nexus of US military and political power by top-ranking diplomats and politicians.

Where the British were deliberate, the Irish found themselves in a special relationship almost by default. While many American and Irish politicians have fondly evoked the close ties between Ireland and the US, few have sought to explicitly define this relationship, and fewer still have until recently successfully mobilised it in their favour (Sinn Féin and the IDA being notable). The Irish Question has always been a live issue in American politics,[53] but the truth is that British influence in Washington has usually trumped efforts to involve America on the side of the Irish. Andrew Jackson was the first American President to have his arm twisted by the Irish, although to little ultimate effect. Ireland then had to wait for the Clinton presidencies to find an American leader who would devote large amounts of political energy to it.

Thirdly, events on a grander scale inevitably impinge upon the special relationship. In particular, the Cold War that followed the Second World War meant that London was the first port of call in the outside world for proud Irish-Americans such as Kennedy and Reagan. Their involvement in Irish politics rarely rose above the sentimental, again largely because it never served their political interests to do so.

In this respect, the case of Germany is interesting, especially for the way in which the potential for a special relationship exists but has yet to be acted on. Although Irish-Americans are popularly thought of as being the largest ancestral grouping within the US population, German-Americans number over 46 million. However, unlike the Irish in America, who promote and celebrate their heritage, it seems that German-American is the ancestry that dare not speak its name. There are clear reasons for this, principal amongst them being the two world wars.

The Hiberno-German writer Hugo Hamilton[54] offers some clues as to why Irish people do and Germans do not express their identities when overseas, and why, 'unlike the Irish, Germans abroad tend to forget where they come from. There is no German enclave in New York as there used to be. Where the Irish and the Italians always longed to be on the map, to he heard and not forgotten, the Germans longed to be invisible.'

Germany can take some comfort from the fact that, although Irish-Americans have been more visible and vocal than German-Americans, it is only recently that Ireland has worked out how to use the special relationship to produce discernible outcomes. Making the special relationship with the US work to your advantage depends heavily on geo-political events. Some countries like Mexico (the first country George W. Bush visited after he was first elected) have seen their special relationship with the US turn to a forgotten one as soon as the attention of the world focused on the Middle and Far East.[55]

The final lesson, and one that is especially relevant to Ireland's neutrality, is that participation in a special relationship with a country as powerful as the US results in a forfeiture of some independence. Britain's relationship with the US increasingly appears to draw it away from European politics, as events before and after the second Gulf War have shown. Moreover, fifty years of close military ties with the US have left the British armed services heavily dependent on the Americans for intelligence, logistics and nuclear arms.[56] Ireland too faces a number of dangers from its growing reliance on the US, such as the role of American multinationals in the Irish economy. A wider concern is that the growing perception of the US as a hegemony can make its allies unpopular by association.

In summary, as discussed in the previous sections, two broad trends will make it more difficult for Ireland to remain strictly neutral in the future. The first is the rise of new and dangerous security threats, notably the increased sophistication of organised crime. The second relates to how the two most powerful regions of the world, Europe and the US, are reacting to the new geo-strategic order.[57] In Europe, the pace of EU military co-operation is increasing and at some stage is likely to draw Ireland firmly into its reach. At the same time, the US, with whom Ireland has a close relationship, is proving a more singular but at times unpopular player on the world stage. The influence of these factors necessitates a thorough reassessment of Ireland's policy of neutrality.

Part IV – The 'micro' power

More than its European counterparts, Irish neutrality has been eroded by domestic and international events over the past ten years. If a foreign policy based on neutrality remains of value to Ireland then it must be overhauled and imbued with a rigour that has been lacking in recent years, or else it will merely wither away. The relative success of this policy so far and the high esteem in which it is held in Ireland suggest that it should be revitalised in an imaginative way.

There are already signs that globalisation and its effects are prompting debate about neutrality within Europe's neutral states, and in time it may be a catalyst towards either a more scrupulous practice of neutrality or alternatively a growing acceptance that it is a policy whose time has passed. It seems that two options present themselves. The first is that smaller neutral European countries admit their place in the westernised world and fall into line in the gathering pan-European defence force. An alternative and more demanding option is to follow the example of the Swiss, and to an extent the Norwegians, and build a constructive form of neutrality that uses factors like culture and past experience in conflict resolution as soft assets to facilitate a role as an intermediary, or most optimistically as an international peace-maker.

Good deeds, good offices

A starting-point in revitalising a policy of neutrality is a more focused practice of good deeds and good offices. 'Good deeds' refers to acts ranging from foreign aid and peace-keeping to sensible contributions to the global debate on the environment. The term 'good offices' is best typified by the Swiss and Norwegian governments, who are well known for using their diplomatic apparatus as the means of mediating between conflicting parties.

An approach guided by the principles of good offices and good deeds is not without its difficulties. The first is that this niche is a pretty crowded one. A second and related difficulty for Europe's neutrals is that non-neutrals like Norway and the Netherlands seem to perform the perceived duties of neutral states better than the neutrals themselves.

Norway is often pointed to as a model country, particularly in terms of its contribution to international affairs, notably its role in Israeli/Palestinian relations. Its reach stretches beyond the Middle East; for example, in 2004 and 2005 Norway mediated between Tamil Tiger rebels and Sri Lankan government officials.[58] The Sri Lankan peace process (like that in East Timor) is an area to which the Irish government has committed resources, although on this occasion the opportunity to broker a political agreement was seized by the Norwegians, not the Irish. Norway's practice of diplomatic mediation is a good example of how small countries can have a positive impact on conflicts in developing regions, although it seems that gaining influence through intermediation is becoming an increasingly competitive space.

Aid

The difficulty of constructing a distinctive foreign policy is underlined by the issue of aid. Like many of the smaller European countries, Ireland has traditionally sought to occupy the space of well-intentioned neutral, and the domestic opinion of Irish peace-keeping and aid efforts is high. However, when compared to the development policies of other countries, Ireland's contribution is not as impressive as many think.

An attempt to quantify the various types and amounts of aid given by developed countries to the developing world has been undertaken by the Center for Global Development[59] and *Foreign Policy* magazine, who have created a Commitment to Development Index (CDI) that ranks 21 of the world's richest nations according to how much their governments' policies contribute to the economic and social development of poor countries.

In assessing developed countries' aid policies, the CDI rewards benevolent aid-giving, hospitable immigration policies, significant contributions to peace-keeping operations, and foreign direct investment (FDI) in developing countries. The index penalises financial assistance to corrupt regimes, obstruction of imports from developing countries and policies that harm shared environmental resources. For instance, with regard to aid, the CDI improves upon traditional measures such as total aid relative to GDP by considering the quality of aid and penalises 'tied' aid. Denmark, Sweden, the Netherlands and Norway give the best quality aid.

Overall, the Netherlands emerges as the top-ranked nation in the index, thanks to its strong performance in aid, trade, investment and environmental policies. Two other small European countries, Denmark and Portugal, follow in 2nd and 3rd place, respectively. New Zealand finishes 4th, due to a healthy showing in migration and peace-keeping policies. Ireland ranked 15th out of 21 countries. Although this is a new survey, it is wide-ranging and underlines the fact that Ireland is being outshone by quite a few other small European states.[60]

Ireland spends about 0.4% of GNP on overseas aid, with much of this going to Uganda, Mozambique and Ethiopia. Over the past five years the government has a stated target level of aid spending of 0.7% of GNP, but this figure is unlikely to be committed to in the next couple of years.

Irish government aid spending is matched by the activities of a number of well-known NGOs. These congregate under the umbrella group Dochas, and are very active in areas like aid and human rights. In addition, the Department of Foreign Affairs (DFA) has a dedicated human rights unit as one of its eight functional parts, as well as a joint committee of DFA personnel and those from NGOs that campaign in this field. Reflecting this, human rights is often a prominent part of Irish diplomats' engagements with larger developing countries like China, although there have also been some lapses on its watch.

A recent example of Ireland's failure to act aggressively on human rights abuses is the appalling case of ethnic cleansing of black Sudanese in western Sudan by Arab militia acting for the government in Khartoum. This was made public during Ireland's term as President of the European Union. For example, in June 2004 USAid had warned that up to 1 million displaced Sudanese were at risk from the violence, disease and hunger that had resulted from the attacks by the government-supported militia. Ireland's diplomatic response to the crisis in Darfur was criticised as 'timid'[61] by some senior European politicians, and probably marks a lost opportunity to have acted in a more responsive and meaningful way.

The reality of Ireland's contribution in the area of human rights, and particularly aid, falls short of not only the generally positive perception of it, but of the contributions made by many other small European nations. This gap between perception and reality is emblematic of Ireland's policy of neutrality, and can only heighten the need for a more focused and committed foreign policy.

A sharper focus on soft power

In economic terms, the ability to prosper in a globalised world is broadly defined by a country's comparative advantage, or a corporation's competitive advantage. This refers to the ability to do something that others cannot do, or to do something that others already do but to do it better and more distinctively. In a similar manner to the challenge posed to Ireland's economy by globalisation, foreign policy needs to become more distinctive and specialised. A former French foreign minister, Hubert Védrine, defined America's role in the post-Communism world as a 'hyper-power' (*hyper puissance*). Consistent with this classification, the role that Ireland could carve out in a globalised world is of a niche power, or a 'micro' power. This role would be based on a defined identity, undertaking diplomatic tasks that fit its background and build its international influence and that are consistent with a meaningful form of neutrality.

In international politics, power is traditionally conceived of in either military or financial terms and Ireland cannot be considered powerful in these ways. However, in the increasingly peaceful globalised western world, a country's foreign policy as well as its identity is less dependent on hard military power and more on soft power. A broader definition of power, and one that is more relevant to Ireland, is provided by the political scientist Joseph Nye: 'simply put, power is the ability to effect the outcomes you want and, if necessary to change the behaviour of others to make this happen'. He refers to the ability to get others to want what you want as soft power, saying that it 'co-opts people rather than coerces them. Soft power rests on the ability to set the political agenda in a way that shapes the preferences of others.'[62]

Soft power can be drawn from many sources and relies more on diplomacy, identity and culture than military power. Again, as Nye points out, 'some countries such as Canada, the Netherlands and the Scandinavian states have political clout that is greater than their military and economic weight, because of the incorporation of attractive causes such as economic aid or peacekeeping into their definitions of national interest'.[63]

A related perspective on soft power concerns the identity of the state as described by Peter Van Ham: 'Singapore and Ireland are no longer merely countries on an atlas. They have become "brand states", with geographical and political settings that seem trivial compared to their emotional resonance among an increasingly global audience of consumers.'[64] A recent example is the success of Ireland's Presidency of the European Union in the first half of 2004. In addition to brokering several complicated intergovernmental agreements, the Irish government machine was generally perceived as being well run, a factor that should encourage global institutions and other nations to take it seriously as a player on the diplomatic stage.

In contrast, America's prosecution of the war on terror has seen it lose soft power. In September 2004, a report from the Defence Science Board, a federal committee of strategists and academics formed to give independent advice to the Defence Secretary, held that:

> US strategic communication must be transformed. America's negative image in world opinion and diminished ability to persuade are consequences of factors other than failure to implement communications strategies . . . Mistakes dismay our friends and provide enemies with unintentional assistance. The United States is engaged in a generational and global struggle about ideas, not a war between the West and Islam . . . We must think in terms of global networks, both government and non-government.[65]

In general, the rise of soft power means that developed countries will increasingly do battle through technocracy rather than in military terms. In addition, in the battles of the future the prizes will not be territorial but will come in the form of prestige, tourism and investment flows. When developed countries do mobilise their military, it is more often to come to the aid of the weak, or to counter security threats as opposed to classical threats to defence. Economic, cultural and technocratic power, as well as a willingness to help other nations, have assumed greater roles within the arsenal of diplomacy.

Ireland cannot aim to compete with most other nations on the basis of hard power, but the growing importance of soft power offers it an avenue towards increased influence in a globalised world. Soft power, like economic competitive advantage, is difficult to create from scratch, though a good starting-point can be a country's past. Ireland's past is full of experiences that can be put to use around the world. The challenge is to institutionalise them and apply them to specific international political issues. Using its diplomatic know-how, there are several independent roles that Ireland can play and capabilities that it can develop – mediator, techno-politics, military specialisation in asymmetric warfare, its special relationship with the US and strategic partner to emerging nations.

Military specialisation
A significant part of Ireland's identity is derived from its struggle for independence from Britain and from the more recent Troubles. As a result of these episodes, traditions of guerrilla warfare[66] and more recently of political reconciliation exist in Ireland. Consistent with this, Ireland's military, though of little consequence in terms of its size or hardware,[67] is better versed than many other European armies in guerrilla warfare. The proposal here is that guerrilla and counter-insurgency warfare should be made the specialisation of the Irish army. The creation of a guerrilla warfare and counter-terrorism institute would significantly enhance Ireland's ability to independently monitor and defend against security threats. Other improvements could follow from this. In particular, the army needs more specialists in areas like information technology, a decent rapid airlift capability and, though the Army Ranger Wing numbers close to 120, this could be increased to match new threats and the relative size of other specialist units.[68]

The new global security threats such as cyber crime, drug and people trafficking are much more likely to be tackled using the techniques and lessons of counter-terrorist warfare than conventional means. This in turn increases the need to broaden the training of Irish military personnel to a wider range of skills, such as special combat situations, languages and computer-based tasks, and might also involve the recruitment of former IRA activists into the Irish army. This would not be an unprecedented move, as for example the French[69] and British secret services maintain close contact with mercenary groups staffed by former soldiers and irregulars, while there is also mounting evidence of collusion between loyalist terrorists in Northern Ireland and the British army. It would have the advantage of preserving the knowledge of some able guerrilla warfare specialists, while aiding the managed demobilisation of the IRA and diminishing the risk that its operatives might turn to crime, as some have already done.

Diplomatic specialisation

An emphasis on specialised pro- and counter-guerrilla warfare skills by the military can also be mirrored in the diplomatic arena. The two great successes of Irish foreign policy, EU membership and the Good Friday Agreement, underline the professionalism of Irish diplomats and their abilities in negotiation. The Irish experience in conflict resolution can profit other disputes, although these would need to be chosen carefully. One suggestion is that a ninth unit of the Department of Foreign Affairs be established to offer mediation in civil wars or in disputes between nations. The cases that this unit would take up would be carefully selected, and restricted to issues that are not intractable and where some advantage to Ireland could be gained. As a template, this unit could take the same approach as the teams sent by the likes of the World Bank and IMF to country-specific crises.

This approach would have the advantage of flexibility and of allowing civil servants and politicians to select situations where the Irish experience could be profitably brought to bear. At the moment, many Irish diplomats seem drawn to the Israeli/Palestine conflict, which, though worthy of their attention, seems intractable at the best of times and is a conflict more likely to be brought to a close by another foreign government (i.e. the US or Norway) than Ireland.

Irish diplomatic resources should be diverted to other areas where they can be more effective. A case in point is Iran, which, following the second Gulf War, the re-election of George W. Bush and the relaunching of Iran's nuclear research project, looks likely to become one of the leading issues in international relations. Iran, and its relationship (or lack of it to be more accurate) with the US, presents a very ambitious case of how Irish diplomacy can be brought to bear on international events. The election of Mahmoud Ahmadinejad as President of Iran lowers the probability that a dialogue between American and Iran will succeed, though it also increases the need for intermediation.

Ireland's involvement

The case of Iran presents several opportunities to Irish foreign policy. The first and most important is that there is a clear need for an 'honest broker' to set up a channel of communication between Tehran and Washington, which could in time lead to the establishment of a full diplomatic relationship between them but in the short term would serve the need for them to exchange views and thus minimise misunderstandings. A resolution of the issue of Iran's nuclear research programme by military means would produce no winners and would probably up the scale of violence in Iraq and the wider Middle East. In this respect, repairing the broken relationship between Iran and the US by diplomatic means is a prize worth fighting for. Merely establishing a channel[70] of communication between Tehran and Washington would be an achievement.

The second challenge is to help the US understand and accept EU policy towards Iran, and in doing so bridge the fissure that was opened up over the second Gulf War. Though the countries of the EU 3, especially the UK,[71] are more likely to fulfil this role, Ireland does not have any vested interests in Iran that might impair its role as intermediary.

The third challenge for Ireland is to safeguard the Nuclear Proliferation Treaty (NPT). During Ireland's very active period at the UN in the 1950s and 1960s it was one of a group of countries whose diplomatic efforts formed the basis of today's NPT, starting in 1958. In addition to nuclear armed states like Russia, the US and France, a number of other countries, notably Egypt, Brazil, Argentina, Sweden, Taiwan and South Korea, are thought to have considered the construction of nuclear weapons programmes, although their adherence to the NPT is thought to have been an important factor in not deciding to pursue fully fledged nuclear weapons programmes.

Unlike other nuclear powers such as India, Pakistan and Israel, Iran is a signatory of the NPT and therefore its adherence to the treaty is an important test case. By ensuring that Iran is not forced to discard the treaty and that it can safeguard its security within the strictures of the treaty, Irish diplomacy could play an important role in maintaining the credibility of an important international agreement, especially when the issue of the proliferation of weapons of mass destruction is prominent.

Efforts were made to overhaul the NPT at the UN during 2005, but a number of difficulties persist.[72] The first is that, as in the case of Pakistan, a country can sign up to the NPT while secretly developing a nuclear weapons programme and, once that programme is operational, opt out of the treaty. A second difficulty is that, with the emergence of China as a major military power, the strategic case for developed countries like Japan to possess nuclear weapons becomes a more compelling one. Finally, the NPT does not cover the proliferation of biological and chemical weapons (which has its own convention),[73] threats that cannot be ruled out, particularly given that more states possess these weapons than nuclear ones. Above all, the challenge for the NPT is to support the cause of diplomacy and to show that military intervention in the fashion of the second Gulf War is neither necessary nor desirable in the fight against the spread of weapons of mass destruction.

Techno-politics

Related to reform of the NPT is the wider issue of UN reform. Amongst the large 'world' institutions, the UN is the most important to Irish diplomacy. It is an arena where Irish diplomats have performed well in the past and honed the techno-political skills referred to at the end of the previous chapter. Dermot Ahern, Minister for Foreign Affairs and a UN Special Envoy, has referred to the UN as 'the cornerstone of Ireland's foreign policy',[74] and to a large extent the UN is revered by some politicians and policy-makers in Ireland. However, although it is a necessary organisation it is also a flawed one. The invasion of Iraq, controversies surrounding it (i.e. the death of Sergio Vieira De Mello)[75] and the ongoing genocide in Sudan have exposed its shortcomings, and the matter of the $20 billion being siphoned off the oil for food programme has not helped either.

Plenty of challenges lie ahead for the UN. Emerging issues presenting themselves are global trade talks (e.g. the 2006 Doha round) as well as headline-grabbing issues like managing terrorism, preventing proliferation and arguably more important humanitarian issues like disease (Aids and malaria), natural disasters and climate change. All of these issues represent opportunities for Ireland to become closely involved in the reform of the UN, but it needs to do so in a less uncritical manner than previously.

Protégé countries

In addition to investing diplomatic resources in international institutional politics, Ireland's influence abroad and the impact of its experiment with globalisation can be spread by adopting a small number of protégé countries in say Africa or Eastern Europe. Helping the likes of Croatia, Georgia, Uganda, Dubai or Estonia learn the lessons of Irish economic success or focusing the resources of groups like Dochas on specific areas in Africa should achieve more success than if these resources are spread more widely.

At the same time, with an eye on the future and on which countries will grow powerful and wealthy, Ireland should cultivate close relations with a strategic partner state. Numerous countries, from Argentina to

South Korea, and even Ireland at times, have suffered the mantle of 'country of the future'. Today, one of the stock questions in the debate on globalisation is whether China and/or India will be the key geo-strategic region of the future.

China or India?

The large powers are already making strategic choices with respect to China. For instance, the US sells heavy arms to Taiwan and has given undertakings to defend it from Chinese aggression. On the other hand, in 2004 the French navy held the largest ever joint exercise between the Chinese navy and a western power. France recently affirmed its close political ties to China, with former foreign minister Michel Barnier stressing their 'global strategic partnership'.[76]

China has been the target of a number of high-profile visits by Irish politicians in recent years,[77] with reciprocal visits by Chinese politicians and diplomats. Though it is very difficult to deny the growing importance of the role that China plays in the world's economic and political affairs, China's path from post-Communism to modernisation is likely to be a long one, strewn with the wreckage of economic crises (which, like the case of the Asian Tigers, is a consequence of economic growing pains) and disputes over democracy, the environment and human rights and it could prove an unpopular friend in the future for several reasons.

First, it is likely to remain at the centre of a growing number of human rights disputes,[78] with a significant number of Taiwanese demanding full independence, and ongoing protests by the pro-democracy movement in Hong Kong. Second, as a number of books have recently underlined, the growth of the Chinese economy is likely to have wide-ranging and controversial environmental side-effects.[79] Thirdly, China's current banking and industrial systems are still adolescent and will most likely take a volatile route to full maturity. China has historically been through a number of waves of economic and financial development, many of which have ended badly, undermined by poor policy-making, protectionism (often of foreigners) and weak governance.[80] In Ireland's case, it has few intrinsic ties to China and not many business interests there. Given the apparently opaque rewards of a closer engagement with China, it is worth considering whether diplomatic capital could be better invested in another large Asian regional player, such as India.

Ireland has political and historical ties to India that extend beyond their shared language and colonial past.[81] In breaking free from Britain, India adopted the Irish flag and Constitution. Like Ireland, India was partitioned upon independence and remains involved in a low-intensity territorial struggle over Kashmir with Pakistan. Despite the build-up of

nuclear arms between India and Pakistan, and the potential of other border areas to generate trouble, India does not seem as great a threat to the
(western) world order that China does but is nevertheless of significant
geo-strategic importance, a point underlined by the former US Assistant
Secretary of State, Strobe Talbott.[82]

Irish political and diplomatic experience could be employed in
some of the conflicts around India's borders, and the country's very
positive experiences at the heart of the EU could be used to the benefit
of the Indian civil service. At the same time, with the election of a new
government headed by Manmohan Singh (India's equivalent of
T. K. Whittaker), the country is undergoing a great experiment in
policy-making. Over the past ten years it has become more business-
friendly, a move that perhaps leaves it more amenable to importing
some of the lessons from Ireland's economic boom.

Other similarities lie in that both countries have relatively developed
institutional structures and, although Ireland remains a far easier place to
do business than India, economic growth in both countries has been
helped by a more business-friendly approach to regulation. An examination of India's success by Rodrik and Subramanian[83] argues that the 'trig-
ger for India's economic growth was an attitudinal shift on the part of the
national government in 1980 in favour of private business'. They hold
that, 'thanks to its solid democratic institutions and impressive performance in information technology, the country is increasingly vying with,
if not displacing, China as the country of the future in the eyes of many
knowledgeable observers' and attribute this to the pragmatic and pro-
business approach taken by its technocrats.

Conclusion

As the world has become more interdependent and integrated, foreign
policies based on neutrality have lost their edge and their meaning. This
is especially true in Ireland's case. There is a widening gap between the
public image of Ireland's policy of neutrality and the reality of the way in
which it is prosecuted.

Globalisation undercuts Ireland's neutrality in numerous ways. Some
of these are the spread and sophistication of international organised
crime, terrorism and under-development, the prominence of American
military and economic power, bolder initiatives towards common EU
security and defence policies, together with a warmer relationship
between Ireland and Britain.

As befits the role of one of the most globalised countries in the world,
Ireland needs more focused foreign policy, projected globally in order to
enhance the (soft) power it can wield. Neutrality remains a desirable

form for this role, but it needs to be rethought and overhauled. The last part of this chapter outlines a more active and meaningful form of neutrality based on military and diplomatic specialisation and a wider emphasis on techno-political skills and intermediation, in addition to cultivating Ireland's relationships with strategic partners like India and protégé countries such as Estonia, as well as its special relationship with the US.

Chapter Seven

Ireland and the globe

'The new Ireland is still learning the old lessons the hard way, like a brilliant but arrogant boy whose very brilliance acts as a dam against experience, so that he learns everything quickly – except experience.'
Sean O'Faolain[1]

The folly of imitation
The aim of this chapter is to highlight the lessons that other countries, be they globalised or globalising, can learn from Ireland's experience of globalisation. As the quote (written in 1948) at the beginning of the chapter suggests, Ireland itself has many lessons to learn from its embrace of globalisation and from that of other countries too.

Before outlining the lessons that Ireland can offer other nations, it is worthwhile to add a caveat to any recommendations that may follow from the Irish case. A huge chunk of the academic literature on international and development economics, as well as policy-making studies in economics and international relations, is devoted to mapping the experience of one country onto that of another. Policy advisers, academics, business schools, journalists and institutions like the IMF have all made reputations from preaching that one country should adopt the policies of another more successful one.

Well-known examples are the way in which American business academics dissected the 'miracle' of the Japanese manufacturing sector in the 1980s and sought to apply Japanese management techniques to US companies, or the way in which European companies and governments are lectured on the need to be more 'Anglo-Saxon' in their practice of financial policy. It is not unusual for publications like the *Financial Times* to ponder questions like 'can Sweden give Germany fertile ideas to revive its ailing economy'.[2]

Though it is common sense to suspect that a policy that works for one country may not work as well for another, this has not halted the supply of advice based on various 'success stories', nor the demand for it from countries that are eager to advance. Blindly imitating another country's success could prove foolish, because, despite the growing integration of national economies, deep structural economic, cultural and legal differences exist between states. Even within the European Union, which more than any other regional integration project has stripped away social and economic barriers, measures that would be acceptable in, say, Ireland would be found unworkable in France. This is the main reason why the EU's Lisbon Agenda for economic reform has so far proved anything but a success.

The aim of the Lisbon Agenda, to transform the EU into the world's most competitive, knowledge-based economy by 2010 (which incidentally seems to have been adopted verbatim by Irish politicians), has been plagued by problems, such as pensions deficits, the migration of manufacturing capacity to Eastern Europe and Asia and, more worrying, the migration of thousands of European researchers to the US. The overabiding difficulty is that, in policy-making, national preferences and exceptions remain. A good example is the recent Hartz IV reform package, designed to address structural problems in the German labour market and welfare system. This is Germany-specific, and could not be applied to other EU states like Greece or the UK.

So in policy-making the 'country effect' persists, making the transfer of policies that work in one country to another reasonably difficult. In the past, the belief that this was straightforward has been a shortcoming of some global development agencies. One of the main protests of opponents of global institutions like the World Bank is that they are too ready to apply a policy formula that has had success in some developed countries to developing countries, and in doing so take little account of local factors and complex structural differences between nations. This criticism and those mentioned above raise the question: exactly how much of what has worked for Ireland can be applied in other countries?

There is growing curiosity abroad as to how Ireland has moved from relative poverty to wealth. Some indigenous factors cannot be easily replicated, like its English-speaking population, competent Civil Service and close relationship with America. However, other policy measures, such as low taxes, can and are being copied. Of course, the fact that there is no specific 'proprietary' Irish economic model is a bonus for other countries, as it makes Irish policy actions easier to copy. If there were discernible Irish policy characteristics, such as the cross-holding structures found in the Korean, Japanese and German corporate sectors, then these factors would prove difficult and costly to replicate.

A further caution to countries that are keen to import policy from Ireland is that Ireland's experiment with globalisation is only half-baked. So far, the economic side of this engagement is most apparent, but its downside has yet to show itself. The cultural, social and foreign policy challenges that globalisation is presenting to Ireland are as yet neither clear nor well understood.

Why is Ireland's case interesting?

Over the course of the past twenty years, Ireland has gone from being a relatively secluded, poor developed country to a rich developed one with a high international profile. What makes the story of Ireland's journey interesting and hopefully marks out this account of it as more than 'another book on globalisation' is that Ireland does not easily fit the conventional way in which globalisation is debated.

The broad debate on globalisation tends to focus more on unglobalised, developing countries like Brazil, and dwells on issues such as poverty and free trade and on institutions like the WTO. While these important topics touch upon Ireland's experience, they do not fully capture the nature of its economic and social transformation and the problems that it will face in the future. For instance, one of the better accounts of the debate on globalisation[3] makes only four brief mentions of Ireland.

That Ireland occupies a distinct place in the debate on globalisation is made clearer by a thorough report on globalisation prepared for the EU.[4] In concluding, the report poses twelve questions about globalisation and answers each one in turn. These questions are presented here in abbreviated form:

1. Globalisation has caused massive poverty.
2. Globalisation has resulted in an unprecedented degree of inequality.
3. Inequality has increased massively in globalising countries like China.
4. Multinationals are playing governments off against each other, paying less tax and gaining immense power.
5. Multinationals exploit workers in developing countries for sweatshop pay and in appalling conditions in order to cut costs in their home base.
6. The big US multinationals are imposing US culture on the rest of the world for the sake of the profits made by big brands.
7. Globalisation harms the environment in countless ways.
8. Farmers in developing countries switch to cash crops that despoil the local environment and mean they can no longer feed themselves in case of a crisis, all in order to satisfy the whims of northern consumers.
9. The international institutions that are supposed to govern the world economy act solely in the interests of the rich countries, especially the US. They impose policies that are unsuitable for developing countries, such as over-rapid financial liberalisation.
10. Aid spending is pitifully low.

11.   The WTO sets the rules to favour big multinationals so they can do things like patent traditional remedies or block access to cheap drugs.

12.   The WTO is secretive, undemocratic and unfair, with an extreme free-market agenda.

Although this report was written for the European Commission, these questions are clearly more relevant to second and Third World countries. Some issues, such as foreign aid and environmental damage, are also relevant to the Irish case but are given scant attention by policy-makers. The issues that are central to the Irish case of globalisation are the role of large multinationals, financial (i.e. bond) markets and the policies of world institutions like the WTO. Contrary to popular wisdom, and most certainly the views of anti-globalists, Ireland's experience of these factors has been, on balance, a positive one.

Who can learn? – Ireland's peers
Different countries, of varying size and development, will be able to draw different conclusions from Ireland's encounter with globalisation. Ireland shares common factors with both large and small countries, as diverse as Finland and India. However, amongst the ranks of the world's most globalised countries[5] there is a discernible small-country effect. There are several reasons for this. In the past century, many more small countries have gained independence than large ones. In fact, it is the break-up of large countries like the former Soviet Union and Yugoslavia that has spawned new, small nations. Countries like Estonia, Slovenia and Hungary are therefore amongst the most likely candidates to learn from and adopt some of the lessons of Ireland's success.

Compared to large established nations like Germany, small countries tend to have more open economies and need to trade more, as they are not self-sufficient in all manufacturing and service areas. Small countries like Ireland are less mighty in terms of hard power and military and financial mass and therefore tend to be more actively involved in world institutions like the UN. In recent years small countries have proved to be leaders in certain policy areas, such as Norway in foreign policy, New Zealand in monetary policy and Finland in the technology sector. Most importantly, the impact of globalisation on small countries is more likely to be greater than on large ones. The key role of small developed countries in the globalisation debate makes the Irish case all the more relevant and there is a wide range of small developing countries, from Croatia, Georgia and Estonia to the Arab Emirates, that could learn from Ireland's experience of globalisation.

On the other hand, Ireland's experience of globalisation can be mapped onto some large developing countries, especially when, like India, they share common historical and political factors with Ireland. At the very least, under-developed countries can take heart from the fact that so much has been done in Ireland in terms of the poor physical infrastructure and lack of competitive advantage, and also from the fact that geographic location now matters less as a determinant of wealth in the globalised world.

Lessons from Ireland and the Global Question
The scope of this book is confined to examining the relationship between globalisation and the Irish economy, and its effects on society, and to considering how foreign policy must adapt to a changing world order.[6] As highlighted in the first chapter, the broad conclusion is that the economic globalisation of Ireland seems to have gone as far as it can go, such that new goals and a new approach to policy-making are required if economic growth is to be sustained. The side-effects of globalisation on society appear to be going too far and need to be buffered by a bigger and more responsible role for the state. Finally, the globalisation of foreign policy has not gone far enough, and it needs to be projected globally in a more defined way.

The common thread that runs through the issues discussed here and draws the individual strands of Ireland's Global Question together is the question of independence, whether globalisation frees nation states to pursue their own destinies or whether it dominates them. All other countries, be they large or small, have this dilemma in common. In the light of this, the sections below highlight some of the lessons that can be gleaned from the Irish experience of globalisation.

Lesson 1: Be more pragmatic and inventive
Ireland's contribution to the debate on globalisation is manifold, though the best known is the economic aspect. The secret of Ireland's success lies not in a distinctive Irish model of development, but more in the combination of favourable external circumstances with the pragmatic adoption of a set of economic policies that closely resembles the much-maligned Washington consensus,[7] namely fiscal discipline, tax reform, streamlined public expenditure and a business-friendly approach to regulation. As with many of the Latin-American countries to which the Washington consensus was applied, Ireland implemented these measures at a time when its economic performance could arguably not have been weaker, and was fortunate to have the common monetary project to act as a policy framework and political cover.

Ireland adopted the above measures more aggressively than its old economic peer group of Greece, Spain and Portugal, largely because politicians, civil servants and other stakeholders like business owners and unions were determined to avoid further economic decline and were highly pragmatic in the way policy was applied. In this respect, Ireland is an example, in economic terms at least, that the Washington consensus works. The main difference between Ireland and other countries that have adopted this policy mix is that it has for a long time enjoyed political stability and a first world institutional apparatus.

The lesson for other countries from Ireland's adoption of the EU version of the Washington consensus (the Brussels consensus really does not sound dynamic enough) is not to let ideology get in the way of pragmatic policy. Countless articles have appeared in respected journals on how 'structural' factors, ideology and country exceptions act as barriers to real economic reform. The example of Ireland suggests that countries that wish to follow Ireland will have to be happy to override concerns over nationalism, labour markets, social models and 'ways of life' in order to implement a more liberal form of economic policy. Many of the other 'New European' states have already done this and exhibit what would ordinarily be recognised as right-wing economic policies. In the future, many of these countries, and Ireland too, will find that pragmatism needs to be complemented with inventiveness, as old problems like inflation have to be dealt with in very new ways, largely because of the strictures of monetary union.

Lesson 2: But don't allow pragmatism to smother strategic planning, or even ideology

However, there is a good reason as to why ideology and national exceptions stand in the way of liberal economic policies in countries like France and Germany. As mature developed economies these countries have sufficient policy experience to realise that blind economic liberalisation leads to an imbalance between society and economy. There is a lesson for Ireland in the fact that some countries have not taken to economic reform as aggressively as it has. This is that liberal economics can breed an illiberal and unequal society. It is unsurprising therefore that there is little sign that globalisation has made Ireland less unequal.

In this respect, the social revolution that has occurred in Ireland bears out the warning that large-scale economic transformations are accompanied by great social changes. The changes taking place in Irish society are profound and have much to offer modernising states by way of a case study. In essence, Irish society has been turned upside down, rebuffing everything that made up pre-globalised Ireland (the Church and trust in institutions, to mention a couple) while embracing all that is new (consumerism, capitalism). Like the post-Communism countries making the transition from totalitarianism to democracy, the change in Irish society seems all the greater by comparison to its past as a marginal, poor nation. Though many of these changes are for the better, the danger is that they go unchecked and produce imbalances, such as large income and wealth inequalities, or deterioration in social fabric.

The triumph of pragmatism over strategic planning in Ireland is demonstrated by the fact that globalisation is lop-sided, skewed towards economic factors, and appears to operate under the assumption that what is good for economic growth is good for society. Under these conditions, a clash between an economy-centric view of the world (broadly speaking, the Anglo-Saxon one) and a society-based one (the European model) seems likely in the future. Overall, there is a sense that in Ireland pragmatism has smothered ideology, or at the very least thrived at the expense of a strategic plan of how society should develop. This is a trap that other countries should be careful not to fall into.

Lesson 3: The role of the state is still very important, especially for small countries
The dramatic changes occurring in Irish society during this period of globalisation and the encroachment of non-state actors like large corporations into the geo-strategic environment are some of a number of reasons as to why the state remains important in this era of globalisation, rather than being made irrelevant by it. Though the breaking down of traditional boundaries and the rush of financial, information and trade flows above the level of the state are part of globalisation, state structures will continue to be important for the way in which they can intermediate and adapt the side-effects of globalisation.

As emerging trends in Ireland are beginning to show, the role of the state as a buffer between society and globalisation is likely to focus on tasks like building new domestic institutions and managing social problems like inequality and racism and spending on physical and human infrastructure. Ireland is unique amongst small, developed, globalised countries in that the role of government (e.g. spending and taxes) is very small. This suggests that it may have to expand as globalisation intensifies and that, by the same token, watching the way in which the state adjusts its role to globalisation should prove instructive for other nations.

Lesson 4: Globalisation is changing the way we think of sovereignty, and new tactics are needed in modern foreign policy
Ireland has historically treasured its sovereignty, but in recent years has happily exchanged it for both peace and prosperity. Specifically, the

Good Friday Agreement and membership of the EU have demonstrated that in a globalised world sovereignty can be interpreted in a more fluid and ultimately profitable manner. The results of this strategy mean that Ireland has gone from a geo-politically secluded nation to one that is much more integrated into the international order. However, operating at this level demands new political tactics if a country is to retain some influence over the way international affairs affect it. In particular, as Chapter Five outlined, an innovative foreign policy focused on building soft power and active membership of transnational institutions is valuable. Several other small developed countries (i.e. those of the Nordic region) have already figured this out and are practising this lesson with great skill.

Another configuration of the argument that sovereignty is changing is what some commentators call 'the death of geography'. While it is an exaggeration to believe that geography no longer counts as a significant determinant of a nation's wealth, Ireland's case does help to sustain the argument that geography is less important. This is especially true when we consider how its geographic isolation and proximity to Britain has been a powerful factor in its political economy. But there are now a number of reasons why geography matters less. As the debate on outsourcing shows, global corporations are nimble and can easily site different parts of their production chain in different continents. The growth of service- and information-based economies also facilities this. In foreign affairs, there is a growing emphasis on 'softer' forms of power that are less dependent on geography, and the increasing importance of global governance also diminishes the role that geography plays in international politics.

Lesson 5: Institution-building is important, both domestically and globally
An extension of lessons three and four is that Ireland's case shows that being able to influence and interact with 'world' institutions like the UN and supra-national ones like the EU is crucial to a country's ability to co-opt power at an international level. Doing so successfully means that diplomats and civil servants need to be skilled in the art of techno-politics. Before the current wave of globalisation, what marked Ireland out as being unusual amongst the less wealthy countries of the world is that it had a relatively developed institutional apparatus in the form of its Civil Service, which allowed it to interact with bodies like the EC and the UN.

The argument that globalising countries should focus their energies on developing the capabilities necessary to engage world institutions is supported by the fact that countries that are not globalised seem to have low-quality institutions. Although the relation between globalisation and the quality of domestic institutions is a hard one to prove, much of the literature appears to support this notion. It is also worth mentioning the fact that, amongst the globalised Asian countries, strong institutional structures rather than democracy has been a defining characteristic. In practical terms, institution-building should focus on tasks like minimising corruption, allowing independent media to develop, building a proficient central bank and finance ministry, and rewarding skills in areas like medicine and education.

Furthermore, once a country has become more globalised, new institutions are necessary to intermediate the effects of the outside world on society. In Ireland today, domestic institution-building is taking place at a rapid pace, largely aimed at building the institutional infrastructure necessary for a growing economy (i.e. National Pension Reserve Fund) and a changing society (i.e. The Equality Authority).

Lesson 6: Beware of bubbles
It is still a moot point amongst central bankers as to whether they can spot and then lance bubbles in asset prices. Being able to do so is critically important because of the damage that these bubbles leave behind them – the equity market crash of 1929, the Japanese property bubble of the 1990s and the more recent equity market bubble being well-known examples.

Although the temptation to let the good times roll can often be overbearing, any hint that asset prices in a particular area of the economy are above where they should reasonably trade warrants scrutiny and potentially stiff medicine. Ireland's property market (in addition to high consumer inflation) has many of the characteristics of a bubble, not least the fever with which people follow the market. The culprit of asset price inflation is usually cheap money, and Ireland is no exception here, with real interest rates often dipping below zero.

Ireland has yet to experience the downside of its property bubble, but when it does the effects will most probably be felt by those who are least prepared for it, those who were drawn in at the top of the bubble and who are heavily indebted. Once asset prices stop rising, high levels of debt will make many people's lives very difficult, and exacerbate income and wealth inequalities.

Yet to be learned – globalisation in the future
In the sense that there has already been an era of globalisation, in the nineteenth century, this generation should be able to learn from it and ensure that the current wave of globalisation is not derailed by nationalism and protectionism. Despite this, the path of globalisation does not seem any clearer, partly because the Anglo-Saxon model, the one that is

the most prominent and criticised form of globalisation, is being challenged by two other emerging models. One is the Asian model of development, as pioneered by the Tiger economies and now adopted as Confucian capitalism by China, and the other centres around the growing role of the EU as a major player in trade, financial markets and world institutions. In this context, Ireland's case is interesting in that by referring to it as a Tiger economy some commentators confuse it with the Asian model, and many Irish people would like to think of it as fitting the European one, but in fact it conforms most closely to the Anglo-Saxon one.

In time, the world may evolve into a tri-polar form along the lines of three chief regions incorporating the EU, the Anglo-Saxon world and Asia (led by China), or, as invoked by George Orwell in *1984*, Oceania, Eurasia and Eastasia. In economic terms, a tri-polar world is not unlikely. Assuming it consolidates economic and foreign policy, Europe will have almost as much economic clout and soft power as the US, and Asia cannot be ignored if countries like Japan and China can be counted on to maintain open markets.

Growing regionalisation could lead to a new form of balance of power politics, just as the emergence of a larger Germany at the end of the nineteenth century led to coalitions between other European powers (back then, America, like China now, was the emerging power). The extent to which this happens is a matter of speculation, but the key lesson from the first wave of globalisation is that a mixture of nationalism, balance of power rivalries, financial market imbalances and creeping protectionism led to the end of globalisation.

Although world institutions like the UN, IMF and WTO are now in place to prevent these types of events recurring, there are plausible scenarios that envisage the end of globalisation. The potential breakdown of the transatlantic relationship between the EU and the US, the rise of immigration and outsourcing as populist political issues, the adolescent Chinese economy and debt-laden US one, the rise of nationalism in countries like the US, Saudi Arabia and Taiwan, and the growing seriousness of environmental catastrophes are just a few of a long list of factors that could derail globalisation as we know it.

The long view of history
Notwithstanding this litany of potential scare stories, globalisation is likely to be around for a while yet as such immense geo-economic trends take time to fade. Still, the risk that globalisation could halt or even change course is one that a highly globalised country like Ireland should consider. This places a premium on strategic thinking and perhaps a long view of history.

As the case of Ireland demonstrates, a long view of history shows that even poor, dominated countries will have their day. The converse of this, and the lesson that must be learned in the future, is that prosperity should not be squandered, but should be built upon and used for the common good. As Ireland was claiming its independence in the early twentieth century, a prominent politician stated:

> So it is with the nation: we must prepare the ground and sow the seed for the rich ripeness of maturity; and bearing in mind that the maturity of the nation will come, not in one generation but after many generations, we must be prepared to work in the knowledge that we prepare for a future that only other generations will enjoy.[8]

These words remain relevant today. Lessons from other countries and different experiences of globalisation show that only careful strategic planning and an unselfish eye on the future will enable a country in Ireland's position to resolve its Global Question.

Notes and References

Introduction
1. J. J. Lee, *Ireland 1912–1985, Politics and Society* (Cambridge: Cambridge University Press, 1989), p. 631.
2. For example, the National Competitiveness Council's (NCC) Annual Competitiveness Reports show Ireland to rank ahead of its peers in terms of exports relative to GDP, imports relative to GDP, foreign direct investment, and economic freedom (www.forfas.ie/ncc).
3. A good starting-point in tracking these changes is the CSO publication *Ireland and the EU, 1973–2003* (www.cso.ie).
4. 'Bulgarians Dream of Emulating the Celtic Tiger in Enlarged EU', *Irish Times,* 1 June 2004
5. China's Premier Wen Jiabao has held that Ireland's economic success has lessons for China (*Irish Times,* 29 April 2004).
6. P. Beresford-Ellis (ed.), *James Connolly: Selected Writings* (London: Pluto Press, 1997), p. 140.
7. C. O'Clery, *Ireland in Quotes: A History of the 20th Century* (Dublin: O'Brien Press, 1999), p. 97.
8. Philip Pettit, *Republicanism* (Oxford: Oxford University Press, 1997), p. 5.
9. Jagdish Bhagwati, *In Defence of Globalization* (Oxford: Oxford University Press, 2004), p. ix.
10. Charles MacKay, *Extraordinary Popular Delusions and the Madness of Crowds* (PA: Templeton Foundation Press, 1989).
11. Dani Rodrik, *Has Globalisation Gone Too Far?* (Washington: Institute for International Economics, 1997).
12. Ibid., p. 9.

Chapter One
1. Karl Marx and Friedrich Engels, *Ireland and the Irish Question* (Moscow: Progress Publishers, 1986), p. 59.
2. Demographics remain favourable to Ireland. It has the lowest old age dependency ratio of any EU country, with the population over 65 and above as a percentage of the working age population at 16.4% in 2003, and expected to tally 17.3% in 2010. The EU averages for these periods are 25.5 and 27.3% respectively (www.cso.ie).
3. House of Lords Economic Affairs Committee, *First Report on Globalisation* (London: House of Lords, 16 January 2003) (www.parliament.the-stationery-office.co.uk/pa/ld200203/ldselect/ldeconaf/5/501.htm).
4. Available at www.unctad.org.

5. Stanley Fischer, 'Globalization and Its Challenges', *American Economic Review Papers and Proceedings*, May 2003, p. 2.

6. Kevin O'Rourke and Jeremy Williamson, 'When Did Globalization Begin?', *European Review of Economic History*, vol. 6, 2002, p. 24.

7. House of Lords Economic Affairs Committee, chapter two, paragraph 30.

8. Joseph Nye, 'Globalization's Democratic Deficit: How to Make International Institutions More Accountable', *Foreign Affairs*, vol. 80, no, 4, July/August 2001.

9. J. Donahue, and J. Nye, *Governance in a Globalizing World* (Washington: Brookings Institution Press, 2000), p. 1.

10. Jan-Aart Scholte, 'What is Globalization? The Definitional Issue – Again', *University of Warwick CSGR Working Paper*, no. 109/02, December 2002, p. 3.

11. Ibid., p. 8.

12. Theodore Levitt, 'The Globalization of Markets', *Harvard Business Review*, May/June 1983, p. 2.

13. Joseph Stiglitz, *Globalization and Its Discontents* (New York: WM Norton & Co., 2003). In a reply to Stiglitz's book, Thomas Dawson, a Director at the IMF, points out that 'The *Economist* said in its review that a more accurate title for the book would have been 'The IMF and My Discontent'. In addition he notes that Stiglitz's book has some 64 references to globalisation, whereas references to the IMF total 340 (http://www.imf.org/external/np/speeches/2002/061302.htm).

14. This argument is taking hold amongst the European left, in publications such as Lionel Jospin's *Le monde comme je le vois* (Paris: Gallimard, 2005).

15. NAFTA (North American Free Trade Agreement), MERCOSUR ('Mercado Comun del Sur' – common market of the South), ASEAN (Association of Southeast Asian Nations), APEC (Asia Pacific Economic Co-operation).

16. Pope Leo XIII, 'Rerum Novarum', *Papal Encyclical*, 15 May 1891.

17. Papal address to Pontifical Academy of Social Sciences, 27 April 2001 (www.catholic-forum.com).

18. A study commissioned by the US bishops' National Review Board, and published on 27 February 2004, found that over 4% of priests ministering between 1950 and 2002 were accused of sexual abuse of a minor, with 68% of this alleged abuse taking place between 1950 and 1979 (www.usccb.org/nrb).

19. Daniel Cohen, *La mondialisation et ses ennemis* (Paris: Grasset, 2004).

20. Jared Diamond, *Guns, Germs and Steel: The Fates of Human Societies* (New York: WM Norton & Co., 1999).

21. D. Flynn, and A. Giraldez, 'Path Dependence, Time Lags and the Birth of Globalization: A Critique of O'Rourke and Williamson', *European Review of Economic History*, vol. 8, 2004, pp. 81–108. These authors hold that globalisation began in 1571, and outline a series of 'silver cycles' that have taken place since then. The response to this paper by O'Rourke and Williamson (2004), 'Once More: When Did Globalization Begin?', *European Review of Economic History*, vol. 8, 2004, pp. 109–117, aggressively dismisses many of the arguments in the Flynn paper.

22. Severe Acute Respiratory Syndrome.

23. R. Rajan and L. Zingales, 'The Great Reversals: The Politics of Financial Development in the Twentieth Century', *Journal of Financial Economics*, vol. 69, no. 1, 2003, pp. 5–50.

24. Kevin O'Rourke, 'Europe and the Causes of Globalization, 1790 to 2000', in H. Kierkowski (ed.), *From Europeanization of the Globe to Globalization of Europe* (Hampshire: Palgrave, 2002).

25. Rodrik, *Has Globalisation Gone Too Far?*, p. 7.

26. J. M. Keynes, *The Economic Consequences of the Peace 1919* (New York: Dover Publications, 2004), p. 4.

27. R. Baldwin and P. Martin, 'Two Waves of Globalisation: Superficial Similarities, Fundamental Differences', *NBER Working Paper*, no. 6904, 1999, p. 4.

28. Soros, whose outlook on life is greatly influenced by the philosopher Karl Popper, has himself attempted to address some of the problems posed to the world by both capitalism and globalisation. For example, 'The Capitalist Threat', *Atlantic Monthly*, May 1995, 'Towards a Global Open Society', *Atlantic Monthly*, January 1998, and *George Soros on Globalization* (New York: Perseus Books, 2002).

29. P. Masson, 'Globalization: Facts and Figures', *IMF Policy Discussion Paper*, no. 01/4, October 2001.

30. F. Bourguignon et al., 'Making Sense of Globalization: A Guide to the Economic Issues', *Centre for Economic Policy Research (CEPR) Policy Paper*, no. 8, July 2002.

31. Ibid., p. 67.

32. P. Lindert and J. Williamson, 'Does Globalization Make the World More Unequal?', *NBER Working Paper*, no. 8228, April 2001, p. 1.

33. Ibid., p. 1.

34. D. Dollar, 'Globalization, Poverty, and Inequality since 1802', *World Bank Policy Research Working Paper*, no. 3333, June 2004, p. 7.

35. Ibid., p. 40.

36. United Nations Development Program – 'Investing in Development: A Practical Plan to Achieve the Millennium Development Goals' (www.undp.org).

37. R. Wade, 'Is Globalization Reducing Poverty and Inequality?' *World Development*, vol. 32, no. 4, 2004, pp. 567–589.

Chapter Two

1.	D. Irwin, *Against the Tide: An Intellectual History of Free Trade* (Princeton: Princeton University Press, 1996), p. 19.
2.	Official Statistics in the New Millennium, Central Statistics Office, 1999 (www.cso.ie).
3.	Population and Migration Estimates, April 2004 (www.cso.ie).
4.	Department of Social and Family Affairs (www.welfare.ie). CSO population estimates in April 2005 only picked up approximately 12,000 Poles coming to Ireland in the previous twelve months (www.cso.ie/releasespublications/documents/population/current/popmig.pdf).
5.	Available at www.foreignpolicy.com.
6.	The 2005 AT Kearney/*Foreign Policy* globalisation report saw Ireland drop from first place to second in the globalisation league table, replaced by Singapore. The primary reason for this was the dip in Irish GDP from 7% in 2002 to 1.8% in 2003. In addition, Singapore has become more politically globalised, increasing spending on aid and its contribution to the UN (it runs a large peace-keeping force in East Timor – where some Irish troops are also stationed).
7.	Figures from the 2005 AT Kearney/*Foreign Policy* report.
8.	Available at www.hdr.undp.org/reports/global/2004/.
9.	Inequality, for instance, in terms of share of income amongst the richest 10% of the population, Ireland ranks very high, with almost 28% of income/consumption being shared amongst the richest 10%. Only the chief Anglo-Saxon countries, the UK and US, are higher in the western developed world.
10.	Ireland ranked first, ahead of Switzerland, Norway, Luxembourg and Sweden. The UK was in 29th place and the US was 13th.
11.	The EIU use material wellbeing (GDP per capita), health (life expectancy), political stability and security, family life (divorce rate), community life (i.e. church attendance, trade union membership), climate and geography, job security (unemployment rate), political freedom and gender equality.
12.	The fact that there is an 83% correlation between the ranking of a country's quality of life and its GDP per capita suggests that the results of the EIU's quality of life index are driven by rising incomes.
13.	B. Frey and A. Stutzer, 'What Can Economists Learn from Happiness?', CESifo Working Paper, no. 503, June 2001; A. Oswald, 'Happiness and Economic Performance', *Economic Journal*, vol. 107, 1997; Di Tella et al., 'The Macroeconomics of Happiness', *Review of Economics and Statistics*, vol. 85, no. 4; R. Easterlin, 'Explaining Happiness', Proceedings of the National Academy of Sciences, vol. 100, September 2003.
14.	Although the study of utility/happiness in economics goes back a long way, at least as far as the work of Bernoulli in the seventeenth century.
15.	Richard Easterlin, 'Explaining Happiness', *Proceedings of the National Academy of Sciences*, vol. 100, September 2003, p. 11177.

16. Lionel Robbins Memorial Lectures, 'Happiness: Has Social Science a Clue?', February 2003, Lecture 1, p. 13. Layard is also the author of *Happiness: Lessons from a New Science* (London: Penguin, 2005).

17 Available at www.cso.ie.

18. The alarming rise in the suicide rate in Ireland has prompted the Health Service Executive (HSE) to plan the establishment of a national office on suicide prevention.

19. Available at www.mentalhealthireland.ie.

20. Available at www.aware.ie.

21. According to the National Taskforce on Obesity, 39% of Irish people are overweight and 18% are obese. Over 300,000 Irish children are thought to be obese (www.healthpromotion.ie/topics/obesity/).

22. Angus Deaton, 'Health in an Age of Globalization', Research Program in Development Studies, Center for Health and Wellbeing, Princeton University, July 2004, p. 6.

23. Ibid., p. 15.

24. OECD, *Statistical Profile of Ireland*, 2005.

25. A. Oswald, 'Happiness and Economic Performance', *Economic Journal*, vol. 107, 1997, p. 1816.

26. Eurobarometer, *Globalisation*, Flash Eurobarometer 151b, November 2003 (http://europa.eu.int/comm/public_opinion/index_en.htm).

27. A later Eurobarometer survey, in July 2005, confirmed this. Irish people were unique in Europe for the very high number (87%) of respondents who believed that membership of the EU is beneficial (in Denmark, for example, the number is only 50%).

28. J. Hale, *The Civilisation of Europe in the Renaissance* (London: Harper Collins, 1993), p. 56.

29. T. Todorov, *Le nouveau desordre mondial: reflexions d'un Européen* (Paris: Robert Laffont, 2003), pp. 88–89.

30. *Financial Times*, 25 November 2004.

31. Cohen, *La mondialisation*, p. 149.

32. The European School Survey on Alcohol and other Drugs found that in 2003 a third of Irish teenagers admitted to binge drinking, making Ireland the worst EU country for teenage binge drinking. Irish students were also twice more likely than the EU average to use other drugs, like cannabis (www.espad.org).

33. Liam Brady, perhaps.

34. For instance, the UK and Ireland have the lowest level of total investment in infrastructure relative to GDP in the developed world (www.forfas.ie).

35. S. Partridge, 'The British–Irish Council: The Trans-Islands Symbolic and Political Possibilities', British Council Looking into England Papers, 2003.

36. See www.britishcouncil.org/ireland.htm.

Chapter Three

1. Quoted as 'Si au lieu de l'expéditon d'Egypte j'eusse fait celle d'Irlande, que pouvait être l'Angleterre aujhourd'hui', in Thomas Pakenham's *The Year of Liberty: The History of the Great Irish Rebellion of 1798* (London: Panther Books, 1992), p. 336.

2. Data comes from Angus Maddison's database (www.eco.rug.nl/~Maddison/).

3. As Marx and Engels also note, little love was lost between the English workers and their Irish counterparts, 'the ordinary English worker hates the Irish worker as a competitor', K. Marx and F. Engels, *Ireland and the Irish Question* (Moscow: Progress Publishers, 1986), p. 392.

4. E. Mossner and I. Ross (eds.), *The Correspondence of Adam Smith* (Indianapolis: Liberty Fund, 1987), p. 242.

5. Ibid., p. 242.

6. D. Rodrik, 'Trading in Illusions', *Foreign Policy,* March/April 2001, p. 4.

7. Mossner and Ross, *Correspondence of Adam Smith*, p. 243.

8. Ibid., p. 242.

9. Ibid, p. 241.

10. Emmet Larkin, *Alexis de Tocqueville's Journey in Ireland, July–August 1835* (Dublin: Wolfhound Press, 1990), p. 88.

11. Ibid., p. 3.

12. Ibid., p. 39.

13. Ibid., p. 55.

14. Ibid., p. 24.

15. Ibid., p. 21.

16. Marx and Engels, *Ireland and the Irish Question*.

17. Ibid., p. 62.

18. Ibid., p. 84.

19. D. McLellan, *The Thought of Karl Marx*, second edition (Papermac, 1980).

20. Marx and Engels, *Ireland and the Irish Question*, p. 36.

21. Ibid., p. 48.

22. Ibid., p. 148.

23. Ibid., p. 35.

24. Ibid., p. 436.

25. Ibid., p. 245.

26. Ibid., p. 93.

27. Ibid., p. 388.

28. Ibid., p. 103.

29. Ibid., p. 24.

30. Ibid., p. 57.

31. Ibid., p. 107.

32. Ibid., p. 59.

33. Ibid., pp. 66–67.

34. Ibid., p. 391.

Chapter Four

1.   Marx and Engels, *Ireland and the Irish Question*, p. 372.

2.   Even in recent years, 1999–2004, the only developed countries to better Ireland's GNP growth were South Korea and Hungary
(www.oecd.org). Over a longer time period, 1994–2004, Ireland had
easily the best average growth in GDP (7.9%) amongst the OECD
countries.

3.   'The performance of Irish productivity and Irish employment since
the mid-1980s is very impressive. I do not know the rules by which
miracles are officially defined, but this comes close', Olivier Blan-
chard, p. 61, in P. Honohan and B. Walsh, 'Catching up with the Leaders', *Brookings Papers on Economic Activity*, vol. 1, 2002.

4.   Board of Governors of the Federal Reserve System, 'Preventing Deflation: Japan's Experience in the 1990s', *International Finance Discussion
Papers*, no. 729, 2002.

5.   It remained close to 16% until 1988, falling to 13% in 1990. Still, by
1993 it was again close to 16% (www.oecd.org).

6.   J. J. Lee, *Ireland 1912–1985: Politics and Society* (Cambridge: Cambridge University Press, 1989), p. 514.

7.   Ibid., p. 521.

8.   Cormac O'Grada, 'Is the Celtic Tiger a Paper Tiger?', *UCD Centre for
Economic Research Working Paper Series*, January 2002, p. 3.

9.   Such as R. MacSharry and P. White, *The Making of the Celtic Tiger: The
Inside Story of Ireland's Boom Economy* (Cork: Mercier Press, 2001).

10.   For instance, the Chairman of the Board of Governors of the US Fed-
eral Reserve, Alan Greenspan, 'The Critical Role of Education in the
Nation's Economy', 20 February 2004, Greater Omaha Chamber of
Commerce 2004 Annual Meeting (www.federalreserve.gov/).

11.   Available at www.cso.ie.

12.   Available at www.forfas.ie/ncc.

13.   'The Social Situation in the European Union', European Commission
2004 (www.europa.eu.int).

14.   Programme for International Student Assessment (PISA) survey published in December 2004 by the OECD (www.pisa.oecd.org).

15.   Available at www.cid.harvard.edu/ciddata/ciddata.htm.

16.   R. Cohen, *By the Sword* (London: Random Books, 2003), p. 390.

17.   Available at http://ed.sjtu.edu.cn/rank/2004/Statistics.htm.

18.   Very little investment capital was available, owing to poor government
finances, entrepreneurship was low and the research and development
base needed to spawn indigenous growth did not exist to any critical
degree.

19.   A. Murphy and F. Ruane, 'Foreign Direct Investment in Ireland: An
Updated Assessment', *Central Bank of Ireland Annual Report*, 2003
(www.centralbankofireland.com).

20.   'Globalisation Divided? Global Investment Trends of US Manufacturers', Deloitte, May 2004 (www.deloitte.com).

21.   In particular, youth unemployment fell from 24% in 1994 to 8% in 2004. It was 24% in Italy and 23% in France in 2004 (OECD, *Statistical Profile of Ireland*, 2005).

22.   M. De Freitas, 'Quantity versus Quality: The Growth Accounting in Ireland', *Economic Bulletin Banco de Portugal*, March 2000; L. Ferreira and P. Vanhout, 'Catching the Celtic Tiger by Its Tail', *European Investment Bank Economic and Financial Report*, 2002/01.

23.   M. Cassidy, 'Productivity in Ireland: Trends and Issues', *Central Bank of Ireland Quarterly Bulletin*, Spring 2004.

24.   'Annual Competitiveness Report', National Competitiveness Council, September 2005, pp. 34–35.

25.   Denis O'Hearn, *Inside the Celtic Tiger: The Irish Economy and the Asian Model* (London: Pluto, 1998).

26.   Geraldine Slevin, 'Is There a "New Economy" in Ireland?', Central Bank of Ireland Technical Research Paper, June 2002.

27.   This phenomenon is now an integral part of economic globalisation as a two-part *Financial Times* (FT) investigation has shown, *Financial Times*, 21–22 June. The *FT* journalists showed how multinationals are using highly complex strategies, and how they fund foreign ventures out of debt or equity, so as to incur their tax liabilities in the most favourable jurisdictions.

28.   Incidentally, the rate of return that US companies earn in Ireland (20%) easily outstrips the rates they earn in other countries, like the UK (7.6%) and France (6%), (www.forfas.ie/ncc).

29.   *The Economist*, January 1988.

30.   L. Alfaro, K. Sebnem and Volosovych, V. 'Why Doesn't Capital Flow from Rich to Poor Countries? An Empirical Investigation', Harvard Business School Working Paper Series, no. 04-040, 2004.

31.   Ireland had joined the IMF and World Bank in 1958, and the IDA was set up in 1959.

32.   J. Kelly and M. Everett, 'Financial Liberalisation and Economic Growth in Ireland', in *Central Bank and Financial Services Authority of Ireland Quarterly Bulletin*, Autumn 2004, pp. 91–112.

33.   Ibid., p. 96.

34.   B. Connolly, *The Rotten Heart of Europe* (London: Faber & Faber, 1995).

35.   Christopher Bartlett and Sumantra Ghoshal, *Managing Across Borders: The Transnational Solution* (Boston: Harvard Business Review Books, 1989).

36.   Forfas, *International Trade and Investment Report 2004* (www.forfas.ie). 2003 was the first time ever that Britain was not the main export destination for goods coming from Ireland.

37.   Available at www.cso.ie.

38.   D. Addison-Smyth, 'Ireland's Revealed Comparative Advantage', *Central Bank of Ireland Quarterly Bulletin*, vol. 1, 2005, p. 4.

39.   Available at www.cso.ie.

40.   Available at www.forfas.ie/esg/.

41.   Will Hutton's *The State We're In* (London: Vintage, 1996) is a good example.

42.   Although the first such agreement was hammered out in 1979 as the National Understanding for Economic and Social Development, the first really successful effort came with the Programme for National Recovery (1988–1990), followed by the Programme for Economic and Social Progress (1991–1993), then the Programme for Competitiveness and Work (1994–1997), the Partnership for Inclusion (1997–2000), and lately the Programme for Prosperity and Fairness (2000–2003).

43.   Available at www.forfas.ie/ncc/.

44.   OECD (*OECD in Figures*, 2005) data for 2004 show that both total government expenditure and total government revenue amount to close to 35% of GDP, one of the lowest in the OECD. In addition, total tax receipts as a proportion of GDP are very low.

45.   Available at http://www.heritage.org/research/features/index/downloads.htm.

46.   A more elegant classification has been suggested by Honohan and Walsh, who state that 'we prefer Aesop's hare, long somnolent, dashing to catch up with the slow and steady tortoise, as a metaphor for the Irish economy's recent performance over the more widely touted 'Celtic tiger'. The latter is zoologically improbable, whereas the hare is one of the largest wild animals actually native to Ireland' ('Catching up with the Leaders', *Brookings Papers on Economic Activity*, vol. 1, 2002, p. 3).

47.   Lindert and Williamson, 'Does Globalization Make the World More Unequal?', p. 26.

48.   Some economists like Edward Prescott (http://minneapolisfed.org/research/prescott/) have suggested that the influence of monetary policy on larger economies is overestimated.

49.   This is not just an Irish problem. For instance, Latvia, whose currency is now pegged to the euro and which had the strongest economic growth of any EU economy in 2005, also suffers from high inflation. The June 2005 edition of the Latvian Central Bank's monthly report stated that 'Latvijas Bank does not have at its disposal any mechanisms to control inflation' (www.bank.lv).

50.   Martin Feldstein, *The Economic Problems of Ireland in Europe* (Dublin: ESRI Publications, 2001), p. 4.

51.   Ibid., p. 5.

52.   Central Bank and Financial Services Authority of Ireland, *Financial Stability Review*, 2004, p. 11.

53.   *The Economist*, 11 September 2004.

54.   Based on data from www.economist.com, www.cso.ie and www.centralbankofireland.com.

55.   J. Kelly and A. Reilly, 'Credit Card Debt in Ireland: Recent Trends', *Central Bank of Ireland Quarterly Bulletin*, vol. 1, 2005.

56. Central Bank and Financial Services Authority of Ireland, *Quarterly Bulletin*, Spring 2004, p. 45.

57. K. O'Rourke and R. Thom, 'Irish Inflation: Appropriate Policy Responses', *Irish Banking Review*, Winter 2000, pp. 33–47.

58. In this respect, it is a blessing that Irish house prices only enter into the consumer inflation numbers in the form of mortgage costs, and not as the actual inflation in house prices. Some studies, like Cornede (2005) and Reis (2005), that include factors like house prices and asset prices in measures of inflation highlight the point that many 'conventional' measures tend to understate inflation (B. Cornede, 'House Prices and Inflation in the Euro Area', OECD Economics Department Working Paper, no. 450, October 2005; R. Reis, 'A Cost of Living Dynamic Price Index, with an Application to Indexing Retirement Accounts', Princeton University Economics Department, October 2005).

59. It is estimated that by 2015 only 13% of the Irish population will be over the age of 65, compared to 22% in Italy and 21% in Germany (www.forfas.ie/ncc).

60. Some estimates put the impact of paying out public pension schemes at 8% of GDP by 2050 (it is currently close to 3%).

61. Set up in 1996, the Norwegian Fund is now worth over $140 billion.

62. International Institute for Management Development (IMD), *World Competitiveness Report*, Lausanne, 2005.

63. On this particular topic, Ireland slipped down the rankings in Transparency International's Corruption Perceptions Index (2005), and is now ranked below most other European countries and falls well behind other small EU states.

64. Available at www.weforum.org.

65. A less pessimistic view on the competitiveness of Irish industry is presented by Eoin O'Malley, 'Competitive Performance in Irish Industry', *ESRI Quarterly Economic Commentary* (Dublin: ESRI Publications, 2004).

66. Forfas, *Business Expenditure on Research and Development (BERD) Ireland 2003/4*, Forfas Science and Technology Indicators Unit, April 2004 (www.forfas.ie).

67. Alan Greenspan, 'The Euro in Wider Circles', European Banking Congress, Frankfurt, 19 November 2004 (www.federalreserve.gov).

68. Central Bank and Financial Services Authority of Ireland, *Quarterly Bulletin*, April 2004, p. 6.

69. Forfas Enterprise Strategy Group, *Ahead of the Curve: Ireland's Place in the Global Economy* (Forfas, July 2004), p. 35 (www.forfas.ie/esg/).

70. For example, Slovakian wages are about 20% of those in Austria, a factor that is driving its role as one of the car manufacturing centres of Europe – Volkswagen, Hyundai and Peugeot have plants there.

71. M. O'Sullivan, 'How to Keep the Irish Lucky', *Wall Street Journal Europe*, 4 January 2004.

72. Dollar, 'Globalization, Poverty and Inequality', p. 29.

73.   S. Wei and M. Amiti, 'Fear of Service Outsourcing: Is It Justified?', NBER Working Paper, no. 10808, October 2004.
74.   In the July 2005 Eurobarometer (63) survey, Irish people said that the most important domestic political issues were public transport and the healthcare system.

Chapter Five

1.   Robert Savage (ed.), *Ireland in the New Century* (Dublin: Four Courts Press, 2003), p. 109.
2.   Pettit, *Republicanism*, p. 5.
3.   He is more popularly known for views such as 'it is a sound maxim that reprehensible actions may be justified by their effects, and that when the effect is good it always justifies the action', *The Discourses* (London: Penguin Books, 1983), p. 132.
4.   The claim that Cromwell's Glorious Revolution in England led to the first form of republican government in Ireland is a difficult one to make to an Irish audience, as the conduct of Cromwell and his supporters in Ireland did everything to refute the basic principles of republicanism.
5.   Benjamin Franklin, Letter to Joshua Babcock, 13 January 1772, in *The Writings of Benjamin Franklin*, vol. III (http://www.historycarper.com).
6.   Norman Porter (ed.), *The Republican Ideal* (Belfast: Blackstaff Press, 1998), p. 66.
7.   Thomas Pakenham's account of the rebellion of 1798, *The Year of Liberty* (London: Panther Books, 1992), is one of the better ones available.
8.   Marx and Engels, *Ireland and the Irish Question*, p. 22.
9.   Dorothy MacArdle's *Tragedies of Kerry 1922–1923* (Dublin: Irish Freedom Press, 1988) is a good example of some of the terrifying violence enacted by Irishman on Irishman.
10.   Often nationalism is so strong that it trumps other socio-political distinctions such as class. For example, Fintan Lane explains that 'Ireland was unlike other western European countries in which mass working class parties did develop . . . socialism in Ireland was faced with a competing and potent oppositional ideology in the form of nationalism', p. 227 in F. Lane, *The Origins of Modern Irish Socialism, 1881–1896* (Cork: Cork University Press, 1997).
11.   J. Hutchinson and A. Smith, *Nationalism* (Oxford: Oxford University Press, 1994), p. 18.
12.   Conor O'Clery, *Ireland in Quotes*, p. 107.
13.   The 2004 UN Human Development Report specifically refers to the case of Northern Ireland as one where significant inequalities can fuel tension and conflict. The report underlines the fact that 'Catholics in Northern Ireland have suffered economic and political deprivations since the 16th century' (p. 41), and more broadly speaking states that a study of 233 groups in 93 countries strongly supports the hypothesis that such inequalities between groups are liable to lead to violence.

14.   Fareed Zakaria, *The Future of Freedom* (New York: WM Norton & Co., 2003), p. 156.

15.   Also, Ireland does not fall into the category of illiberal democracy. Though it has only recently become liberal, it is a highly democratic state, with a very representative and open electoral system and a stable locally focused political system. Over the last five years the Freedom House survey, 'Freedom in the World', has given Ireland (as well as most other developed western countries) its highest rankings in terms of civil liberties and political rights. Compared to 1974, when it ranked only 25% of countries as 'free', it now holds that up to 44% of countries (89 out of 192) are free. Close on 27% are rated as 'not free' (www.freedomhouse.org). In addition, the 2005 UNDP Human Development Report (p. 20) shows that 59% of all governments in 2003 were democracies, compared to only 39% in 1990, and only 18% were autocracies, compared to 39% in 1990.

16.   One of the best known is the Austrian social scientist Karl Polanyi's work, *The Great Transformation*, published in the US in 1944.

17.   For instance, Mikheil Saakashvili, 'Europe's Third Wave of Liberation', *Financial Times*, 20 December 2004.

18.   Peadar Kirby, *The Celtic Tiger in Distress: Growth with Inequality in Ireland* (Hampshire: Palgrave, 2002), p. 159.

19.   R. Wade, 'Is Globalization Reducing Poverty and Inequality?' *World Development*, vol. 32, no. 4, 2004, p. 583.

20.   'Overall income inequality and inequality in the distribution of earnings rose sharply during the 1980s and 1990s in a number of industrialised countries, notably the UK and the USA', p. 346 in B. Nolan and B. Maitre, 'A Comparative Perspective on Trends in Income Inequality in Ireland', *Economic and Social Review*, vol. 31, no. 4, October 2000.

21.   Robert Wade comments that 'Canada excepted, all the countries of English settlement, led by the United States, have experienced big increases in income inequality over the past 20–30 years . . . the Unites States is now back to the same level of inequality of income as in the decades before 1929, the era of the "robber barons" and the "Great Gatsby"' ('On the Causes of Widening World Income Inequality, or Why the Matthew Effect Prevails', *New Political Economy*, vol. 9, no. 2, 2004, p. 12).

22.   Nolan and Maitre, 'A Comparative Perspective on Trends in Income Inequality in Ireland', p. 348.

23.   Nolan and Smeeding, 'Ireland's Income Distribution in Comparative Perspective', December 2004 (http://ssrn.com/abstract=646024), p. 30.

24.   Ibid., p. 11.

25.   *The Social Situation in the European Union*, European Commission 2004 (www.europa.eu.int).

26. Ibid., p. 69. Other studies of income inequality such as the Luxemburg Income Study do not show as big a drop in inequality in Ireland over the same period. Also the 2005 Annual Competitiveness report of the NCC quotes a rather high Gini co-efficient for Ireland of 35.9 (Denmark and Hungary have co-efficients of 24, for example).

27. D. O'Neill and O. Sweetman, 'Poverty and Inequality in Ireland 1987–1994: A Comparison Using Measures of Income and Consumption', *Economics Department Working Paper series*, no. 860399, Department of Economics, NUI Maynooth, March 1999.

28. Defined as below 60% of the median income including social transfers. The findings of the ESRI's Trends in Welfare for Vulnerable Groups report support this view.

29. Defined as low income in 2001 and at least two of the three previous years.

30. Combat Poverty Agency, 'Mapping Poverty: National Regions and County Patterns', August 2005 (www.cpa.ie).

31. T. Callan, 'Why Is Relative Income Poverty So High in Ireland?', *ESRI Policy Research Series*, September 2004, p. 2.

32. These trends were highlighted in greater detail in a recent NESC report, *The Developmental Welfare State*, NESC 2005 (www.nesc.ie).

33. The UNHDR focuses on gender inequality in key areas of economic and political participation and decision-making, and it tracks the share of seats in parliament held by women, the number of female legislators, senior officials and managers, and female professional and technical workers, as well as gender disparities in earned income.

34. Available at www.cso.ie.

35. C. Whelan and R. Layte, 'Economic Change, Social Mobility and Meritocracy: Reflections on the Irish Experience', *ESRI Quarterly Economic Commentary*, September 2004, pp. 89–108.

36. Ibid., p. 2.

37. Ibid., p. 15.

38. For example, the mean score for 15-year-olds in a combined reading literacy test was higher for private schools than for public ones in the US, UK and Canada, though less so in the cases of Japan and South Korea (*The Economist*, 3 July 2004).

39. The NESC report on the Developmental Welfare State in Ireland mentions the fact that the number of pupils in fee-paying schools in Dublin increased as a proportion of all secondary students from 24% in 1983/4 to 32% by 2002/3, p. 163.

40. NESC, *The Developmental Welfare State*, p. 149.

41. J. K. Galbraith, *The Culture of Contentment* (London: Sinclair-Stevenson, 1992), p. 10.

42. P. Kirby, L. Gibbons and M. Cronin, *Reinventing Ireland: Culture, Society and the Global Economy* (London: Pluto Press, 2002), p. 2.

43. Andre Sapir ('Globalisation and the Reform of European Social Models', Background Document for ECOFIN Informal Meeting, 9 September 2005, Breugel Research Institute) takes the distinction between the Anglo-Saxon and European models to a more detailed level and highlights four European social models – Anglo-Saxon (UK and Ireland), Mediterranean, Nordic and European. Of these four models, the Nordic countries have the highest levels of social protection expenditure and universal welfare provision, Mediterranean countries are heavily focused on spending on old-age pensions, the European countries rely more on insurance-based, non-employment benefits and old-age pensions, while the Anglo-Saxons countries tend to focus on social assistance of the last resort in terms of labour and social policies. In general, the Anglo-Saxon model is more efficient than the other ones but the least equitable. In the context of globalisation, Sapir stresses the fact that the economic challenges posed to European countries by it will necessitate more flexible approaches to labour market and social policies.

44. The recent EU report on the Social Situation in the EU found that civic participation (defined as the percentage of people participating in at least one organised activity) in Ireland is close to the EU average. It is particularly high in the Nordic region and low in Spain and Portugal.

45. The number of homicides recorded has been rising steadily in tandem with the pace of globalisation. In 1991, there were 15 homicides recorded in Ireland, but by 2001 this was closer to 55 (www.cso.ie).

46. The Irish are, after Luxembourg and Hungary, the biggest consumers of alcohol per capita in the world (*The Economist*, 3 July 2004).

47. The National Drug Treatment Centre Board's 2003 annual report showed an increase in drug abuse, especially those using cocaine, which had been flooded onto the Irish market by dealers in the previous two years. Most of the Drug Centre users in 2003 were aged 20 to 29, while 6% of those attending the centre were aged from 10 to 19. Some 20% of clients were registered as homeless (www.addictionireland.com).

48. *Irish Times*, 19 May 2004.

49. Available at www.cso.ie.

50. Between May 2004 and April 2005, 40,973 Poles, 18,063 Lithuanians, 9,207 Latvians, 7,190 Slovakians, 4,447 Czechs, 2,693 Hungarians, 2,260 Estonians, 85 Slovenians, 166 Maltese and 30 Cypriots registered for PPS (Personal Public Service) numbers (Department of Social and Family Affairs).

51. 'Population and Labour Force Projection 2006–36', December 2004 (www.cso.ie).

52. See www.equalitytribunal.ie

53. The CSO estimates that Ireland's labour force needs about 45,000 immigrants each year over the next thirty years. As these immigrants come to Ireland, social security, unions, housing and welfare rights will have to be adapted to accommodate them.

54.   J. Bayliss and S. Smith, *The Globalization of World Politics*, second edition (Oxford: Oxford University Press, 2001), p. 21.
55.   Belfast at least did enjoy the fruits of industrialisation in terms of the development of the textile, brewing and ship-building industries and a steady rise in trade.
56.   Interestingly, a recent study of values on both sides of the border (Fahey, Hayes and Sinnott, *Conflict and Consensus*, IPA, 2005) held that religion is a source of cultural similarity as well as division between the two communities, and that because of strong religious beliefs in the Catholic and Protestant communities they are more alike in their thinking on a range of issues, such as family life and morality, than other European societies (Britain included).
57.   J. Bradley and E. Birnie, *Can the Celtic Tiger Cross the Irish Border* (Cork: Cork University Press, 2001), p. 60.
58.   Ibid., p. 81.
59.   Fareed Zakaria's book, *The Future of Freedom*, makes this point convincingly.
60.   United Nations Conference on Trade and Development (UNCTAD) (www.unctad.org).
61.   Available at www.dochas.ie.
62.   Some others include Combat Poverty Agency (1986), Pensions Board (1990), Family Support Agency (2001), Comhairle (2000), National Council on Ageing and Older People (1997), National Qualifications Authority (2001), Human Rights Commission (2002), Refugee Appeals Tribunal (2000), FÁS (1986) and Local Drugs Task Forces (1997). An impressively long list of new Irish institutions is given on page 93 of the NESC report of the Developmental Welfare State (www.nesc.ie).
63.   A federal approach to government is commonplace in other European countries, existing in various forms in Switzerland, Belgium and Spain. In Germany, a commission has been set up to resolve legislative conflicts between the sixteen regions and the federal government. Conflict between the Bundesrat and Bundestag, and the ability of individual regions to set taxes and negotiate with the EU, are some of the factors that have slowed the German economy and Germany's ability to react to changes in the world around it.

Chapter Six
1.   Conor O'Clery, *Ireland in Quotes: A History of the Twentieth Century* (Dublin: O'Brien Press, 1999), p. 60.
2.   G. John Ikenberry's article 'Illusions of Empire: Defining the New American Order' in *Foreign Affairs*, March/April 2004, is a good review of the debate on America's empire.
3.   For example, Joe Lee writes that before the Second World War 'Ireland had already intellectually isolated herself in large measure since independence. Her links with the outside world were mainly confined to Britain and the Vatican' (Lee, *Ireland 1912–1985*, p. 261).

4. Daniel Keohane, 'Realigning Neutrality: Irish Defence Policy and the EU', EU Institute for Security Studies (ISS), Occasional Paper 24, March 2001.

5. J. Bowman, *De Valera and the Ulster Question: 1917–1973* (Oxford: Oxford University Press, 1989), p. 218.

6. The 1938 Constitution of Ireland and the creation of the External Relations Act in the same year effectively marked the conception of Ireland's policy of neutrality. The treatment of neutrality in law is based primarily on the Fifth and Thirteenth Hague Conventions of 1907. In this sense, neutrality is effectively taken to mean non-involvement in wars with and between other states.

7. Irish police and army intelligence agents co-operated extensively with their British and US counterparts during the Emergency (Lee, *Ireland 1912–1985*, pp. 244–245; Eunan O'Halpin, *Defending Ireland: The Irish State and Its Enemies Since 1922* (Oxford: Oxford University Press, 1999)).

8. Ibid., p. 349.

9. P. Keatinge, *A Singular Stance: Irish Neutrality in the 1980s* (Dublin: Institute of Public Administration, 1984), p. 22.

10. Ibid., p. 22.

11. M. Moynihan, *Speeches and Statements by Eamon De Valera 1917–1973* (Dublin: Gill & Macmillan, 1980), p. 32.

12. The case of Sweden also demonstrates that other countries practised it in a pragmatic fashion. During the Cold War the Swedes spied on Russia with the intention of gauging the strength of Russian forces and prospective battle formations were a conventional war to break out on Sweden's borders. However, when a Swedish double agent, Stig Wennerstrom, alerted the Russians to the fact that the Swedes were passing the results of their spying missions to NATO, the Russians responded by shooting down a Swedish DC-3 off the coast of what is now Latvia in June 1952. Although the Swedes protested that the aircraft was on a training mission, it was in fact supplied with sophisticated listening equipment. Wennerstrom was arrested and jailed in 1963 (*Courier International*, 6 April 2004).

13. Bowman, *De Valera and the Ulster Question*, p. 207.

14. Ibid., p. 255.

15. Lee, *Ireland 1912–1985*, p. 236.

16. It is probably fair to say that both sides regarded Ireland as a member of the western world, and therefore neither one saw much value in trying to formally co-opt Ireland.

17. AT Kearney/*Foreign Policy*, 'Measuring Globalisation Index 2005' (www.foreignpolicy.com).

18. Department of Defence, White Paper on Defence, 2001, p. 13 (www.defence.ie).

19.   Low-intensity violence continues, with punishment beatings in particular grabbing the headlines. Figures from the PSNI estimate that there have been 1,700 punishment beatings in Northern Ireland since 1998, two-thirds of which have been carried out by loyalist paramilitaries (*Irish Times*, 13 May 2004, and www.psni.police.uk).

20.   A good assessment of neutrality within these countries is provided by the Finnish Institute of International Affairs (UPI) entitled 'Neutrality and Non-Alignment in Europe Today', 2003, available through www.upi-fiia.fi.

21.   In strict terms, Ireland failed the recent test of its neutrality during the second Gulf War, when it permitted over 100,000 American troops to land in Ireland, whereas both Austria and Switzerland closed their airspace to the US military. Ireland is also alone amongst Europe's neutrals in that it does not have the military hardware to mount any form of defence of its sovereignty.

22.   Available at www.un-globalsecurity.org.

23.   *Irish Times*, 14 December 2004.

24.   Piracy, especially in South Asia, has risen threefold over the past ten years. An article in the November/December 2004 edition of *Foreign Affairs* by Luft and Korin underlines the increasing sophistication of pirates, stating that today's pirates are often trained fighters aboard speedboats equipped with satellite phones and global positioning systems and armed with automatic weapons, antitank missiles, and grenades. Given that 80% of the world's trade is transported by sea, this trend is worrying, more so as many pirates have close links to terrorists.

25.   Jason's Burke's book *Al Qaeda: Casting a Shadow of Terror* (London: IB Taurus, 2003) is a good read. An article written by the same author in the May/June 2004 edition of *Foreign Policy* entitled 'Al Qaeda: Think Again' is also worth reading.

26.   Olivier Roy's book *Globalised Islam* (London: Hurst, 2004) is a reference point.

27.   Osama Bin Laden, 'Resist the New Rome', *Guardian*, 6 January 2004.

28.   J. Gray, 'The Era of Globalisation Is Over', *New Statesman*, 24 September 2001.

29.   One estimate from the International Institute of Strategic Studies (IISS) put the number of young Al-Qaeda operatives that were trained in Afghan bases at 18,000, almost twice the size of the Irish army (www.iiss.org).

30.   8,442 people aged 15–64 were surveyed in Northern Ireland and the Republic between October 2002 and April 2003 (http://www.hrb.ie/).

31.   During the current period of globalisation, the rate of homicide in Ireland has increased dramatically from the late 1980s when the annual number of homicides was in single digits to an average of 34 per annum over the period 1998–2003, and currently surpasses 50 (www.cso.ie).

32.   Available at www.emcdda.eu.int.

33. A thorough study of this phenomenon comes from Peter Singer, *Corporate Warriors: The Rise of the Privatized Military Industry* (New York: Cornell University Press, 2003).

34. Felix Rohatyn and Allison Stanger, 'The Profit Motive Goes to War', *Financial Times*, 17 November 2004.

35. The findings of the latest Stevens Inquiry add some light here (www.met.police.uk/commissioner/MP-Stevens-Enquiry-3.pdf).

36. R. Kagan, 'Power and Weakness', *Policy Review*, no. 113, June 2002.

37. Javier Solana, 'A Secure Europe in a Better World', European Council, Thessaloniki, 20 June 2003 (http://ue.eu.int/pressdata/en/reports/76255.pdf).

38. In doing so he referenced a Eurobarometer survey (November 2002) that asked European citizens what they most feared. Their greatest fears were international terrorism (> 80%), organised crime (> 75%), WMD proliferation and a nuclear accident (similarly, the Through Irish Eyes survey of Irish attitudes to Britain highlighted the Sellafield nuclear power plant as the area where interviewees felt that increased co-operation between British and Irish governments was most necessary). The least feared were a conventional war in Europe (< 50%) and a nuclear conflict in Europe.

39. Address to UN Security Council, Dominique de Villepin, French foreign minister, Security Council 19 March 2003: 'Dans un monde ou la menace est asymetrique, ou le faible défie le fort, la capacité de convaincre, la faculté de faire évoluer les esprits comptent autant que le nombre de divisions militaires' (www.un.int/france).

40. 'China Ponders New Rules of "Unrestricted War"', *Washington Post*, 8 August 1999.

41. The most prominent task taken on by the directoire of France, Germany and the UK has been their efforts as the 'EU-3' to mediate the progression of Iran's nuclear research project.

42. 'Common Foreign and Security Policy: An Overview' (http://europa.eu.int/comm/external_relations/cfsp/intro/).

43. To safeguard common values, fundamental interests, the independence and integrity of the Union in conformity with the principle of the UN Charter; to strengthen the security of the EU; to preserve peace and strengthen international security; to promote international co-operation; to develop and consolidate democracy and the rule of law, and respect for human rights and fundamental freedoms.

44. 'A European Way of War', Centre for European Reform, May 2004 (www.cer.org).

45. *Irish Times*, 31 March 2004.

46. Irish Presidency of the European Union, 'Action against Organised Crime', Informal meeting of the Justice and Home Affairs Ministers, Dublin, 22–23 January 2004, p. 3 (www.eur02004.ie).

47.   Eunan O'Halpin's book *Defending Ireland* adds considerable detail to the close co-operation between security forces in Ireland and Britain over the past seventy years. He details early co-operation on issues like immigration and passport issuance in which Ireland 'had a discrete adoption of the outlook and assumptions of the British state' (p. 80), the founding of the Air Corps and Navy and the exchange of intelligence.

48.   For example, when the EU took over military responsibility for Bosnia from NATO in December 2004, all that most soldiers had to do was change insignia.

49.   Participation in EU military operations operates under what is called the 'triple lock' mechanism, where approval is granted by the UN, government and the Oireachtas. In some cases, such as potential Irish involvement in an EU peace-keeping mission to Macedonia, UN approval has been difficult to obtain (in the case of Macedonia, China blocked UN approval of Irish involvement).

50.   A Eurobarometer survey (no. 63, July 2005) showed that 87% of Irish people think that EU membership is beneficial, compared to the average of 55%. In the UK, people are more pessimistic, with only 40% thinking that it is a good thing. In Ireland, support for a common foreign policy was below average at 61%, while support for a common security and defence policy comes in at 58%, which is low by comparison to the EU average of 77%. In Austria, Sweden and Finland, support for a common defence and security policy is marginally lower than in Ireland. A previous Eurobarometer survey (Attitudes to the EU, 2004) suggested that, to an extent, Irish people's dim view of greater foreign policy co-operation is reflected in the views of its EU neighbours, as only 47% of Europeans believed that neutral countries should have a say in EU foreign policy.

51.   The term is widely accepted to have originated in Winston Churchill's 'Sinews of Peace' address, March 1946.

52.   Available at www.census.gov.

53.   Benjamin Franklin declared that 'the cause of America was the cause of Ireland. The cause of Ireland was the cause of America'; R. Savage (ed.), *Ireland in the New Century* (Dublin: Four Courts Press, 2003), p. 101.

54.   Hugo Hamilton, 'The Loneliness of Being German', *Guardian*, 7 September 2004.

55.   Jorge Castaneda, 'The Forgotten Relationship', *Foreign Affairs*, May/June 2003.

56.   Roderic Braithwaite, 'End of the Affair', *Prospect*, May 2003.

57.   Gerard Chaliand's sketch of the new world order is worth a read in this respect; G. Chaliand, *Atlas du Nouvel Ordre Mondial* (Paris: Robert Laffont, 2003).

58.   In a similar way, Finland took a high-profile role as a mediator between the Indonesian government and the Free Aceh Movement (GAM) in 2005.

59. Available at www.cgdev.org.

60. According to the CDI/*Foreign Policy* aid report, Ireland ranks 15th out of 21 countries overall. It scores well on the quality of its trade with the developing world (a score of 6.6 out of 10, compared to 6.9 for the UK and 4 for Switzerland) and migration (a score of 4.5, compared to 1.8 for Spain and 8.1 for Germany). It does poorly on the environment because of its high level of fishing subsidies and relatively high greenhouse gas emission (a score of 1.6 compared to 4.9 for France and 5.7 for the Netherlands). In peace-keeping, Ireland scores 3.7, which is above that of other neutrals – Austria (2.6), Finland (2.9), Sweden (1.3) and Switzerland (0.1) – but below that of other smaller active countries like Norway (7.4) and Denmark (7.1). The quality of Irish investment in the developed world does not rate highly, at a score of 2.3, compared to 9 for Portugal and 8.2 for Spain, but it is still better than the likes of Greece (0), Italy (1.5) and Australia (1.6). Similarly, the amount of money that Irish people give to charities is not as great as some would think. Ireland only ranks 12th out of 20 countries in terms of 'volunteering and giving' relative to GDP. A survey by the Johns Hopkins Institute (www.jhu.edu/~ips/) in the US measured private philanthropy as a proportion of GDP between 1995 and 2000, with Irish people giving 0.55% of GDP, compared to 1% in the US and 0.62% in the UK.

61. Emma Bonino and William Shawcross criticised the diplomatic response of the EU President (Ireland) in the *Financial Times*, 20 May 2004.

62. J. Nye, 'The Limits of American Power', *Political Science Quarterly*, vol. 117, no. 4, p. 549.

63. Ibid., p. 554.

64. Peter Van Ham, 'The Rise of the Branded State', *Foreign Affairs*, vol. 80, no. 5, p. 1.

65. See http://www.acq.osd.mil/dsb/reports/2004-09-Strategic Communication.pdf, p. 9.

66. Tom Barry's *My Guerrilla Days in Ireland*, Earnan O'Maille's *On Another Man's Wound* and Sean Moylan's *Sean Moylan in His Own Words* being examples.

67. O'Halpin refers to it as having been a 'supplier of public order and pageantry' (O'Halpin, *Defending Ireland*, p. 150).

68. For example, almost 5% of the US army's personnel are in the special forces, numbering a total of close to 45,000. The increased focus on specialisation is also evident in Britain, where the government has proposed downsizing traditional infantry regiments but creating a new ranger regiment to support the SAS and SBS.

69. *Le Monde Diplomatique*, December 2003.

70. What contact there has been so far has been through the offices of the Swiss foreign sevices, the EU 3 (France, Germany and the UK) and several informal brokers.

71.   As suggested by Timothy Garton Ash in his recent book, *Free World: Why a Crisis of the West Reveals the Opportunity of Our Time* (London: Penguin, 2004).

72.   M. Levi and M. O'Hanlon, *The Future of Arms Control* (Washington: Brookings Institution Press, 2004).

73.   Biological and chemical weapons are much more easily developed and proliferated then nuclear weapons technologies.

74.   *Irish Times*, 14 December 2004.

75.   Alexander Casella, 'After the Bomb', *Prospect*, September 2004.

76.   *Le Monde*, 7 July 2004.

77.   The most recent being a trade mission to China in mid-January 2005, led by An Taoiseach.

78.   Minxin Pei's account, 'Time to Reflect on How Far China Has to Go', *Financial Times*, 19 January 2005, is a good example of this argument.

79.   Elizabeth Economy, *The River Runs Black: The Environmental Challenge to China's Future* (New York: Cornell University Press, 2004).

80.   William Goetzmann, 'China and the World Financial Markets 1870–1930: Modern Lessons from Historical Globalization', Yale ICF Working Paper, no. 00-62, 2001.

81.   The works of Nicholas Mansergh are outstanding for the way they track the political links between Ireland and India.

82.   Strobe Talbott, *Engaging India: Diplomacy, Democracy and the Bomb* (Washington: Brookings Institution Press, 2004).

83.   D. Rodrik and A. Subramanian, 'From "Hindu Growth" to Productivity Surge: The Mystery of the Indian Growth Transition', IMF Working Paper, no. 04/77, May 2004.

Chapter Seven

1.   Sean O'Faolain, *The Irish* (London: Penguin, 1980), p. 139.

2.   *Financial Times*, 20 October 2004.

3.   Martin Wolf, *Why Globalization Works* (New Haven: Yale University Press, 2004).

4.   F. Bourguignon, 'Making Sense of Globalization', pp. 104–107.

5.   For instance, there are seven 'small' countries in the top ten of the AT Kearney/*Foreign Policy* globalisation rankings – Ireland, Singapore, Switzerland, Finland, New Zealand, Austria and Denmark – four of which are neutral and five in the euro-zone.

6.   There are plenty of other worthwhile issues, like the environment, that are unfortunately ouside the scope of this book.

7.   Jeremy Williamson, 'What Should the World Bank Think about the Washington Consensus', *World Bank Research Observer*, vol. 15, no. 2, pp. 251–264.

8.   Terence McSwiney, *Principles of Freedom* (Cork: Cork City Libraries, 2005), p. 7.

Bibliography

Addison-Smyth, D. 'Ireland's Revealed Comparative Advantage', *Central Bank of Ireland Quarterly Bulletin,* vol. 1, 2005.

Alfaro, L., Sebnem, K., and Volosovych, V. 'Capital Flows in a Globalized World: The Role of Policies and Institutions', Harvard Business School Working Paper Series, no. 05–054, 2004.

——. 'Why Doesn't Capital Flow from Rich to Poor Countries? An Empirical Investigation', Harvard Business School Working Paper Series, no. 04-040, 2004.

Allen, K. *Fianna Fail and Irish labour* (London: Pluto Press, 1997).

Arthur, P. *Special Relationship: Britain, Ireland and the Northern Ireland Problem* (Belfast: Blackstaff Press, 2000).

Avi-Yonah, R. 'Globalization, Tax Competition and the Fiscal Crisis of the Welfare State', Harvard Law School Working Paper, no. 004, Spring 2000.

Baldwin, R., and Martin, P. 'Two Waves of Globalisation: Superficial Similarities, Fundamental Differences', NBER Working Paper, no. 6904, 1999.

Barrett, A. 'Irish Migration: Characteristics, Causes and Consequences', IZA Discussion Paper, no. 97, December 2004.

Barro, R., and Lee, J-W. 'International Data on Educational Attainment: Updates and Implications', Center for International Development at Harvard University Working Paper, no. 42, April 2000.

Barry, T. *My Guerrilla Days in Ireland* (Dublin: Anvil Books, 1995).

Bartlett, C., and Ghoshal, S. *Managing Across Borders: The Transnational Solution* (Boston: Harvard Business Review Books, 1989).

Basu, K. *India's Emerging Economy* (Cambridge, MA: The MIT Press, 2004).

Bavarez, N. *La France qui tombe* (Paris: Perrin, 2003).

Bayliss, J., and Smith, S. *The Globalization of World Politics*, second edition (Oxford: Oxford University Press, 2001).

Benevenisti, E. 'Exit and Voice in the Age of Globalisation', *Michigan Law Review,* vol. 98, no. 1, October 1999.

Beresford-Ellis, P. (ed.). *James Connolly: Selected Writings* (London: Pluto Press, 1997).

Berlin, I. *The Crooked Timber of Humanity* (Princeton: Princeton University Press, 1990).

Bhagwati, J. 'Coping with Antiglobalization', *Foreign Affairs*, vol. 81, no. 1, January/February 2002.

——. *In Defence of Globalization* (Oxford: Oxford University Press, 2004).

Bin Laden, O. 'Resist the New Rome', *Guardian*, 6 January 2004.

Board of Governors of the Federal Reserve System. 'Preventing Deflation: Japan's Experience in the 1990s', Federal Reserve System International Finance Discussion Papers, no. 729, 2002.

Bordo, M., Eichengren, B., and Irwin, D. 'Is Globalization Today Really Different than Globalization a Hundred Years Ago?', NBER Working Paper, no. 7195, June 1999.

Bourguignon, F. 'Making Sense of Globalization: A Guide to the Economic Issues', Centre for Economic Policy Research (CEPR), Policy Paper, no. 8, July 2002.

Bowman, J. *De Valera and the Ulster Question: 1917–1973* (Oxford: Oxford University Press, 1989).

Bradley, J., and Birnie, E. *Can the Celtic Tiger Cross the Irish Border?* (Cork: Cork University Press, 2001).

Braithwaite, R. 'End of the Affair', *Prospect*, May 2003.

Brender, A. *La France facé a la mondialisation,* fifth edition (Reperes, 2004).

British Council, 'Through Irish Eyes: Irish Attitudes towards the UK', The British Council, February 2004.

Burke, J. *Al Qaeda: Casting a Shadow of Terror* (London: IB Taurus, 2003).

Callan, T., Nolan, B., O'Neill, D., and Sweetman, O. 'Female Labour Supply and Income Inequality in Ireland', Paper for Irish Economic Association Annual Conference, April 1998.

Casella, A. 'After the Bomb', *Prospect*, September 2004.

Cassidy, M. 'Productivity in Ireland: Trends and Issues', *Central Bank of Ireland Quarterly Bulletin,* Spring 2004.

Castaneda, J. 'The Forgotten Relationship', *Foreign Affairs,* May/June 2003.

Central Bank and Financial Services Authority of Ireland, *Quarterly Bulletin,* Spring 2004.

——. *Financial Stability Report*, Spring 2004.

——. *Financial Stability Report*, November 2004.

Central Statistics Office (CSO). *Measuring Ireland's Progress: Indicator's Report*, vol. 1, Central Statistics Office, 2003.

——. *National Accounts Statistics* (www.cso.ie).

Centre for European Reform. *A European Way of War* (London: CER Publications, May 2004).

Chaliand, G. *Atlas du nouvel ordre mondial* (Paris: Robert Laffont, 2003).

Chubb, B. *Government of Ireland*, second edition (London: Longman, 1982).

Cohen, D. *La mondialisation et ses ennemis* (Paris: Grasset, 2004).

Cohen, R. *By the Sword* (London: Random Books, 2003).

Connolly, B. *The Rotten Heart of Europe* (London: Faber & Faber, 1995).

Cornede, B. 'House Prices and Inflation in the Euro Area', OECD Economics Department Working Paper, no. 450, OECD, October 2005.

Council on Foreign Relations. *Iran: Time for a New Approach – Report of an Independent Task Force* (Washington: Council on Foreign Relations, 2004).

Crotty, W., and Schmitt, D. *Ireland on the World Stage* (London: Longman, 2002).

Deaton, A. 'Health in an Age of Globalization', Research Program in Development Studies, Princeton University Center for Health and Wellbeing Paper, July 2004.

De Freitas, M. 'Quantity versus Quality: The Growth Accounting in Ireland', *Economic Bulletin Banco de Portugal,* March 2000, pp. 59–70.

Department of Enterprise, Trade and Energy. *Building Ireland's Knowledge Economy: The Irish Action Plan For Promoting Investment in R&D to 2010*, August 2004 (www.entemp.ie/publications/enterprise/2004/knowledgeeconomy.pdf).

Dervis, K. *A Better Globalization: Legitimacy, Governance and Reform* (Washington: Centre for Global Development, 2005).

Desai, M. 'India and China: An Essay in Comparative Political Economy', Paper for IMF Conference on India/China, Delhi, November 2003.

Diamond, J. *Guns, Germs and Steel: The Fates of Human Societies* (New York: WM Norton & Co., 1999).

Di Tella, R., MacCulloch, R., and Oswald, A. 'The Macroeconomics of Happiness', *Review of Economics and Statistics*, vol. 85, no. 4, November 2003, pp. 809–827.

Dollar, D. 'Globalization, Poverty, and Inequality since 1802', World Bank Policy Research Working Paper, no. 3333, June 2004.

Donahue, J., and Nye, J. *Governance in a Globalizing World* (Washington: Brookings Institution Press, 2000).

Easterlin, R. 'Explaining Happiness', Proceedings of the National Academy of Sciences, vol. 100, September 2003, pp. 11176–11183.

Economist Intelligence Unit (EIU). *The World in 2005: The Economist Intelligence Unit's Quality of Life Index* (EIU, 2005).

Economy, E. *The River Runs Black: The Environmental Challenge to China's Future* (New York: Cornell University Press, 2004).

Eichengreen, B., and Sussman, N. 'The International Monetary System in the (Very) Long Run', IMF Working Paper, no. 00/43, March 2000.

Eichengreen, B., and Bordo, M. 'Crises Now and Then: What Lessons from the Last Era of Financial Globalisation', NBER Working Paper, no. W8716, 2002.

Errera, P. 'Three Circles of Threat', *Survival,* vol. 47, no. 1, Spring 2005, pp. 71–88.

Eurobarometer. Public Opinion Surveys (http://europa.eu.int/comm/public_opinion/).

——. *Public Opinion in the EU,* Spring 2004, Eurobarometer 61.

——. *Globalisation,* Flash Eurobarometer no. 151b, November 2003.

——. *Country Report – Ireland,* Autumn 2004.

Everts, S., and Keohane, D. 'The European Convention and EU Foreign Policy: Learning from Failure', *Survival,* vol. 45, Autumn 2003, pp. 167–186.

Fahey, T., Hayes, B., and Sinnott, R. *Conflict and Consensus: A Study of Values and Attitudes in the Republic of Ireland and Northern Ireland* (Dublin: Institute of Public Administration, March 2005).

Fallon, B. *An Age of Innocence: Irish Culture, 1930–1960* (Dublin: Gill & Macmillan, 1998).

Feldstein, M. *The Economic Problems of Ireland in Europe* (Dublin: ESRI Publications, 2001).

Ferreira, L., and Vanhout, P. 'Catching the Celtic Tiger by Its Tail', *European Investment Bank Economic and Financial Report,* European Investment Bank 2002/01.

Fischer, S. 'Globalization and Its Challenges', American Economic Review Papers and Proceedings, May 2003, pp. 1–32.

Fitzsimons, E., Hogan, V., and Neary, P. 'Explaining the Volume of North–South Trade in Ireland: A Gravity Model Approach', *Economic and Social Review,* vol. 30, no. 4, October 1999, pp. 381–401.

Flynn, D., and Giraldez, A. 'Path Dependence, Time Lags and the Birth of Globalization: A Critique of O'Rourke and Williamson', *European Review of Economic History,* vol. 8, 2004, pp. 81–108.

Forfas Enterprise Strategy Group. *Ahead of the Curve: Ireland's Place in the Global Economy* (Forfas, July 2004).

——. *Business Expenditure on Research and Development (BERD) Ireland 2003/4,* April 2004, Forfas Science and Technology Indicators Unit.

Frankel, J. 'Globalisation of the Economy', NBER Working Paper, no. W7858, 2000.

Frey, B., and Stutzer, A. 'Happiness, Economy and Institutions', CESifo Working Paper, no. 246, January 2000.

Frey, B., and Stutzer, A. 'What Can Economists Learn from Happiness?', CESifo Working Paper, no. 503, June 2001.

Fukuyama, F. 'Social Capital and the Global Economy: A Redrawn Map of the World', *Foreign Affairs,* vol. 74, no. 5, September/October 1995.

——. 'The End of History?', *The National Interest,* Summer 1989.

Galbraith, J. K. *The Affluent Society*, second edition (London: Penguin, 1999).

——. *The Culture of Contentment* (London: Sinclair-Stevenson, 1992).

——. *The Great Crash 1929* (London: Penguin, 1992).

Garton Ash, T. *Free World: Why a Crisis of the West Reveals the Opportunity of Our Time* (London: Penguin, 2004).

Goetzmann, W. 'China and the World Financial Markets 1870–1930: Modern Lessons from Historical Globalization', Yale ICF Working Paper, no. 00–62, 2001.

Gray, J. 'The Era of Globalisation Is Over', *New Statesman*, 24 September 2001.

——. *Al Qaeda and What It Means to Be Modern* (London: Faber & Faber, 2003).

Hale, J. *The Civilisation of Europe in the Renaissance* (London: Harper Collins, 1993).

Honohan, P. 'Ireland in EMU: Straitjacket or Skateboard?', *Irish Banking Review*, Winter 2000, pp. 15–32.

Honohan, P., and Lane, P. 'Divergent Inflation Rates in EMU', Trinity College Dublin Economic Papers 2003/4, Trinity College Dublin Economics Department.

Honohan, P., and Walsh, B. 'Catching up with the Leaders', Brookings Papers on Economic Activity, vol. 1, 2002, pp. 1–57.

House of Lords Economic Affairs Committee. *First Report on Globalisation* (London: House of Lords, 16 January 2003) (www.parliament.the-stationery-office.co.uk/pa/ld200203/ldselect/ldeconaf/5/501.htm).

Hutchinson, J., and Smith, A. *Nationalism* (Oxford: Oxford University Press, 1994).

Hutton, W. *The State We're In* (London: Vintage, 1996).

Ikenberry, G. J. 'Illusions of Empire: Defining the New American Order', *Foreign Affairs*, March/April 2004.

Irwin, D. *Against the Tide: An Intellectual History of Free Trade* (Princeton: Princeton University Press, 1996).

James, H. *The End of Globalization* (Cambridge, MA: Harvard University Press, 2001).

Jospin, L. *Le monde comme je le vois* (Paris: Gallimard, 2005).

Kagan, R. 'Power and Weakness', *Policy Review*, no. 113, June 2002.

Keatinge, P. *A Singular Stance: Irish Neutrality in the 1980s* (Dublin: Institute of Public Administration, 1984).

Kelly, J., and Everett, M. 'Financial Liberalisation and Economic Growth in Ireland', *Central Bank and Financial Services Authority of Ireland Quarterly Bulletin*, Autumn 2004, pp. 91–112.

Kelly, J., and Reilly, A. 'Credit Card Debt in Ireland: Recent Trends', *Central Bank of Ireland Quarterly Bulletin*, vol. 1, 2005.

Keohane, D. 'Realigning Neutrality: Irish Defence Policy and the EU', EU Institute for Security Studies (ISS) Occasional Paper 24, March 2001.

——. *The EU and Counter-Terrorism* (London: Centre for European Reform, May 2005).

Keohane, R., and Nye, J. 'Power and Independence in the Information Age', *Foreign Affairs*, vol. 77, no. 5, September/October 1998.

Keynes, J. M. *The Economic Consequences of the Peace 1919* (New York: Dover Publications, 2004).

Kirby, P., Gibbons, L., and Cronin, M. *Reinventing Ireland: Culture, Society and the Global Economy* (London: Pluto Press, 2002).

Kirby, P. *The Celtic Tiger in Distress* (Hampshire: Palgrave 2002).

Kissinger, H. *Diplomacy* (London: Wiedenfield, 1994).

Konings, J., and Murphy, A. 'Do Multinational Enterprises Relocate Employment to Low Wage Regions? Evidence from European Multinationals', Central Bank and Financial Services Authority of Ireland, Technical Research Paper, March 2005.

Korin, A., and Luft, G. 'Terrorism Goes to Sea', *Foreign Affairs*, November/December 2004.

Krugman, P. 'Growing World Trade: Causes and Consequences', Brookings Papers on Economic Activity, vol. 1, Brookings Institute, 1995.

Krugman, P. *The Age of Diminished Expectations*, third edition (Cambridge, MA: MIT Press, 1997).

Lane, F. *The Origins of Modern Irish Socialism, 1881–1896* (Cork: Cork University Press, 1997).

Lane, P. 'Ireland and the Deflation Debate', *Irish Banking Review*, Winter 2003, pp. 2–17.

Larkin, E. *Alexis de Tocqueville's Journey in Ireland, July–August 1835* (Dublin: Wolfhound Press, 1990).

Layard, R. 'Happiness Is Back', *Prospect*, March 2005.

——. *Happiness: Lessons from a New Science* (London: Penguin, 2005).

Layte, R., O'Connell, P., Fahey, T., and McCoy, D. 'Ireland and Economic Globalisation: The Experiences of a Small Open Economy', Globalife (University of Bielefeld) Working Paper, no. 21, 2002.

Leddin, A., and Walsh, B. *The Macro-Economy of the Euro-Zone: An Irish Perspective* (Dublin: Gill & Macmillan, 2003).

Lee, J. J. *Ireland 1912–1985, Politics and Society* (Cambridge: Cambridge University Press, 1989).

Legrain, P. *Open World: The Truth about Globalization* (London: Abacus, 2002).

Levitt, T. 'The Globalization of Markets', *Harvard Business Review*, May/June 1983.

Levy, M., and O'Hanlon, M. *The Future of Arms Control* (Washington: Brookings Institution Press, 2004).

Lindert, P., and Williamson, J. 'Does Globalization Make the World More Unequal?', NBER Working Paper, no. 8228, April 2001.

McAleese, D. 'The Irish Economy: Recent Growth, European Integration and Future Prospects', Address at Centro Informacao Europeia Jacques Delors, 12 October 2001.

MacArdle, D. *Tragedies of Kerry 1922–1923* (Dublin: Irish Freedom Press, 1988).

Machiavelli, N. *The Discourses* (London: Penguin, 1983).

MacKay, C. *Extraordinary Popular Delusions and the Madness of Crowds* (Pennsylvania: Templeton Foundation Press, 1989).

McLellan, D. *The Thought of Karl Marx*, second edition (Papermac, 1980).

MacSharry, R., and White, P. *The Making of the Celtic Tiger: The Inside Story of Ireland's Boom Economy* (Cork: Mercier Press, 2001).

McSwiney, T. *Principles of Freedom* (Cork: Cork City Libraries, 2005).

Manseragh, N. *The Unresolved Question* (New Haven: Yale University Press, 1991).

———. *Nationalism and Independence* (Cork: Cork University Press, 1997).

Marquand, D. *Decline of the Public* (Cambridge: Polity, 2004).

Marx, K., and Engels, F. *Ireland and the Irish Question* (Moscow: Progress Publishers, 1986).

Masson, P. 'Globalization: Facts and Figures', IMF Policy Discussion Paper, no. 01/4, October 2001.

Michalet, C-A. *Qu'est ce que la mondialisation?* (Paris: La Decouverte, 2004).

Montesquieu, C. *The Spirit of the Laws* (New York: Hafner Press, 1949).

Mossner, E., and Ross, I. (eds.). *The Correspondence of Adam Smith* (Indianapolis: Liberty Fund, 1987).

Moylan, S. *Sean Moylan in His Own Words* (Aubane Historical Society, 2003).

Moynihan, M. *Speeches and Statements by Eamon De Valera 1917–1973* (Dublin: Gill & Macmillan, 1980).

Murphy, A., and Ruane, F. 'Foreign Direct Investment in Ireland: An Updated Assessment', Central Bank of Ireland Annual Report, 2003.

National Competitiveness Council/Forfas. *Annual Competitiveness Report*, September 2005 (www.forfas.ie/ncc).

———. *Annual Competitiveness Report*, November 2003 (www.forfas.ie/ncc).

———. *The Competitiveness Challenge*, November 2003 (www.forfas.ie/ncc).

National Economic and Social Council (NESC). *The Developmental Welfare State* (Dublin: NESC Publications, May 2005).

——. *National Progress Indicators for Sustainable Economic, Social and Environmental Development* (Dublin: NESC, February 2002).

Nolan, B., and Maitre, B. 'A Comparative Perspective on Trends in Income Inequality in Ireland', *Economic and Social Review,* vol. 31, no. 4, October 2000, pp. 329–350.

Nolan, B., and Smeeding, T. 'Ireland's Income Distribution in Comparative Perspective', December 2004 (http://ssrn.com/abstract=646024).

Nye, J. 'The Limits of American Power', *Political Science Quarterly,* vol. 117, no. 4, Winter 2002/3, pp. 454–559.

Nye, J. 'Globalization's Democratic Deficit: How to Make International Institutions More Accountable', *Foreign Affairs,* vol. 80, no. 4, July/August 2001.

Obstfeld, M. 'Globalization and Capital Markets', NBER Working Paper, no. W8846, 2002.

O'Clery, C. *The Greening of the White House* (Dublin: Gill & Macmillan, 1996).

——. *Ireland in Quotes: A History of the 20th Century* (Dublin: O'Brien Press, 1999).

O'Faolain, S. *The Irish* (London: Penguin 1980).

O'Grada, C. 'Is the Celtic Tiger a Paper Tiger?', Centre for Economic Research Working Paper, January 2002.

O'Halpin, E. *Defending Ireland: The Irish State and Its Enemies since 1922* (Oxford: Oxford University Press, 1999).

O'Hearn, D. *Inside the Celtic Tiger: The Irish Economy and the Asian Model* (London: Pluto, 1998).

Ojanen, H. (ed.). *Neutrality and Non-Alignment in Europe Today* (Helsinki: Finnish Institute of International Affairs, 2003).

O'Malley, E. *Raids and Rallies* (Dublin: Anvil Books, 1982).

——. *On Another Man's Wound* (Dublin: Anvil Press, 1997).

O'Malley, E. 'Competitive Performance in Irish Industry', *ESRI Quarterly Economic Commentary,* ESRI Publications, December 2004.

O'Neill, D., and Sweetman, O. 'Poverty and Inequality in Ireland 1987–1994: A Comparison Using Measures of Income and Consumption', Economics Department Working Paper series, no. 860399, Department of Economics, NUI Maynooth, March 1999.

O'Rahilly, T. F. *Early Irish History and Mythology* (Dublin: Dublin Institute of Advanced Studies, 1971).

Organisation for Economic Co-operation and Development (OECD). *The World Economy: A Millennial Perspective* (Paris: OECD, 2001).

——. *Ireland – Country Survey* (Paris: OECD, 2003).

——. *Statistical Profile of Ireland* (Paris: OECD, 2005).

——. *OECD in Figures* (Paris: OECD, 2005).

O'Rourke, K. 'Europe and the Causes of Globalization, 1790 to 2000', in H. Kierkowski (ed.), *From Europeanization of the Globe to Globalization of Europe* (Hampshire: Palgrave, 2002).

O'Rourke, K., and Thom, R. 'Irish Inflation: Appropriate Policy Responses', *Irish Banking Review,* Winter 2000, pp. 33–47.

O'Rourke, K., and Williamson, J. 'When Did Globalization Begin?', *European Review of Economic History*, vol. 6, 2002, pp. 23–50.

——. 'Once More: When Did Globalization Begin?', *European Review of Economic History,* vol. 8, 2004, pp. 109–117.

——. 'Around the European Periphery 1870–1913: Globalization, Schooling and Growth', NBER Working Paper, no. W5392, 1995.

Oswald, A. 'Happiness and Economic Performance', *Economic Journal,* vol. 107, 1997, pp. 1815–1831.

O'Sullivan, M. 'How to Keep the Irish Lucky', *Wall Street Journal Europe*, 4 January 2004.

O'Toole, F. *After the Ball* (Dublin: New Island, 2003).

Padoa-Schioppa, T. *The Euro and its Central Bank* (Cambridge, MA: MIT Press, 2004).

Pakenham, T. *The Year of Liberty: The History of the Great Irish Rebellion of 1798* (London: Panther Books, 1992).

Partridge, S. 'The British–Irish Council: The Trans-Islands Symbolic and Political Possibilities', British Council Looking into England papers, 2003.

Pei, M. 'Time to Reflect on How Far China Has to Go', *Financial Times*, 19 January 2005.

Pettit, P. *Republicanism: A Theory of Freedom and Government* (Oxford: Oxford University Press, 1997).

Pollin, R. 'Globalization, Inequality and Financial Instability: Confronting Marx, Keynes and Polanyi, Problems in Advanced Capitalist Economies', University of Massachusetts Amherst, Political Economy Research Institute Working Paper, no. 8.

Porter, N. (ed.). *The Republican Ideal* (Belfast: Blackstaff Press, 1998).

Prasad, E., Rogoff, K., Wei, S., and Kose, M. 'Effects of Financial Globalisation on Developing Countries', International Monetary Fund Occasional Paper, no. 220, 2003.

Primakov, Y. *A World Challenged: Fighting Terrorism in the 21st Century* (Washington: Brookings Institution Press, 2004).

Rajan, R., and Zingales, L. 'The Great Reversals: The Politics of Financial Development in the Twentieth Century', *Journal of Financial Economics,* vol. 69, no. 1, 2003, pp. 5–50.

Reis, R. 'A Cost of Living Dynamic Price Index, with an Application to Indexing Retirement Accounts', Princeton University Economics Department, October 2005.

Rodriguez, F., and Rodrik, D. 'Trade Policy and Economic Growth: A Skeptic's Guide to the Cross-National Evidence', NBER Working Paper, no. 7081, 1999.

Rodrik, D. *Has Globalisation Gone Too Far?* (Washington: Institute for International Economics, March 1997).

——. 'Trading in Illusions', *Foreign Policy,* March/April 2001.

Rodrik, D., and Subramanian, A. 'From "Hindu Growth" to Productivity Surge: The Mystery of the Indian Growth Transition', IMF Working Paper, no. 04/77, May 2004.

Rohatyn, F., and Stanger, A. 'The Profit Motive Goes to War', *Financial Times*, November 2004.

Roy, O. *Globalised Islam: The Search for a New Ummah* (London: Hurst, 2004).

Saakashvili, M. 'Europe's Third Wave of Liberation', *Financial Times*, 20 December 2004.

Sapir, A. 'Globalisation and the Reform of European Social Models', Background Document for ECOFIN Informal Meeting, 9 September 2005, Breugel Research Institute.

Savage, R. (ed.). *Ireland in the New Century* (Dublin: Four Courts Press, 2003).

Scholte, J-A. 'What Is Globalization? The Definitional Issue – Again', University of Warwick, CSGR Working Paper, no. 109/02, December 2002.

——. *Globalisation: A Critical Introduction* (Hampshire: Palgrave, 2000).

Sciolino, E. *Persian Mirrors: The Elusive Face of Iran* (New York: Free Press, 2000).

Singer, P. *Corporate Warriors: The Rise of the Privatized Military Industry* (New York: Cornell University Press, 2003).

Skinner, Q. *Machiavelli* (Oxford: Oxford University Press, 1996).

Slaughter, A. 'The Real New World Order', *Foreign Affairs*, September/October 1997.

Slevin, G. 'Is There a "New Economy" in Ireland?', Central Bank of Ireland Technical Research Paper, June 2002.

Solana, J. 'A Secure Europe in a Better World', European Council, Thessaloniki, 20 June 2003 (http://ue.eu.int/pressdata/en/reports/76255.pdf).

Soros, G. 'The Capitalist Threat', *Atlantic Monthly,* May 1995 (www.theatlantic.com).

——. 'Towards a Global Open Society', *Atlantic Monthly,* January 1998 (www.theatlantic.com).

——. *George Soros on Globalization* (New York: Perseus Books, 2002).

Stiglitz, J. 'Globalization and Growth in Emerging Markets and the New Economy', *Journal of Policy Modelling,* vol. 25, 2002, pp. 505–524.

——. *Globalization and Its Discontents* (New York: WM Norton & Co., 2003).

Stulz, R. 'The Financial Limits of Globalization', ECGI Working Paper Series in Finance, no. 75, March 2005.

Talbott, S. *Engaging India: Diplomacy, Democracy and the Bomb* (Washington: Brookings Institution Press, 2004).

Teschke, B. *The Myth of 1648* (London: Verso, 2003).

Todorov, T. *Le nouveau desordre mondial: réflexions d'un Européen* (Paris: Robert Laffont, 2003).

Wade, R. 'On the Causes of Widening World Income Inequality, or Why the Matthew Effect Prevails', *New Political Economy*, vol. 9, no. 2, 2004, pp. 163–188.

——. 'Is Globalization Reducing Poverty and Inequality?' *World Development*, vol. 32, no. 4, 2004, pp. 567–589.

Walsh, B. 'What's in Store for the Celtic Tiger?', *Irish Banking Review*, Spring 1999.

Walt, S. 'International Relations: One World, Many Theories', *Foreign Policy,* Spring 1998.

Wei, S., and Amiti, M. 'Fear of Service Outsourcing: Is It Justified?', NBER Working Paper, no. 10808, October 2004.

Whelan, C., and Layte, R. 'Economic Change, Social Mobility and Meritocracy: Reflections on the Irish Experience', *ESRI Quarterly Economic Commentary,* September 2004, pp. 89–108.

Whelan, C., Nolan, B., and Maitre, B. 'Trends in Welfare for Vulnerable Groups, Ireland 1994–2001', *ESRI Publications,* August 2005.

Williamson, J. 'What Should the World Bank Think About the Washington Consensus?' *World Bank Research Observer,* vol. 15, no. 2, pp. 251–264.

——. 'Globalisation and Inequality Past and Present', NBER Working Paper, no. 5491, 1995.

Wolf, M. *Why Globalisation Works* (New Haven: Yale University Press, 2004).

World Competitiveness Yearbook 2003 (www.IMD.com).

Zakaria, F. *The Future of Freedom* (New York: WM Norton & Co., 2003).

Index